Simulation Foundations, Methods and Applications

More information about this series at http://www.springer.com/series/10128

Okan Topçu • Umut Durak • Halit Oğuztüzün
Levent Yilmaz

Distributed Simulation

A Model Driven Engineering Approach

 Springer

Okan Topçu
Department of Computer Engineering
Turkish Naval Academy
Istanbul, Turkey

Halit Oğuztüzün
Department of Computer Engineering
Middle East Technical University
Ankara, Turkey

Umut Durak
Department of Flight Dynamics
and Simulation
DLR Institute of Flight Systems
Braunschweig, Germany

Levent Yilmaz
Department of Industrial
and Systems Engineering
Auburn University
Auburn, AL, USA

ISSN 2195-2817   ISSN 2195-2825   (electronic)
Simulation Foundations, Methods and Applications
ISBN 978-3-319-79136-4   ISBN 978-3-319-03050-0   (eBook)
DOI 10.1007/978-3-319-03050-0

Springer International Publishing AG Switzerland is part of Springer Science+Business Media
(www.springer.com)

To Oğuz and Tuğçe with love.
You make it all worthwhile.
Okan Topçu

To my wife, my sailmate, Rabia.
Without you, I could not navigate the high seas.
Umut Durak

To Serpil, Çerağ and Ozan.
My circle of love.
Halit Oğuztüzün

To my mentors and teachers who inspired and motivated me to keep expanding my horizons.
Levent Yilmaz

Foreword

The impressive and imposing stature of contemporary "simulation" is in contrast with its humble beginnings at the fourteenth century. At the beginning, the word "simulation" used to mean "an imitating, feigning, false show, or hypocrisy." Currently, hundreds of types of simulation can be grouped under two categories: performing *experiments* and gaining *experience* by using models of dynamic systems.

Performing experiments – as the essence of the scientific method – was promoted by Francis Bacon in his "Novum Organum" early seventeenth century (1620) in contrast to Aristotelian rhetoric. The well-known advantages of performing experiments on models (i.e., simulation) over performing experiments on real systems are numerous and are augmented by the fact that in several cases, experiments on real systems cannot or should not be done. This last aspect lets simulation to be the only possibility to perform experiments. Performing simulation experiments while real system is running – in tandem or in sequence – has additional advantages that no other technique can provide.

Gaining experience by simulation can enhance three types of skills (i.e., motor, decision making, and operational skills), or can be entertaining. Use of simulation to enhance motor, decision making, and operational skills correspond to virtual, constructive, and live simulations. Gaming simulation to provide experience for entertainment purposes is technically so advanced that some of its techniques are used for serious games.

Advancements of all types of simulation lead to *simulation-based methodologies* and provide infrastructure for a multitude of application areas and disciplines, including *simulation-based engineering* as well as *simulation-based science*. An important type of simulation is distributed simulation to provide several types of training and assessment possibilities for complex systems. In fact, *distributed simulation* has been the de facto approach to tackle several types of complex problems.

At an abstract level, any type of simulation is a model-based knowledge processing activity, and due to vital role of models, the terms simulation and modeling are often used together as *modeling and simulation*. Accordingly, several concepts around models have been developed; they include, in addition to hundreds of types of models, modeling – including static and dynamic model composition – building, maintaining, and searching model bases and relevant activities and concerns, such as model integrity, and many types of model processing – including model transformations and checking. Accordingly, *model-driven approaches* have gained well-deserved and very important momentum in many disciplines, including science and engineering. *Model-driven engineering* is already an important and fundamental concept and practice.

The volume "Distributed Simulation: A Model Driven Engineering Approach" by Topçu, Durak, Oğuztüzün, and Yilmaz is an important contribution for the advancement of modeling and simulation. It is the first book to cover all aspects of distributed simulation from the model-driven engineering perspective. Some of the topics covered in detail include: model-driven engineering, high level architecture, distributed simulation engineering, conceptual modeling, simulation environment design, federate architecture, scenario management, implementation and execution, simulation evolution, and modernization. The advantages of the synergies of model-driven engineering and agents, which provide a very powerful computational paradigm, are also covered for the future advancements. Three case studies are given to provide ample clarification of the concepts presented. The volume provides practitioners a powerful way to tackle complex problems.

University of Ottawa   Tuncer Ören
Ottawa, ON, Canada
September 10, 2015

Preface

Purpose of the Book

Both distributed simulation (DS), an area of modeling and simulation (M&S), and model-driven engineering (MDE), an area of software engineering, are fields with their distinct body of knowledge. This book builds on the premise that developments in one field can provide new avenues for advancing the theory, methodology, and the practice in the other field. Therefore, it provides a comprehensive view on DS from the MDE perspective by illustrating how MDE affects the overall lifecycle of the simulation development process.

Rationale

Software engineering aims to improve the quality and efficacy of software intensive systems engineering processes. In software engineering, one of the major problems is the gap between the high-level design and the application code deployed on a platform. MDE, as an up-and-coming approach, allows increasing the abstraction level to models to address both the platform and the application complexity. By automating transformations across models at different levels of resolution, an MDE-based process model supports the technology, engineering, and management of software development via tool-based automation and code generation and hence increases both productivity and quality.

DS applications can be regarded as software-intensive systems. The high level architecture (HLA), which is a standard for DS, has been around for over 20 years, and it has already proven its worth in many distributed simulation applications. The synergy between DS, particularly the HLA, and the MDE methodology has been promoted as a viable solution to improve productivity, reuse, and longevity of simulation models. However, both DS and MDE require substantial domain expertise due to their sophisticated and technical body of knowledge. Moreover, the principles and best practices in both fields are dispersed across many publications. In the light of these observations, this book presents a comprehensive reference bringing together the principles, concepts, and development processes of DS from the point of view of the MDE perspective by covering a wide spectrum of topics from conceptual modeling to simulation modernization.

The book supplements the theoretical overview with practical case studies to demonstrate the utility and applicability of the methodology. Multiple case studies are presented to demonstrate the technological aspects of engineering and management of models. Most of the case studies and models presented in this book are developed with public-domain tools that can be downloaded from their project websites.

Book Overview

The book is structured as follows. Chapter 1 presents an introduction to the essential concepts of modeling and simulation, while highlighting DS as the focal area of interest. Chapter 2 provides an overview of the fundamental concepts, principles, and processes of MDE. Chapter 3 gives an introduction to the HLA. These three chapters together lay the technical background for linking two distinct disciplines, DS and MDE. Chapter 4 presents a road map for building and deploying a distributed simulation system in accordance with the MDE perspective, and it introduces a process model based on the principles and best practices of MDE. Chapters 5, 6, 7, 8, 9 and 10 elaborate on the process model presented in this chapter. Chapter 5 treats conceptual modeling from the MDE perspective, and it presents a methodology and a technical framework to develop conceptual models. Chapter 6 introduces the concept of federation (simulation environment) architecture. By demonstrating the formalization of a federation architecture using the metamodeling concepts, we promote automated code generation and semi-automated model validation over the machine processable specifications of a federation architecture. Chapter 7 focuses on federate architectures and presents a practical approach to the design of federations (i.e. simulation member design) by applying a well-known architectural style, the layered architecture. After introducing the model-driven scenario development process, Chapter 8 explains the major concepts of simulation scenarios and discusses the main activities related to scenario management in a distributed simulation. Chapter 9 delineates the nature of MDE-based implementation activities, including model development, model checking, code generation and integration, and testing. Chapter 10 introduces simulation evolution and modernization. It presents and adopts the software modernization approaches, particularly architecture-driven modernization (ADM) for simulation modernization. Finally, Chapter 11 brings the agent paradigm to the fore and examines potential synergies among the agent, DS, and MDE methodologies, pointing to avenues of future research and development at the intersection of these three fields.

Final

We believe that the most prominent contribution of this book is its unique frame of reference in presenting the principles, concepts, and development processes of distributed simulation (DS) from the model-driven engineering (MDE) perspective. As the only book so far that builds on the synergies of DS and MDE, it explains the theoretical underpinnings of DS and MDE and demonstrates the utility and effectiveness of MDE principles in developing DS applications. In this respect, the book covers *de facto* DS standard, namely, High Level Architecture (HLA) (also a *de jure* standard IEEE 1516-2010) in order to illustrate theoretical issues and serve as a testbed to substantiate the role of MDE for DS. We hope that this book gives a direction for the readers, who are interested in adopting MDE principles and practices for developing complex DS systems.

Istanbul, Turkey   Okan Topçu
Braunschweig, Germany   Umut Durak
Ankara, Turkey   Halit Oğuztüzün
Auburn, AL, USA   Levent Yilmaz

Supplementary Material

Software Tools	URL (Web Address)
SimGe	https://sites.google.com/site/okantopcu/simge
RACoN	https://sites.google.com/site/okantopcu/racon
FAMM	https://sites.google.com/site/okantopcu/famm
NSTMSS	https://sites.google.com/site/okantopcu/navysim
DeCoAgent	https://sites.google.com/site/okantopcu/decoagent

Acknowledgments

We would like to thank our colleagues Gürkan Özhan, Mehmet Adak, Deniz Çetinkaya, Vijdan Kızılay, Thorsten Pawletta, Artur Schmidt, Torsten Gerlach, Jürgen Gotschlich, and Robert Siegfried for their contribution in creating some material that found its way into this book. Also we would like to acknowledge Dr. Tuncer Ören for providing an insightful foreword and our associate editor Simon Rees for smooth editorial assistance.

Okan would like to thank his parents, Selime and Bekir, for their boundless support and his graduate students for their worthy feedback.

Umut is grateful for Dr. Holger Duda for his invaluable support. His special thanks go to Simulation Technologies Group in DLR Institute of Flight Systems for the comfort and understanding.

Halit would like to thank all his graduate students; he learned a lot from them.

For various chapters of this book, we have adapted parts of the following articles:

Topçu, O., Adak, M., & Oğuztüzün, H. (2008, July). A metamodel for federation architectures. *Transactions on Modeling and Computer Simulation (TOMACS)*, *18*(3), 10:1–10:29. Parts adapted and reprinted with permission from ACM. Appears in Chap. 6.

Topçu, O., Adak, M., & Oğuztüzün, H. (2009). Metamodeling live sequence charts for code generation. *Software and Systems Modeling (SoSym)*, *8*(4), 567–583. Parts adapted and reprinted with permission from Springer. Appears in Chap. 6.

Topçu, O., & Oğuztüzün, H. (2010). Scenario management practices in HLA-based distributed simulation. *Journal of Naval Science and Engineering*, *6*(2), 1–33. Parts adapted and reprinted with permission from DEBIM. Appears in Chap. 8.

Topçu, O., & Oğuztüzün, H. (2013, March). Layered simulation architecture: A practical approach. *Simulation Modelling Practice and Theory*, *32*, 1–14. Parts adapted and reprinted with permission from Elsevier. Appears in Chap. 7.

Topçu, O. (2004). *Development, representation, and validation of conceptual models in distributed simulation.* Halifax, NS, Canada: Defence R&D Canada – Atlantic (DRDC Atlantic). Parts adapted and reprinted with permission from DRDC-Atlantic. Appears in Chap. 5.

Durak, U., Schmidt, A., & Pawletta, T. (2015). Model-based testing for objective fidelity evaluation of engineering and research flight simulators. In *AIAA modeling and simulation technologies conference.* Dallas, TX Parts adapted and reprinted with permission from DLR and Hochschule Wismar. Appears in Chap. 9.

Durak, U., Topcu, O., Siegfried, R., & Oguztuzun, H. (2014). Scenario development: A model-driven engineering perspective. In M. S. Obaidat, J. Kacprzyk, & T. Ören (Eds.). *Proceedings of the 4th international conference on simulation and modeling methodologies, technologies and applications.* Vienna, Austria: SCITEPRESS. Parts adapted and reprinted with permission from SCITEPRESS. Appears in Chap. 8.

Gerlach, T., Durak, U., & Gotschlich, J. (2014). Model integration workflow for keeping models up to date in a research simulator. In M. S. Obaidat, J. Kacprzyk, T. Ören (Eds.). *Proceedings of the 4th international conference on simulation and modeling methodologies, technologies and applications.* Vienna, Austria: SCITEPRESS. Parts adapted and reprinted with permission from SCITEPRESS. Appears in Chap. 9.

Schmidt, A., Durak, U., Rasch, C., & Pawletta, T. (2015). Model-based testing approach for MATLAB/Simulink using system entity structure and experimental frames. In *Proceedings of 2015 Spring Simulation Multi-Conference.* Alexandria, DC. Some figures are reprinted with permission from SCS.

Özhan,G., & Oğuztüzün, H. (2015). Transformation of conceptual models to executable high level architecture federation models. In L. Yılmaz (Eds.). *Concepts and methodologies for modeling and simulation – A tribute to Tuncer Ören* (pp. 135–173). Basel, Switzerland: Springer. Some figures and text are reproduced with permission from Springer. Appears in Chap. 5.

Contents

List of Symbols/Abbreviations/Acronyms/ Initialisms

A

ACM	(Field) Artillery Conceptual Model
ACMM	ACM Metamodel
ADM	Architecture Driven Modernization
ALSP	Aggregate Level Simulation Protocol
AMG	Architecture Management Group
AMMA	ATLAS Model Management Architecture
AOP	Aspect Oriented Programming
API	Application Programming Interface
ARPA	Advanced Research Projects Agency
ATL	ATLAS Transformation Language
ASTM	Abstract Syntax Tree Metamodel

B

BM	Base Model
BMM	Behavioral Metamodel
BOM	Base Object Model
BPMN	Business Process Model and Notation

C

CASE	Computer Assisted Software Engineering
CBD	Causal Block Diagrams
CGF	Computer Generated Force
ChatFdApp	Chat Federate Application
CFF	Call For Fire
CIM	Computation-Independent Model

CM	Conceptual Model
COTS	Commercial off-the-shelf
CSSL	Continuous System Simulation Language

D

DARPA	US Defense Advanced Research Projects Agency
DAVE-ML	Dynamic Aerospace Vehicle Exchange Markup Language
DDM	Data Distribution Management
	Detailed Design Model
DeCoAgent	Deliberative Coherence Driven Agent
DeCoAgentLib	DeCoAgent Library
DeMo	Discrete Event Modeling and Simulation Ontology
DIF	Data Interchange Format
DIN	Deutsches Institut für Normung
DIS	Distributed Interactive Simulation
DLC	Dynamic Link Compatibility
DLL	Dynamic Link Library
DLR	German Aerospace Center
DMAO	DSEEP Multi-Architecture Overlay
DMSO	U.S. Defense Modeling and Simulation Office
DoD	US Department of Defense
DSEEP	Distributed Simulation Engineering and Execution Process
DSL	Domain-Specific Language
DSM	Domain-Specific (Meta)Modeling
DSML	Domain-Specific Modeling Language

E

EF	Experimental Frame
EM	Executable Model
EMF	Eclipse Modeling Framework
EnviFd	Environment Controller Federate
ESA	European Space Agency
ExMFd	Exercise Manager Federate

F

FA	Field Artillery
FAM	Federation Architecture Model
FAME	Federation Architecture Modeling Environment

FAMM	Federation Architecture Metamodel
FCO	First Class Object
FDC	Fire Direction Center
FDD	FOM Document Data
FEAT	Federation Engineering Agreements Template
FED	Federation Execution Details
FEDEP	Federation Development and Execution Process
FedMonFd	Federation Monitor Federate
FEPW	Federation Execution Planner's Workbook
FFE	Fire For Effect
FFL	Federation Foundation Library
FRG	Federation Rapid Generation
FMI	Functional Mock-up Interface
FMU	Functional Mock-up Unit
FMUFd	FMU Federate
FOM	Federation Object Model
FSMM	Federation Structure Metamodel

G

GASTM	Generic Abstract Syntax Meta-Model
GME	Generic Modeling Environment
GPL	General-Purpose Language
GpML	General-purpose Modeling Languages
GReAT	Graph Rewriting and Transformation
GRT	Generic Real-time Target
GUI	Graphical User Interface

H

HDefLib	IEEE1516.2 HLA Defaults Library
HFMM	HLA Federation Metamodel
HIL	Hardware-in-the-Loop
HLA	High Level Architecture
HMOMLib	IEEE 1516.1 Management Object Model Library
HMSC	High Level MSC
HOMM	HLA Object Metamodel
HSMM	HLA Services Metamodel
HTML	HyperText Markup Language

I

IDE	Integrated Development Environment
IEEE	Institute of Electrical and Electronics Engineers
IF	Interface Specification
IMLib	Methods Library for IEEE 1516.1
ITU	International Telecommunications Union

J

JC3IEDM	(NATO's) Joint C3 Information Exchange Data Model

K

KDM	Knowledge Discovery Metamodel

L

LHS	Left Hand Side
LMM	LSC Metamodel
LSC	Live Sequence Chart

M

M0	Physical Level
M1	Model
M2	Metamodel
M2M	Model-to-Model
M2T	Model-to-Text
M3	Meta-Metamodel
MAAB	MathWorks Automotive Advisory Board
MATE	Model Advisor Transformation Extension
MB	Model Base
MBT	Model-Based Testing
MDA	Model-Driven Architecture
MDE	Model-Driven Engineering
MDRE	Model-Driven Reverse Engineering
MDS	Model-Driven Science
MDScD	Model-Driven Scenario Development
MEE	Model Experiencing Environment
MetaGME	GME Metamodel

MIC	Model Integrated Computing
MIL	Model-in-the-Loop
MiLEST	Model-in-the-Loop for Embedded System Test
MIM	MOM and Initialization Module
MMM	MSC Metamodel
MMT	Model-to-Model Transformation
MOF	Meta Object Facility
MOM	Management Object Model
MS	Microsoft
M&S	Modeling and Simulation
MSC	Message Sequence Chart
MSDL	Military Scenario Definition Language
MUT	Model Under Test

N

| NFL | NSTMSS Foundation Library |
| NSTMSS | Naval Surface Tactical Maneuvering Simulation System (pronounced as 'NiSTMiSS') |

O

OM	Object Model
OCL	Object Constraint Language
OLMECO	Open Library for Models of Mechatronic Components
OME	Object Model Editor
OMG	Object Modeling Group
OMT	Object Model Template, Object Modeling Technique
OOA&D	Object Oriented Analysis and Design
OOW	Officer of the Watch
OWL	Web Ontology Language
OSE	Officer Scheduling the Exercise
OTC	Officer in Tactical Command

P

PDU	Protocol Data Unit
PES	Pruned Entity Structure
PIM	Platform-Independent Model
POC	Point of Contact
P-Process	PROMELA Process

PROMELA	Process Metalanguage
P/S	Publish/Subscribe
PSM	Platform-Specific Model
PSML	Platform-Specific Modeling Language
PSMM	P/S Metamodel

Q

QVT	Query/View/Transformation

R

RACoN	RTI Abstraction Component for .Net
RHS	Right Hand Side
RPR	Real-time Platform-level Reference
RID	RTI Initialization Data
RTI	Runtime Infrastructure

S

SASTM	Specialized Abstract Syntax Meta-Models
SBVR	Semantics of Business Vocabulary and Rules
SCM	Simulation Conceptual Model
ScOM	Scenario Object Model
SDEM	Simulation Data Exchange Model
SDL	Scenario Definition Language
SES	System Entity Structure
SES/MB	System Entity Structure and Model Base
ShipFd	Ship Federate
SimGe	SIMulation Generator
SIMNET	Simulation Networking
SISO	Simulation Interoperability Standards Organization
SIL	Software-in-the-Loop
SKDM	Simulation KDM
SM	Scenario Management
SMDL	Simulation Model Definition Language
SME	Subject Matter Expert
SMP2	Simulation Model Portability 2
SOAP	Service-Oriented Access Protocol
SOM	Simulation Object Model
StationFd	Station Federate
STMS	Strait Traffic Monitoring Simulation
SysML	Systems Modeling Language

T

TCP/IP	Transmission Control Protocol/Internet Protocol
TENA	Test and Training Enabling Architecture
TLC	Target Language Compiler
TSONT	Trajectory Simulation Ontology

U

UI	User Interface
UML	Unified Modeling Language
US DoD	United States Department of Defense

V

V&V	Verification and Validation
VV&A	Verification, Validation, and Accreditation

W

W3C	World Wide Web Consortium

X

XML	Extensible Markup Language
XMI	XML Metadata Interchange

Part I
Foundations

Chapter 1
Introduction

This chapter provides an introduction to the essential concepts of modeling and simulation (M&S) keeping distributed simulation (DS) in focus. Our purpose in this chapter is to familiarize the reader with the terminology and concepts used frequently in subsequent chapters. First, we introduce the basic concepts from the theory of M&S, and then present a historical perspective on DS and related standards. The chapter concludes with an outline of the book chapters.

1.1 M&S Concepts

In this section, we would like to clarify some fundamental concepts that we use throughout this book. Concepts such as model, simulation, system keep occurring in our discussions, so we need to be clear about them.

A model is construed as a representation of reality, and modeling as the activity of creating a model. Admittedly, this formulation is rather terse. We need to be a bit more explicit about what our notion of "reality" is, what kinds of "representation" are admissible, and what sort of processes can be followed to come up with representations that will be useful for a certain purpose, and how we can put them into use.

By the term reality, we may mean the world that exists independently of our minds, or the imagined or hypothetical world that exists only in our minds, or any mixture of the two. In other words, the reality we are referring to can be objective, subjective, or any combination thereof. Consider, for example, the hydrodynamics model of an existing ship and that of a ship being designed. They would be indistinguishable as representations. Further, suppose we are planning modifications to an existing ship, say, by upgrading its engine, then the future ship is a mixture of the existing one (so that we can keep its geometric model) and the envisioned one (so that we have a new propulsion model reflecting the new engine capabilities).

© Springer International Publishing Switzerland 2016
O. Topçu et al., *Distributed Simulation*, Simulation Foundations,
Methods and Applications, DOI 10.1007/978-3-319-03050-0_1

Therefore, the notion of reality that is subject to modeling does not necessarily have a material counterpart.

At any moment, we are concerned with only a confined part or a certain aspect of reality, because we have a particular purpose. We have a particular problem to solve, or decision to be made, or, more basically, we need a better understanding of what the situation is. Thus, we have to limit the scope of our modeling effort accordingly. Perhaps, for example, the navigation system of the ship is not of immediate concern; then, it is out of our modeling scope. For the same reason, we need to put a limit on the level of detail we can have in our models. For example, the wear and tear of the ship's engine may be ignorable if we are only interested in the maximum torque it can produce. After all, we cannot duplicate reality. This means, in modeling, we are after some deliberately simplified view of reality.

Abstraction refers to the fact that a model explicitly represents those aspects of reality that are of interest to us while omitting other aspects that are not of concern. Suppose we are interested in studying the maneuverability of a ship. Then, parameters related to its mass, geometry, propulsion, and rudder will be taken into consideration while the material used in its construction can be safely ignored.

What is subjected to modeling, the part of reality which is known as the simuland, can involve entities, systems, events, and processes. The term entity is used in quite a generic sense, meaning any recognizable and identifiable thing, tangible or intangible, in the domain of application, such as a wheel of a car model or percept of a sensor. An entity can have attributes, states, and functional behavior, just like an object in the sense of object-oriented programming.

A *system* is an organized collection of components that interact with each other according to a pattern in order to achieve some purpose or functionality. A *component* is any entity that is capable of exhibiting an input-output behavior through a well-defined interface. A *system's purpose* is realized through its interactions with its environment. The *environment of a system* is the part of reality that the system receives input from and provides output to. Consider, for example, the driver and passengers of a car which it carries as well as the road it moves on and the air that it goes through.

In the context of discrete-event systems (Cassandras and Lafortune 2010), an *event* refers to an indivisible action, whereas a process is a sequence of events. For modeling purposes, an event is usually thought of as being instantaneous while a process as consuming time. Hence, we may want to assign a time instant to an event and a time interval to a process.

It is often undesirable to experiment with reality directly; in many cases, too dangerous or plainly impossible. Suppose we would like to study the wave actions that might cause our ship to capsize. This is when the use of models becomes indispensable. We can experiment with models safely in our offices.

From the perspective of usage, a model can be viewed as being descriptive or prescriptive. The descriptive view is adopted when studying the properties of an existing system, while the prescriptive view is adopted when building a new system. In general, the descriptive view of a model is prevalent in reverse engineering, while prescriptive view in forward engineering.

The intended uses of a model constitute its purpose. There are several kinds of practical uses for models, which can take place in a descriptive or prescriptive viewpoint: First, perhaps the most common, use is communication among stakeholders. It is easier to share our ideas and intuitions about reality if we are referring to the same model. Second, the model can be subjected to rigorous analysis, using computational methods, for example. This way we can answer questions about a system's performance. Third, the purpose we are particularly interested in this book, is generating the behavior of the system from the system's model. The behavior of a system is some ordering (possibly, partial) of the system's actions over time. An action typically consists of taking some inputs and producing some outputs. The inputs come from the system's environment and the outputs create some effect on the system's environment.

A method of generating system behavior from the system model is known as *simulation*. Thus, simulation amounts to a mechanism to move a model over time, given input data. Evidently, a computer-based or software-intensive system is the most common way of realizing a simulation. Figure 1.1 depicts the basic notions and relationships that we have discussed thus far.

Modeling and simulation revolves around certain concepts, such as reality, model, simulation, computer, and results and relations among these elements. Figure 1.1 depicts the basic elements, relations, and processes of the modeling and simulation enterprise.

The simulation user, who could be an analyst, researcher, decision maker, trainer or trainee, has an interest in a real world issue, say, the maneuverability of a certain class of ship. He (or she) builds a mathematical model of the ship that accounts for the significant factors that can affect the maneuverability of the ship. He implements this model in a mathematical programming language, say, MATLAB. The simulation in MATLAB runs on a computer getting inputs in accordance with a scenario. The user examines the results produced by the simulation run, or multiple runs, and hopefully gains an understanding of the maneuverability of the ship under the conditions dictated by the scenario – without actually handling the ship.

The description of the above steps reveals several issues that need to be addressed in a simulation study: What are the input, output and control variables and system parameters to be studied and what is the objective of our study: comparison, optimization? What is the required level of accuracy (fidelity)? Did we include all factors that matter to achieve the objectives (level of detail)? Did we implement the mathematical model faithfully as a program (verification)? Is the scenario adequate given the objectives (input data analysis)? How far can we rely on the outputs produced by the simulation runs (results validation)? Trying to discuss these issues adequately in this book would divert us from our main objective, which is to show how to apply model-driven engineering principles in the construction of distributed simulation systems. Fortunately, several excellent books are available for the readers who want to build a strong foundation on M&S, such as Law (2007), Sokolowski and Banks (2010), and Banks et al. (2010).

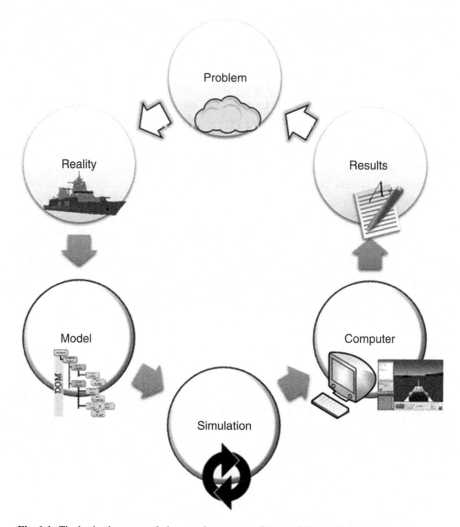

Fig. 1.1 The basic elements, relations, and processes of the modeling and simulation endeavor

Behavior of a system involves its outputs in response to its inputs. In many systems of interest, the input-output relationship can change with time. We call such systems as dynamic systems (Luenberger 1979). In such systems the output of the system at time t, in response to its inputs at time t will depend on its state at time t. The state of the system will undergo changes as it receives more inputs from its environment as time passes. In contrast, we may consider static systems that provide a fixed input-output relationship. Consider, for example, a damage assessment service that computes the damage to a car in good shape in the event of its crash with a barrier. Given all the parameters of the crash event, the damage assessment will be the same no matter when it occurs.

In some cases, it is easy to distinguish the model and the simulation. For example, the model could be in a mathematical form, say, as a linear system of ordinary differential equations, and the simulation could take the form of software that implements a solver for this system of equations. Given the power and prevalence of software, the distinction between a model and simulation is not always clear. In many cases, the model is directly expressed in an executable form, say, in a general purpose programming language such as Java, simulation-oriented programming language such as SIMSCRIPT III (Rice et al. 2005), a mathematical programming language, such as MATLAB (Chapman 2015), or a language with development and execution environment specifically designed for simulation such as SIMAN/ARENA (Kelton et al. 2014). In such cases, the model does not have a separate representation, but embodiment as the source code. Then, people may refer to that code as a simulation model. When it is not important or not practical to separate the model and the simulation you may hear people using the terms model and simulation interchangeably. In this book, we will be following this convention. In the context of MDE, however, it is crucial to be clear about the separation between the model and the simulation.

The generation of behavior requires that the model is provided with input data over time. This is where the notion of scenario comes in. A scenario specifies the initial data and the data to be fed to the model in a timely manner, or at least a prescription of how that data will be generated. It is the job of the simulation engine to enact the scenario.

A particular instance of applying a simulation (as a method) with a given set of input data is known as a simulation run (or simulation execution). A simulation run, therefore, consists of events that take place over the time axis. In everyday usage, the terms simulation and simulation run (or execution) are often used interchangeably. In this book, however, we take care to keep the distinction clear.

1.2 Type of Models and Simulations

What kinds of models can we have? A model is, first and foremost, a representation. Naturally, we should be concerned about the language (or notation) in which a representation is expressed. To start with a familiar example, a Java program is a representation of some computation, a process that takes place on an actual computer. We have the Java language, defined syntactically by means of a grammar, in which this source program is expressed. Also consider UML (OMG 2015), a graphical modeling language for software systems (to be) constructed in an object-oriented way. In principle, any language, defined with sufficient precision using well-defined rules, can serve as a representation or modeling language.

Modeling languages can be textual or graphical. Some languages, such as Simulink, combine graphical and textual elements. In fact, text vs. graphics is a concrete syntax issue, which concerns human users, and becomes irrelevant as soon as the specification text or the diagram is translated into an abstract syntax representation by the (front end of) language processor for further processing.

In this book, we emphasize language-based aspects of modeling and simulation as they underlie the model-driven approach. The model and simulation are expressed in appropriate languages, possibly custom designed. Nevertheless, researchers in engineering and science fields build and experiment with physical models as well. Consider, for example, wind tunnel experiments carried out on scaled-down physical models of an aircraft or its parts. The flow of air over the aircraft in flight is simulated by generating a controlled air flow over the physical model of aircraft geometry and making measurements.

The language-based view of models is at the heart of the model-driven approach that is promoted in this book. When we consider metamodels in Chap. 6, we shall see that a metamodel defines a modeling language, just like a grammar defines (the syntax of) a language, say, a programming language.

As the language plays an enabling role in the modeling endeavor, the precision of the language definition comes into play. This brings up the issue of formalism. Traditionally, people use context-free grammars to define the syntax of programming languages. However, grammars need to be supplemented by additional constraints, such as typing rules, so that non-context-free aspects of the programming language syntax can be accounted for. By and large, we have powerful formal notations to represent the syntax of textual languages. Many modeling notations, however, are graphical, such as UML and SysML (OMG 2012). Grammars for graphical languages, known as *graph grammars* (Rozenberg 1997), are a much lesser known subject, and the use of graph grammar formalism for the definition of practical graphical notations is restricted. Definitions of UML graphical notations, for example, rely on verbal descriptions and examples (OMG 2015).

One may question the necessity of formalism in defining languages. After all, are not we all right with intuitively defined notations using verbal means? Ambiguity inherent in natural languages can be tolerated, can even be desirable, in human-to-human communication. However, to bring in tool support our notations should be interpreted by machines unequivocally. Thus, arises the need for formal definitions.

To be sure, one may form models following the tradition of scientific papers. Their delivery for the most part relies on a mixture of natural language and mathematical formulation, possibly supplemented with graphics, figures, pictures, tables, and so on. Even though rigorous, such informal models do not fully support the model-driven approach, which relies on precisely defined models. Informal models still play an important role by promoting communication among the model stakeholders and providing a basis for formal models.

Beyond syntax, further consideration of semantics reveals deeper challenges. The semantics of programming languages is a subject of sustained research effort in the programming languages community. Precise mathematical/logical descriptions of programming language semantics are important for practical reasons. For example, consider the question of whether a certain translation of a given source code to object code must be regarded correct. Such questions are important not only for compiler and interpreter writers but also for ordinary programmers.

Similar concerns are overwhelming in the case of modeling languages. One would like to generate executable code from a model. Then the semantical matters must have been settled so that manipulations of models would result as prescribed, and different model-based tools have a common ground for agreement. Precise semantical description of modeling notations is in a premature stage compared to programming languages (Bryant et al. 2011).

The point is that the language-based underpinnings of model-driven methodology are formally grounded only to a certain, mostly syntactical, extent, but to enable a complete and satisfactory treatment the practitioners need semantical dimension as well. The upshot is that given the state-of-art language technology, there is a great deal of benefit to be obtained by adoption of language-based techniques, such as metamodeling, as demonstrated in this book. Looking into future, we may expect deeper integration of tools and models drawing from a semantical background.

1.3   Model to Simulate, Model to Build

In M&S, we model systems to simulate them. In software and systems engineering, we model systems to build them. The modeling activity is common to most scientific and engineering endeavors though each subject area has its own conventions and traditions in regard to modeling techniques and tools. Beyond the subject area, the difference in purposes can lead to a big difference in modeling approaches. The model of the ship hull to be constructed by engineers, and the model of the ship to be analyzed for its certain structural properties, say, its radar cross-section, or behavioral properties, say, its stability, would look drastically different. This is no surprise as we know that any model is a *purposeful* abstraction of reality. If we have an account of the similarities and differences between these two models we can leverage the techniques and tools available in MDE.

When we start building models to simulate systems, we face the issue of fidelity. Fidelity can be defined as the degree of accuracy of a model (Cross 1999) compared with the actual system. In other words, it is a measure of how accurately the model represents the reality. The level of detail is one aspect of fidelity. Which control surfaces are represented in an aircraft aerodynamics model is a level of detail issue, for example. Resolution is another aspect. The number of cells represented in the finite grid of certain dimensions is a matter of resolution. In any case, the fidelity required of a model depends on the intended uses of the model. In a formation flight training scenario, for example, we would probably need a higher fidelity level for our own aircraft compared to our wingmen's aircraft.

We may want to measure the fidelity of a model by comparing the results from the simulation runs with the data obtained by observing the real world, provided, of course, that such data, called the *referent*, is available. This activity can be a part of a validation process – results validation, to be more specific. One must be aware of the numerical precision and instability problems that might be introduced as the model is implemented as simulation software.

Fidelity requirements of simulations are often in conflict with an important constraint, namely, the cost of both development and operation. Deciding what the right level of fidelity is in any simulation project is tricky. The situation is even more complicated when we need to reuse legacy simulation components with varying degrees of fidelity.

When we start building models to build operational systems, the accuracy and precision requirements are unequivocally derivable from system requirements. Therefore, the level of detail or resolution that the system must support for its correct operation can be determined similarly to other derived requirements.

By and large, the fidelity issue is what separates simulation software from operational software; the issue is much less clear in simulation. Overlapping with the fidelity issue, the range of possibilities for the notion of time also sets simulations apart from other kinds of software. Operational systems, such as control systems, normally operate in real-time while for simulations real-time is just one of the possibilities. The smallest time step for the simulation clock is clearly a matter of resolution.

The simulation conceptual model, as we shall discuss in Chap. 5, is the most appropriate place to settle the fidelity and time issues. A simulation conceptual model also involves the domain entities, along with their attributes and actions, and the relationships between the entities in a level of detail in accordance with the targeted level of fidelity. These must carry over to the model of the simulation software to be developed. Taking an object-oriented view, for example, the tangible and intangible entities in the field may map to classes and the whole-part relationships between entities to aggregations between classes and so on. Armed with the techniques and tools of MDE, we can find a way of transforming the simulation conceptual model to a design model for the simulation system. For the logical data model part of design, the mapping can be easier to see as we can use our object oriented analysis and design (OOA&D) experience. For the behavioral part of design, however, the transition is less straightforward, and we may need help from conceptual scenarios. Chapter 8 shows how to put this intuition into practice.

As simulation engineers, we are interested in building simulation systems, which are the systems whose functionality is to unfold a model over time. Therefore, we would be interested in modeling the simulation systems themselves. This is the case when the part of reality that we target for modeling is the simulation itself as a software application, or a computer-based system, in general.

Modeling of digital systems has long been an area of active research and industrial practice. Modeling of computer and network systems for the purpose of performance evaluation, for example, has a long history (Kleinrock 1976). Modeling digital systems as finite-state machines for the purpose of model checking for safety and liveness properties turned out to be important to achieve reliability (Clarke et al. 1999). Modeling of object-oriented software for analysis and design purposes goes back to the earlier work by object-oriented methodologists that culminated in the development of UML (OMG 2015). Requirements of the modeling of computer-based or software-intensive systems that involve not only software but also hardware, people, and process elements led to the development of SysML (OMG 2012).

Many simulation systems today, such as training simulators for operators of all sorts of platforms and equipment, embedded simulators, and war games, fall into the category of software-intensive systems. Engineering of such systems requires more of a systems engineering effort, rather than a purely software engineering effort. Development of simulation systems can obviously benefit from the modeling technology available for software-intensive systems. Rewards would be even bigger when systems modeling is linked with simulation conceptual modeling.

The stepwise-refinement (also known as the top-down development) paradigm has a long pedigree in the history of software development (Wirth 1973). One might argue that there is a difference between specifying a system to be built and modeling a system to be built. A specification is a statement of the properties that the system to be built has to satisfy. Formally, it is an expression in some system of logic, for example, first-order logic or temporal logic. A model, on the other hand, is a blueprint for the system to be built. It is an expression in some modeling language. While the specification sets the problem, the model outlines the solution. Taking a pragmatic approach, in this book we leave out formal specification in the sense of logical statement, rather, we take a high-level abstract model as the starting point in simulation system development. For a reader with an interest in the formal methods connection, a correct-by-construction approach such as Event-B (Abrial 2010) is recommendable due to its support for the refinement of both data and behavioral aspects of state-based system descriptions with proofs of refinement steps.

Referring back to Fig. 1.1, we need to dig deeper into the relationship between the model of reality, which we want to simulate, and the model of the simulation software, which we want to run on a computer. The essence of applying MDE for simulation is to capture the relationship between these two models – one for simulation, one for construction, as model transformation.

1.4   Distributed Simulation

Often, the subject reality (simuland) inherently involves multiple interacting entities. Imagine a fleet of drones flying in formation. We can of course have one monolithic simulation model including all the drones and their interactions with each other and with the physical environment. An alternative might be to have individual models of each drone and the environment, and let these models interact with each other via a well-defined and agreed-upon interface. The second approach might be preferable for several reasons. First, the load of simulation can be shared by multiple processors. These processors can be distributed over a network, or can be housed on a single host computer. Roughly speaking, the latter leads to parallel simulation while the former leads to distributed simulation.

What distinguishes parallel simulation from distributed simulation in the M&S jargon is the former's emphasis on speed, which can be measured by the number of events processed per second. The speed-up is the ratio of the speed of parallel or distributed simulation to that of the sequential simulation. The primary concern for parallel simulation implementers is to speed up simulation execution to the extent possible with the available high-performance computing technology. Physical distribution usually works against performance as the processors need to communicate by exchanging messages over the network and the network is usually the bottleneck (rather than the processors). However, in situations where the message traffic is not overwhelming, which could be the case when we have loosely coupled models to run together, or replicated runs of the same model, the load sharing argument can win.

Mind you that being distributed is largely a point of view. Two flight simulators, located in faraway facilities, flown by pilot trainees in a coordinated flight exercise, no doubt constitute a distributed simulation. When we consider an individual flight simulator, we can see a single unitary aircraft simulator or a distributed structure with specialized models of the mission computer, sensors, controls, aerodynamical models, image generators for a variety of displays and so on, exchanging data and commands over a bus or local network. Hierarchical composition of systems is a well-known idea, and at which level in the hierarchy we start to have a distributed view of the system is up to the simulation engineer.

The second, perhaps more fundamental, reason to go distributed is that the nature of our models is distributed. The simuland is readily decomposable by its nature; all we need to do is let the simulation system architecture follow the structure of the simuland. This is quite apparent in a gaming situation, such as a war game, where the players interact with models and other players in their own workstations, connected through a network. In general, human-in-the-loop simulations for the purpose of team training tend to be distributed.

In some cases, some simulation components require special hardware located in certain hosts on a network. Visualization needs, location of certain databases and related services (say, message format conversion), location of required storage (e.g. large disks for logging), all lead to a distributed configuration for the simulation system.

An additional advantage of working with composite models rather than big monolithic models is reusability. In many cases, some dependable models are already existing and we would like to reuse them in a new setting. To be sure, composition of models can take place in a centralized setting as well. By and large, distribution promotes the loosely coupled approach that facilitates model development by modules and composition of those modules.

Distributed simulation promotes heterogeneity and dispersion, linking simulation components of various types (e.g. discrete vs. continuous) at multiple locations to create a virtual environment (battlefields, multi-player games, multi-agent systems, virtual factories, supply chains, etc.) with a common notion of space and time. Networked virtual environments are early examples of distributed simulation systems (Singhal and Zyda 1999).

In general, engineers can leverage the known benefits of distributed systems, such as fault tolerance, for simulation. However, they must face the known challenges, too, such as interoperating heterogeneous system components.

In this book, we focus on distributed simulations, which are composite simulations that consist of multiple individual simulations distributed over a network of hosts.

1.5   Time and Change

The reality we are interested in modeling inevitably has a time dimension. For many phenomena in the physical world that we experience directly, time seems to be flowing continuously. Consider, for example, the motion of a ball on a billiards table. The movement of the ball from the instant it is hit by the cue until it stops or falls into one of the holes would seem like a continuous motion. In fact, classical physics-based models of the ball's motion would assume the time as an independent variable ranging over the domain of non-zero real numbers. The smooth motion of the ball would undergo an abrupt change as it hits another ball or bounces off the edge of the table. An observer can record the instants of such events along the time axis. We can define the state of the ball at a time instant t as a vector comprising the ball's position on the table, and its translational and rotational velocity. The state of the ball goes through continuous changes as time flows and instantaneous changes as it experiences events.

When we model such a system we need to account for both continuous developments in state as well as abrupt changes. Such abrupt, instantaneous changes in state are brought about by discrete events. Thus we have the notion of time that keeps increasing continuously (with unit speed) and the system state that is continuously changing with time and instantaneously changing in response to discrete events.

In some cases, one may be able to simplify the situation by ignoring one or the other aspect of time and state change, and arrive at a continuous time model or discrete event model. Continuous time models frequently arise in scientific and engineering domains and differential equations are the modeling technique of choice. Discrete event models frequently arise in the modeling of service and manufacturing systems and social systems; various sorts of state-based formalisms, e.g. Petri nets, are used. Going back to the billiards example, if we are interested in foreseeing when and where two balls will collide we need to maintain the notion of state continuously changing with time but also subject to discrete events that can happen any moment in time. Formal groundwork has been laid for such models, called hybrid automata. We refer the reader to Alur et al. (1993) for the fundamentals of hybrid systems modeling.

Models with continuous time and continuously changing state variables can be quite satisfactory from the modeler's perspective, but from the simulation engineer's perspective there is a problem: A continuous variable is impossible to realize as is on a digital computer due to the limited precision of floating point number representations. Fortunately, an extensive body of knowledge on numerical methods exist that allow the simulation engineers to solve approximately the models expressed as various kinds of differential equations up to desired accuracy, limited by the precision of floating point number representation on the computer, by making the size of time steps sufficiently small.

What if we let the time variable take on integer values only? This can make sense, for example, when we are modeling a synchronous digital circuit, which is driven by a hardware clock. This amounts to deciding to ignore what happens between two successive time instants, say t and $t + 1$. Then the state variables can only be updated at those instants of time, at the clock ticks. Such system models are known as discrete-time models. The mathematical tool of choice to express such models is difference equations (Luenberger 1979).

Once we switch to a discrete notion time, it would seem easier to accommodate discrete events. After all, the ticking of the clock is just another kind of discrete event. The catch is, although ordinary discrete events can occur any time in princi-ple, they can only be processed when the clock tick comes.

Once we have the notion of time progressing in regular intervals we may wonder if the intervals can be allowed to be irregular. Indeed this is possible, in so-called event-driven simulations, quite popular for discrete event system simulation, for example, in queuing system simulations. Instead of letting the time variable (the simulation clock) advance on its own accord, we allow it advance only when an event happens. We leave the thorough treatment of time advancement mechanisms to (Fujimoto 2000).

Most examples in this book assume that an activity scanning mechanism is in place, that is, the time will advance in regular intervals (hence, we have discrete time) and the continuous developments during an interval will be calculated by solving relevant differential equations in smaller step sizes.

1.6 History

The early efforts of US Defense Community on developing distributed simulation technology culminated in the SIMNET (Simulation Networking) project. SIMNET's vision was to create a new generation of networkable simulators. Starting from late 70s till the late 80s, for about a decade, the technological foundations of distributed simulation, from communication protocols to dead reckoning algorithms, were developed (Cosby 1995).

First conceptual demonstration of distributed interactive simulation was con-ducted in 1984 (see Fig. 1.2). Then it was 1985, when the out-of-the-window graph-ics were integrated to the distributed simulation, and in 1986, SIMNET demonstrated a platoon-level scenario. When SIMNET project ended, it was noted that there were 250 simulators installed at 11 sites, seven of which in the US and the rest in Europe (Miller and Thrope 1995).

It was 1993, when the simulation communication protocol, developed in SIMNET to connect simulators, became an industry standard: IEEE 1278 Distributed Interactive Simulation (DIS) Standard Protocols (IEEE 1993). DIS is a message passing protocol standard that defines the messages and the procedures for com-munication among the simulators. It specifies standard message packets called

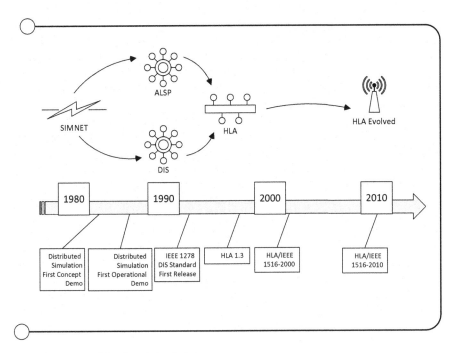

Fig. 1.2 History of distributed simulation

Protocol Data Units (PDUs). PDUs are transmitted over the network from simulator to simulator. Among a number of PDUs specified by the standard, most commonly used ones are Entity State, Fire, Detonation, and Simulation Management PDUs.

Although a lot had been achieved in SIMNET effort, the focus was on linking individual weapon simulators for operator/pilot training, not the aggregate-level combat simulations, which are for high level commander training. These aggregate level simulations had their challenges of being distributed and run in an unprecedented scale. It was 1990, when DARPA (Defense Advanced Research Projects Agency) sponsored another effort, Aggregate Level Simulation Protocol (ALSP), to target distributed simulation of aggregate level simulations. Some of the unique requirements of ALSP were including time management, data management, and architecture independence. ALSP brought many concepts that then became the foundations of High Level Architecture (HLA), such as objects, attributes, interactions, confederation, confederation model, and an infrastructure software (Weatherly et al. 1996) (Wilson and Weatherly 1994).

Further vision was presented in U.S. Department of Defense (DoD) Modeling and Simulation Master Plan (DoD 1995) as creating a common technological framework for simulation development using experience from DIS and ALSP efforts. It was 1995 when developing a high level architecture to facilitate interoperability among simulations as well as operational systems was set as a target. In 1996, initial technical architecture was drafted. The organization that undertook the development of the architecture, called Architecture Management Group (AMG), was composed of major defense modeling and simulation bodies. The HLA effort first focused on developing a baseline that will support early prototyping of developed technologies. By the end of 1996, four prototype federations (protofederations) that ran over the Runtime Infrastructure (RTI) prototype were developed. These were the Platform, Joint Training, Analysis, and Engineering Protofederations (Dahmann et al. 1997). In 1998, HLA became a DoD standard, and the reference RTI implementation for HLA version 1.3 (DMSO 1998) was released. Then in 2000, HLA became an IEEE standard and named as Modeling & Simulation (M&S) High Level Architecture IEEE 1516-2000 Series (IEEE 2000a, b, c).

After the IEEE release, HLA gained wider visibility and acceptance all over the world. It has been employed not only by military projects but also by civilian applications albeit on a much smaller scale (Boer et al. 2009). Alternative implementations, both proprietary and open-source, of RTI are available for the user communities with a wide range of requirements. Simulation Interoperability Standards Organization (SISO) became one of the major platforms that hosts working groups and conducts conferences to discuss and evolve the related standards and recommendations. New generation HLA is called *HLA Evolved*. After years of discussions and constant feedback from the implementers, and in an effort to accommodate the emerging service-oriented computing paradigm, HLA Evolved was published in 2010 as IEEE 1516.2010 series (IEEE 2010a, b, c).

1.7 Standards

DIS (IEEE 1278.1a) protocol is an application protocol originally approved in 1992 by IEEE. All the related IEEE 1278 standards are summarized in Table 1.1. A set of PDUs, used for different purposes, are predefined in the standard. If a new PDU type is required due to changing requirements, then the new PDUs should be defined and added to these standards.

Table 1.1 IEEE 1278 standards

Standard	Explanation
IEEE 1278.1	IEEE Standard for Distributed Interactive Simulation – Application Protocols was approved in 1995. IEEE 1278.1 is a revision and designation of the original 1278 Standard approved in 1992
IEEE 1278.1a	IEEE Standard for Distributed Interactive Simulation – Application Protocols was approved by IEEE in 1998
IEEE 1278.2	IEEE Standard for Distributed Interactive Simulation – Communication Services and Profiles was approved by IEEE in 1995
IEEE 1278.3	IEEE Recommended Practice for Distributed Interactive Simulation – Exercise Management and Feedback was approved by IEEE in 1996
IEEE 1278.4	IEEE Trial-Use Recommended Practice for Distributed Interactive Simulation – Verification, Validation, and Accreditation was approved by IEEE in 1998

Table 1.2 IEEE 1516 standards

Standard	Explanation
IEEE 1516-2010	IEEE Standard for Modeling and Simulation (M&S) HLA Framework and Rules, 18 August 2010
IEEE 1516.1-2010	IEEE Standard for M&S HLA Federate Interface Specification, 18 August 2010
IEEE 1516.2-2010	IEEE Standard for M&S HLA Object Model Template (OMT) Specification, 18 August 2010
IEEE 1516.3-2003	IEEE Recommended Practice for HLA Federation Development and Execution Process, 23 April 2003
IEEE 1516.4-2007	IEEE Recommended Practice for Verification, Validation, and Accreditation of a Federation: An Overlay to the HLA FEDEP, 20 December 2007 (IEEE-1516.4-2007 2007)

Table 1.3 Other HLA standards

Standard	Explanation
SISO-STD-004-2004	SISO Standard for Dynamic Link Compatible (DLC) HLA API Standard for the HLA Interface Specification (version 1.3). Reaffirmed in December 8, 2014
SISO-STD-004.1-2004	SISO Standard for Dynamic Link Compatible HLA API Standard for the HLA Interface Specification (IEEE 1516.1 version). Reaffirmed in December 8, 2014

Table 1.4 DS standards

Standard	Explanation
IEEE Std 1730-2010	IEEE Recommended Practice for Distributed Simulation Engineering and Execution Process (DSEEP), approved September 30, 2010. Revision of IEEE Std 1516.3–2003
IEEE Std 1730.1-2013	IEEE Recommended Practice for Distributed Simulation Engineering and Execution Process Multi-Architecture Overlay (DMAO), approved August 23, 2013

HLA standard comes in three volumes, namely, the HLA Framework and Rules Specification (IEEE 2010a), the HLA Object Model Template (IEEE 2010c), and the HLA Federate Interface Specification (IEEE 2010b). HLA Framework and Rules specifies the elements of systems design and introduces rules for a proper distributed simulation systems design. The second volume, HLA Object Model Template, presents the mechanism to specify the data model – the information produced and consumed by the elements of the distributed simulation. The last volume, HLA Federate Interface Specification, introduces the functional interfaces that enable distributed simulation execution. Thus this standard specifies the capabilities of the software infrastructure of HLA (i.e. RTI). The IEEE standard embodies five related standards shown in Table 1.2.

Moreover, there exist some standards supporting HLA from other organizations. Table 1.3 summarizes those standards.

Later standardization efforts focus on the generalization of some HLA principles to distributed simulation. One is the Recommended Practice for Distributed Simulation Engineering and Execution Process (DSEEP). See Chap. 4 for an overview. Table 1.4 presents those standards.

1.8   Tools

Throughout the book, mainly, we will use a toolset to demonstrate the practical implementation and development aspects of the case studies. Therefore, here we briefly introduce the tools before summarizing the chapters. For a detailed account and use of those tools, please refer their related documentation. The toolset consists of a freeware application, called SimGe, and an open source library, called RACoN. The toolset is specifically developed to support lab activities in a graduate level distributed simulation course. Therefore, the intended use of the toolset is for education, where the students can develop HLA-based simulation projects during a one-semester course.

1.8.1   RACoN

Developing a custom-made abstraction layer (wrapper) over HLA RTI is a popular approach in many HLA-based distributed simulation development projects, since it offers more portable and easier to use methods. In this regard, RACoN (Rti Abstraction COmponent for .Net) is a wrapper targeted for Microsoft .NET environments (Microsoft .NET 2014), where it encapsulates the entire RTI low-level class interface in order to simplify the repetitive, error-prone, and low-level implementation details of the HLA federate interface. With the help of RACoN, any .NET language can be selected to implement an HLA federate (i.e. a simulation component).

The RACoN component is federation independent and can be used in all types of federates, but its current limitation is that it supports only a subset of federate interface specification of HLA 1.3 standard. The RACoN library and its documentation are available at the RACoN website (RACoN 2015).

1.8.2   SimGe

SimGe (SIMulation GEnerator) is a simulation design and development environment for HLA based distributed simulations. SimGe includes an object model editor and a code generator. The editor allows the user to create and modify object models and to import and export HLA related files (i.e. Federation Execution Details (FED),[1] Federation Object Model (FOM) Document Data (FDD)[2]), which contains configuration data for the federation execution. The code generator automatically generates code for the target platform, which is RACoN in our case.

---

[1] FED file is used by RTIs that conform to the HLA 1.3 specification.See Chap. 3.

[2] FDD file is used by RTIs that conform to the HLA 1516 specification. See Chap. 3.

Currently, SimGe can generate all the RACoN compatible classes of a simulation object model using the federation execution configuration files (i.e. FDD/FED). A preview of the tool and sample projects can be obtained from SimGe website (2015).

1.9 Book Outline

1.9.1 Summary of Chapters

The book is structured as follows. This chapter presents an introduction to the essential concepts of modeling and simulation, while highlighting DS as the focal area of interest. Chapter 2 introduces the fundamental concepts, principles, and processes of MDE. Chapter 3 gives an introduction to the HLA. These three chapters together lay the technical background for integrating two different disciplines, DS and MDE. Chapter 4 presents a road map for building and deploying a distributed simulation application in accordance with the MDE perspective, and it introduces a process model based on the principles and best practices of MDE. The Chaps. 5, 6, 7, 8, 9, and 10 elaborate on the process model presented in Chap. 4. Chapter 5 explains conceptual modeling from the MDE perspective, and it presents a methodology and a technical framework to develop conceptual models. Chapter 6 introduces the concept of federation (simulation environment) architecture. By demonstrating the formalization of a federation architecture using the metamodeling concepts, we promote automated code generation and semi-automated model validation over the machine processable specifications of a simulation federation architecture. Chapter 7 focuses on federate architectures and presents a practical approach to the design of federations (i.e. simulation member design) by applying a well-known architectural style called layered architecture. After introducing the model-driven scenario development process, Chap. 8 explains the major concepts of simulation scenarios and discusses the main activities in scenario management in a distributed simulation. Chapter 9 delineates the nature of MDE based implementation activities, including model development, model checking, code generation and integration, and testing. Chapter 10 introduces simulation evolution and modernization and relates it with software modernization approaches. It promotes Architecture Driven Modernization (ADM) for simulation modernization. Finally, Chap. 11 examines potential synergies among the agent, DS, and MDE methodologies, highlighting potential avenues of future research and development at the intersection of these three fields.

1.9.2 Typeface Conventions

This book uses the following typeface conventions:

- All code examples/snippets are printed in Sans serif Font.
- At the first introduction or definition of a major term, the term is shown in *italics*.

- All references to classes, attributes, and other elements of a model are shown in `Courier New` Font.
- *Italics* is used for emphasized words or phrases in running.

1.10 Summary

In this chapter we presented an introduction to the concepts and principles of distributed simulation. We also presented the book structure and introduced the toolset used throughout the book.

References

Abrial, J.-R. (2010). *Modeling in Event-B: System and software engineering.* Cambridge: Cambridge University Press.

Alur, R., Courcoubetis, C., Henzinger, T. A., & Ho, P. H. (1993). Hybrid automata: An algorithmic approach to the specification of hybrid systems. In: *Hybrid systems* (Lecture notes in computer science, Vol. 736). s.l.:Springer-Verlag, pp. 209–229.

Banks, J., Carson, J. S., II, Nelson, B. L., & Nicol, D. M. (2010). *Discrete-event system simulation* (5th ed.). Upper Saddle River: Pearson Education.

Boer, C. A., de Bruin, A., & Verbraeck, A. (2009). A survey on distributed simulation in industry. *Journal of Simulation, 3*, 3–16.

Bryant, B. R., et al. (2011). Challenges and directions in formalizing the semantics of modeling languages. *ComSIS, 8*(2), 225–253.

Cassandras, C. G., & Lafortune, S. (2010). *Introduction to discrete event systems* (2nd ed.). Boston: Springer.

Chapman, S. J. (2015). *MATLAB programming for engineers* (5th ed.). Boston: Cengage Learning.

Clarke, E., Grumberg, O., & Peled, D. (1999). *Model checking.* Cambridge, MA: MIT Press.

Cosby, L. (1995). *SIMNET: An insiders' perspective.* [Online] Available at: http://oai.dtic.mil/oai/oai?verb=getRecord&metadataPrefix=html&identifier=ADA294786. Accessed 19 Dec 2015.

Cross, D. C. (1999). Report from the fidelity implementation study group. *Spring Simulation Interoperability Workshop.* Orlando: SISO.

Dahmann, J. S., Fujimoto, R. M., & Weatherly, R. (1997). *The department of defense high level arhitecture* (pp. 142–149). *Proceedings of the 1997 Winter Simulation Conference.* Atlanta: IEEE

DMSO. (1998). *High level architecture* (1.3 ed.). DMSO.

DoD. (1995). *Modeling and simulation (M&S) master plan.* U.S. DoD

Fujimoto, R. M. (2000). *Parallel and distributed simulation systems.* New York: Wiley.

IEEE. (1993). *Protocols for distributed interactive simulation applications – Entity information and interaction* (1993 ed.). New York: IEEE

IEEE. (2000a). *IEEE standard for modeling and simulation (M&S) high level architecture (HLA) – Framework and rules.* New York: IEEE

IEEE. (2000b). *IEEE standard for modeling and simulation (M&S) high level architecture (HLA) – Federate interface specification.* New York: IEEE

IEEE. (2000c). *IEEE standard for modeling and simulation (M&S) high level architecture (HLA)- Object model template (OMT) specification.* New York: IEEE

IEEE. (2010a). *IEEE standard for modeling and simulation high level architecture (HLA)– Framework and rules.* New York: IEEE

IEEE. (2010b). *IEEE standard for modeling and simulation (M&S) high level architecture (HLA) – Federate interface specification.* New York: IEEE

IEEE. (2010c). *IEEE standard for modeling and simulation high level architecture (HLA) – Object model template (OMT) specification.* New York: IEEE

IEEE-1516.4-2007. (2007). *IEEE recommended practice for verification, validation, and accreditation of a federation: An overlay to the high level architecture federation development and execution process.* New York: IEEE

Kelton, W. D., Sadowski, R., & Zupick, N. (2014). *Simulation with Arena* (6th ed.). McGraw-Hill Education.

Kleinrock, L. (1976). *Queueing systems, volume 2: Computer applications.* New York: Wiley.

Law, A. M. (2007). *Simulation modeling & analysis* (4th ed.). Singapore: McGraw-Hill.

Luenberger, D. G. (1979). *Introduction to dynamic systems: Theory, models, and applications.* New York: Wiley.

Microsoft .NET. (2014). *MS.NET.* [Online] Available at: http://www.microsoft.com/net. Accessed 19 Aug 2015.

Miller, D., & Thrope, J. A. (1995). SIMNET: The advent of simulator networking. *Proceedings of IEEE, 83*(8), 1114–1123.

OMG. (2012). *OMG systems modeling language (SysML) version 1.3.* Object Management Group (OMG).

OMG. (2015). *OMG unified modeling language (OMG UML) version 2.5.* Object Management Group (OMG).

RACoN. (2015). *RACoN web site.* [Online] Available at: https://sites.google.com/site/okantopcu/simge. Accessed 19 Dec 2015.

Rice, S., et al. (2005). The SIMSCRIPT III programming language for modular object-oriented simulation. In: M. E. Kuhl, N. M. Steiger, F. B. Armstrong, & J. A. Joines (Eds.), *Proceedings of the 2005 winter simulation conference.* Orlando: s.n., pp. 621–630.

Rozenberg, G. (1997). *Handbook of graph grammars and computing by graph transformation, volume 1: Foundations.* Singapore: World Scientific.

SimGe. (2015). *SimGe web site.* [Online] Available at: https://sites.google.com/site/okantopcu/simge. Accessed 19 Dec 2015.

Singhal, S., & Zyda, M. (1999). *Networked virtual environments: Design and implementation.* Reading: Addison-Wesley.

Sokolowski, J. A., & Banks, C. A. (2010). *Modeling and simulation fundamentals.* Hoboken: Wiley.

Weatherly, R. M., et al. (1996). Advanced distributed simulation through the aggregate level simulation protocol. In *Proceedings of the twenty-ninth Hawaii international conference on system sciences* (pp. 407–415). IEEE.

Wilson, A. L., & Weatherly, R. M. (1994). *The aggregate level simulation protocol: An evolving system* (pp. 781–787). Winter Simulation Conference Proceedings. IEEE.

Wirth, N. (1973). *Systematic programming: An introduction.* Englewood Cliffs: McGraw-Hill.

Chapter 2
Model Driven Engineering

The objective of this chapter is to introduce the fundamental concepts, principles and processes of Model Driven Engineering (MDE). The role of MDE for code generation in simulation software engineering, interoperability, model replicability and computational reproducibility are discussed. Different modeling levels and operations such as refactoring, refinement and transformation are examined to outline various MDE use cases in simulation software engineering.

2.1 Introduction

Models are abstractions of phenomena, an entity or a system, which serves as the model's referent. Simulation models are dynamic models that define the referent's behavior over time. Simulation is the act of using simulators or simulation engines to generate the dynamic behavior of the referent (Davis and Anderson 2004) using various behavior generation and time-flow management techniques such as discrete-time, discrete-event, activity scanning or process interaction.

Models are paramount to understanding, exploring and analyzing the behavior of complex systems. The MDE methodology (Schmidt 2006; Gaševic et al. 2009) provides a foundation to use models as primary elements in generating and managing a distributed simulation system. Among the potential applications of MDE in simulation engineering include the generation of simulation software code via transformation and stepwise refinement of models, improvement of interoperability among distributed simulation systems via bridge models that serve as transformations or reverse engineering of models to generate platform-neutral abstract representations for analysis and targeted transformation (Atkinson and Kuhne 2003; Sendall and Kozaczynski 2003).

In contrast to other development paradigms such as object-oriented or agent-oriented development where object or agents serve as the building blocks, the MDE

© Springer International Publishing Switzerland 2016

O. Topçu et al., *Distributed Simulation*, Simulation Foundations, Methods and Applications, DOI 10.1007/978-3-319-03050-0_2

methodology uses models and relations among them as the primary artifacts of the development process. Multiple models at different levels, scales and for different aspects of a system co-exist and serve as the key building blocks and constructs of a simulation system. The process heavily relies on the use of models and model engineering allowing principled and systematic production and transformation of models.

The MDE methodology implies that during simulation software engineering it is possible to move from one technical space (Gaševic et al. 2009) to another. A technical space represents the context for the specification, implementation and deployment of simulation applications. Moving from one technical space to another is the core problem in model replication and reproducibility. Transformation across technical spaces requires alignment of concepts in one modeling context to the constructs of the target (Brambilla et al. 2012). Proper alignment of modeling constructs requires explicit specification and use of the syntax and semantics of modeling languages. The MDE methodology promotes meta-modeling as a strategy to facilitate definition of modeling languages. Transformations, which represent the other crucial component of MDE, apply at the meta-modeling level (Gonzalez-Perez and Henderson-Sellers 2008) to allow definition of mappings between different models.

The rest of the chapter is structured as follows. In Sect. 2, we examine the basic concepts and principles of MDE. Section 3 introduces three different types of models and modeling languages within the MDE paradigm. The Model Driven Architecture (Mellor et al. 2002) is overviewed in Sect. 4 as an exemplary MDE framework to explain the abstract concepts outlined in Sect. 2. Section 5 introduces the model transformation concept and its generic process model in detail. In Sect. 6, various applications of MDE are discussed to illustrate how MDE can serve multiple purposes in a simulation system engineering lifecycle. Finally, in Sect. 7, we conclude by summarizing the contributions of the MDE perspective and point out emergent synergies between MDE, distributed simulation and systems engineering.

2.2   The Methodology and the Principles of MDE

MDE provides a structured methodology for simulation system development. Figure 2.1 shows the main aspects of the methodology in a layered structure. The columns in the figure denote the conceptualization dimension, whereas the rows indicate the levels in the implementation dimension.

The *application-level* (Brambilla et al. 2012) in the conceptualization space focuses on the definitions of models, the application of the code generation and transformation mechanisms, and the generation of the code and scripts that use a specific platform (e.g., HLA, DEVS). The *application-domain* focuses on the specification of the modeling language as well as the transformation rules for mapping conceptualization space to the realization (implementation) space. Transformation

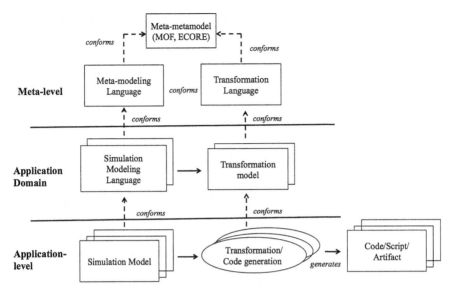

Fig. 2.1 A multi-level view of the MDE methodology

rules can also be defined to map concepts in one technical space (e.g., SimuLink) to another (e.g., DEVS). Similar to the way we define simulation models as abstractions of a phenomena in the real world, *metamodels* are used to conceptualize and define the abstract syntax of modeling languages. That is, a meta-model is yet another abstraction that specifies the properties of the model itself. A model conforms to its meta-model in a way that a program conforms to the grammar of the programming language in which it is developed. The *meta-level* in the conceptualization space provides facilities and languages (i.e., meta-metamodels) used in the specification of the meta-models to which models and transformations conform.

Within the implementation dimension, the *modeling level*, which is represented by the first row, is where the simulation models, meta-models and meta-meta-models are defined. The second level, which is comprised of transformation specifications, languages, and applications, is the *transformation* level that automates the derivation of the artifacts at the realization level. This level includes artifacts such as code, scripts and XML documents. The realization artifacts are deployed on platforms specific to the application domain.

The common strategy in MDE is based on the application of a sequence of transformations starting with application models down to the concrete realization of the simulation system. Besides the reuse of models and deployment of designs in alternative platform, MDE improves the reliability of simulation systems through correctness preserving transformations that allow substantiating the accuracy of realizations with respect to explicit constraints and assumptions defined in the abstract models. To facilitate the application of the MDE methodology shown in Fig. 2.1, models are defined in terms of an explicit modeling language, which in turn is specified in terms of a meta-modeling language. The transformations are executed using a set of rules, which are specified by using the constructs of a specific transformation language such as the Atlas Transformation Language (ATL) (Jouault and Kurtev 2006).

In light of the strategy advocated by the MDE methodology, the main principles underlying an MDE process are the following:

- Models must be defined in a well-defined notation allowing effective communication of their machine-readable abstract syntax.
- Specifications of simulations must be organized around a set of models, meta-models and associated transformations facilitating mappings from their abstract syntax to common standard models that bridge multiple platforms.
- Models of both the abstract syntax and the semantics of simulations must be explicitly defined to formulate meaningful and behavior-preserving mappings.
- For each modeling platform, using dedicated formats, syntactic mappers should inject simulation software as models. Similarly, extractors should be provided to map target abstract syntax onto target simulation software.
- Semantic mappers need to be provided to align the concepts, mechanisms and constraints in the source formalism to the concepts, mechanisms and constraints in the target formalism.

In Fig. 2.1, transformation languages, models and realizations are presented as critical pillars of the MDE methodology within the application-level, application domain and the meta-level of the conceptualization space. While transformations can be used for code generation, they can also be used to translate a model in one language to another language for various purposes, including replication of a simulation model to support cross-validation.

The MDE methodology implies that during simulation software engineering it is possible to move from one technical space to another. A *technical space* represents the context for the specification, implementation and deployment of simulation applications. Moving from one technical space to another is the core problem in model transformation (Sendall and Kozaczynski 2003). Transformation across technical spaces requires the alignment of concepts in one modeling context to the constructs of the target. Proper alignment of modeling constructs requires explicit specification and use of the syntax and semantics of modeling languages. The MDE methodology promotes meta-modeling as a strategy to facilitate definition of modeling languages. Transformations, which represent the other crucial component of MDE, apply at the meta-modeling level to allow definition of mappings between different models.

Figure 2.2 depicts a framework for transforming a model developed in a platform-specific SimuLink environment to an abstract platform-independent representation in Systems Modeling Language (SysML). In this example, a SimuLink model (e.g., RoboSoccer) defined in a specific format (e.g., SLX) is injected into the model management framework to derive a RoboSoccer model that conforms to the meta-model of the SimuLink language. For illustration, we choose the Atlas Model Management Architecture (AMMA) (Salay et al. 2007) to highlight the building blocks of the framework. The meta-model for the SimuLink model needs to be

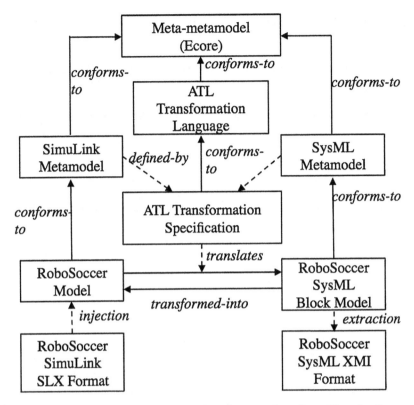

Fig. 2.2 Application of model transformation for cross-formalism (Gonzalez-Perez and Henderson-Sellers 2008) model generation

defined in terms of the meta-meta-model (i.e., ECORE) of AMMA. The injection of SLX-formatted original SimuLink file into the AMMA involves translation of the SLX format into XML Metadata Interchange? (XMI) representation that is consistent with the ECORE-based meta-model.

Similarly, the meta-model for the target SysML (Weilkiens 2011) models need to be defined and encoded within AMMA (Salay et al. 2007) to facilitate translation of constructs in the SimuLink domain to the target SysML constructs. The mapping between the source and target constructs is defined in terms of their meta-models and formally specified using a translation language. The Atlas Transformation Language (ATL) takes XMI representation of the SimuLink model as input and produces XMI specification of the SysML diagram(s) as output. The ATL program is also a model, and it conforms to a meta-model that in turn conforms to the ECORE meta-metamodel. The transformation strategy shown in Fig. 2.2 can be used for various purposes, including model recognition, model refactoring and model (re) generation.

- *Model recognition*: This step involves derivation from the platform-specific source (SimuLink) model an abstract syntax in the form of an XML representation, which in turn is transformed into a Platform- Independent Model (PIM) that captures the essential conceptual and design constructs of the solution that are isolated from the platform constraints.

- *Model refactoring*: Following the generation of PIMs, further refactoring and augmentation of models are necessary to derive abstract models with structural and behavioral constraints that are closer to the target domain. This may involve generation of state-based models for individual entities from multiple activity-flow specifications derived from the platform-specific models during the model recognition phase.
- *Model (re)generation*: The refactored and transformed PIMs in the model refactoring phase are then transformed onto platform-specific models in the target language. This requires extraction from abstract models an abstract syntax (e.g., XMI) that conforms to the metamodel of the target language. This abstract syntax is then translated into concrete syntax of the target language.

2.3   Types of Models, Modeling Languagesand Model Management

Two types of modeling languages are used in MDE: (1) Domain-specific Modeling Languages (DsML) (Van Deursen et al. 2000) and (2) General-purpose Modeling Languages (GpML). In contrast to general–purpose modeling languages, which are broadly applicable to across domains, domain-specific languages are intended for particular application domains. A wide variety of domain-specific languages exist from HTML, which is used in formatting web pages, to domain-specific modeling (specification) languages and domain-specific programming languages. Domain-specific modeling languages often have specific goals in design and implementation. A DsML can be a visual modeling and diagramming language such as those created by the Generic Eclipse Modeling System (e.g., Eclipse Modeling Framework) (Steinberg et al. 2008). Other examples of DSML include VHDL for hardware description languages, MatLab or Mathematica for mathematics and SQL for database access.

GpMLs are used and applied for developing models that can represent systems in a wide variety of domains. The typical example for such languages is the Unified Modeling Language (UML) (Pilone and Pitman 2009), which is a standard modeling language for software systems. Using UML various types of models can be developed to represent static and dynamic aspects of a software system. Similarly, SysML is intended for specifying systems structure and dynamics in a platform-independent manner.

Because modeling inherently involves abstraction, consideration of alternative levels of abstractions and aspects of a system lends itself to classifications of models and modeling languages based on an abstraction hierarchy. At the highest level of abstraction, models are expected to describe the problem domain without any reference to implementation-oriented and application-specific constructs. Next, the structure and behavior of the simulation application needs to be specified in terms of data, algorithms and coordination models without providing technical details pertaining to the implementation platform. At the concrete-level, technological and platform-specific constraints and aspects need to be provided to map abstract solutions onto concrete realizations over desired platforms (e.g., HLA, SimuLink). Separation of concerns in terms of multiple models at different levels of abstractions facilitate definition of transformations for mapping a model at a given abstraction level to another model specified at a different level. In Sect. 4, we illustrate how the Model Driven Architecture (Mellor et al. 2002) standard defined by the Object Management Group (OMG) categorizes models into computation-independent, platform-independent and platform-specific models based on their abstraction levels (Brambilla et al. 2012).

Besides the abstraction levels, models can be classified in terms of the aspects or dimensions of the system they intend to specify. The two dimensions of a system are its static structure and dynamic behavior.

- *Static models*: These models focus on the organizational structure and layout of the system, as well as its conceptual model defined in terms of concepts, attributes and associations (relations). An architectural model provides a specification of the gross organizational layout and style for the system (e.g., layered or client-server), whereas a conceptual model (e.g., UML class model) depicts the classification of concepts in terms of commonalities and differences.
- *Dynamic models*: Behavioral specifications focus on the execution sequence of actions (e.g., activity-flow), the state transitions (e.g., state-charts) and interaction dynamics (e.g., collaboration and sequence diagrams) that depict coordination and cooperation among structural components of the system. Dynamic models explicitly specify the behavior of a system over time in terms of events, activities and processes. Event scheduling models (e.g., event graphs), activity scanning and process interaction models define time flow mechanisms that control the generation of a model's behavior over time.

Although modeling platforms (e.g., UML) provide distinct diagram types that allow specifying different dimensions and aspects of a system, models of multiple aspects are coordinated, facilitating inter-diagram consistency and completeness analysis. Most general-purpose modeling environments provide a suite of languages with coordinated notations complementing each other. A modeling language is defined in terms of three key components: (1) Abstract syntax, (2) Concrete syntax and (3) Semantics (Table 2.1).

Next, we examine the Model Driven Architecture standard promoted by the OMG for designing systems based on the MDE principles and practices.

Table 2.1 Elements of a modeling language

Abstract syntax	Describes the structure of the modeling language in terms of primitives and rules for combining these primitives to form complex model structures. This is similar to the use of a grammar in specifying the syntax of a programming language
Concrete syntax	Defines the specific representation (e.g., textual, visual). For instance, A visual concrete syntax requires using diagrams to build models. There can be multiple concrete syntax representation for a given abstract syntax
Semantics	Specifies the meaning of elements defined in the language as well as the meaning of different ways of composing these elements. Semantics often allows specification of the interpretation of structural elements of the model

2.4   Model Driven Architecture

Model Driven Architecture (MDA) (Mellor et al. 2002) is a system design methodology launched by the OMG for the development of software-intensive systems. Using guidelines to structure and use specification, which are expressed as models, MDA promotes domain engineering and MDE. The premise of MDA is that it supports the principles presented in Sect. 2 and is enabled by existing OMG specifications such as the UML, Meta Object Facility (MOF), the UML profiles such as SysML and the CORBA Component Model.

In MDA, three specific abstraction levels are defined:

- *Computation-Independent Model (CIM)*: The highest level of abstraction of a simulation system includes the specification of the context and the general problem domain specification independent of the computational aspects. CIM serves as a domain vocabulary that indicates the essential and generic concepts that are common among applications in the selected problem domain. It serves as a reference model describing the entities and constraints expected of any solution in that domain of interest. Some of the concepts may not even be transferred into a computational realization, but they serve as artifacts to devise a precise, concise, understandable and valid model of the system of interest. Such domain models facilitate communication and agreement between the stakeholders and simulation software engineers with respect to essential features, constraints and concepts of the problem domain.
- *Platform-Independent Model (PIM):* This is the modeling level where the behavior and structure of the simulation application are defined in a way that is independent of the implementation platform (e.g., HLA, RePast) and environment. The use cases and scenarios of the simulation application are clearly defined and are specified in terms of platform-independent modeling languages (e.g., DEVS, event graphs, UML, SysML). The specification of PIM should exhibit a sufficient degree of independence from the realization environments so that the models can be mapped to one or more concrete implementation platforms.
- *Platform-Specific Model (PSM):* Deployment of a model on a simulation engine and infrastructure requires the provision of information regarding the behavior

and structure of the implementation in terms of the features and constructs of a specific platform. PSMs are technology-aware detailed design and implementation models of a simulation application.

The MDA approach to simulation software engineering involves defining the specification of the problem domain using a CIM and application domain with a PIM specified in terms of either a DSML or a Platform-Specific Modeling Language (PSML). Given a platform model corresponding to a technical simulation infrastructure such as HLA (Dahmann et al. 1997), the PIM is translated to one or more executable PSMs. The transformations are explicitly modeled and executed in terms of formal mappings specified over the meta-models of the selected PIM and PSM.

MDA does not refer to the architecture of the system. Rather, it denotes the architecture of the standards and model specification formalisms that provide the technological basis for the application of MDE principles and practices. In MDA, the key for modeling is the general-purpose modeling language called UML. UML is a suite of languages allowing model builders to specify simulation application's structure and behavior in terms of several different diagram types. A set of domain-specific languages are also defined for addressing specific application domains (e.g., finance, power systems) or technical domains (e.g., service-oriented architectures, web-based simulation) by exploiting either meta-modeling or extensibility features provided through UML. For instance, OMG supports UML extensions through UML profiles and DSML through the use of Meta-Object Facility (MOF), which serves as a meta-metamodel.

2.5 Model Transformations

Along with models, model transformation constitutes the most crucial component of the MDE methodology. By allowing the formalization of the mappings between different models, or a model at different levels of abstraction, model transformations facilitate automation of translation across formalisms and syntax. Transformations are defined at the meta-modeling level and applied to models that conform to those meta-models. MDE environments provide languages for defining model transformations, so that model designers can use optimized, proven, effective strategies for specifying transformations. Transformation templates can be used to map constructs of a source meta-model to equivalent features of the target meta-model. Such templates can be customized and applied upon models by matching rules to constructs and elements of the models.

The strategies for defining such rules can vary depending on the sophistication of the MDE environment. Transformation rules can be produced as a model developed from scratch or can be a refinement of a generic specification template applicable to selected source and target modeling languages. Alternatively, transformation rules can be derived automatically out of higher-level mappings rules between models. This strategy requires (1) defining a mapping of elements of one model to another model (e.g., model weaving) and (2) automating the generation of the actual transformation through an interpreter or matcher that takes as input two model definitions and the mapping rules between them to produce the concrete transformations. The separation of the specification of the mapping from the concrete rule set facilitates application of the same mapping rules to multiple models that conform to the meta-models of the input models. Furthermore, this allows the developers to concentrate on the conceptual aspects and delegate the generation and application of the transformation rules to an automated matcher.

Another critical aspect of the MDE perspective and vision of "everything is a model" is that transformations are represented as models managed in a way similar to other models. That is, they conform to a meta-model, which is referred to as the Model-Transformation Language.

2.6   Applications of MDE

The practical applications of MDE in simulation engineering are diverse. The most widely known scenario is the automation of generation of artifacts, including simulation software in the simulation development lifecycle. However, one can leverage fundamental principles of MDE and its practices in a variety of contexts including system interoperability, reverse engineering, testing, as well as replicability and reproducibility of simulation models and experiments.

2.6.1   Automating Simulation Development

Simulation engineering starts from a high-level problem statement and conceptual domain model that initiates a process for the derivation of a running simulation application through intermediate steps that result in increasingly concrete and detailed artifacts. Representation of each and every artifact as a model and manipulation of these models in accordance with the MDE principles and practices bring many benefits and advantages to the development process.

Models capture and organize shared understanding of the system and facilitate unambiguous communication among team members. Besides, generation of simulation applications from models via model transformations improve the productivity while also reducing inconsistencies during stepwise refinement of the artifacts. However, to generate an executable simulation application from models requires transformation into executable models, which have clear and unambiguous operational semantics. Among the executable model specifications is *Executable UML*, which uses an action language that is similar to imperative pseudocode. The adopted action language for Executable UML (Mellor and Balcer 2002) is known as the Action Language for *fUML* or Alf. Such languages with precise operational semantics facilitate code generation and model interpretation.

The objective of *code generation* is to generate running simulation application code from higher-level models in a way similar to compilers that generate code from a source program defined in a programming language. Hence, model-driven code generation can be viewed as *model compilation*. The process for generating an executable model often involves using rule-based templates that once instantiated with elements in the model, generates the code.

Automated code generation has various advantages. The source-code is provided without sharing the conceptualization and the design, hence protecting the intellectual property of the modeler. The flexibility provided by the ability to map a model onto different platforms alleviates the risk of dependency to a specific vendor. Since simulation application is generated from high-level architectural and design models, the resultant simulation conforms to a selected architectural style, standard or reference model. Such conformance is enforced as a consequence of model-driven nature of simulation application generation. As a result, generated code becomes compliant with IT architectures and policies associated with various quality criteria such as security, reliability and fault-tolerance. Furthermore, models and code generators are much easier to maintain, manage and evolve than the source-code. On the other hand, source-code generated by model transformation may not be as readable as software developed by a programmer, and hence, simulation software engineers may be reluctant to accept and use such applications.

An alternative to code generation is *model interpretation*. Instead of generating code, the model's behavior is generated using an interpreter or simulator. For instance, the behavior of a state-chart model can be generated by a state-machine simulator, which interprets transitions and updates state variables in accordance with the actions associated with a transition. Also, since a model can be updated at run-time on the fly, dynamic model updating and adaptation is easier with model interpretation than with applications derived with code-generation. On the other hand, model interpretation is not as efficient as compiled source-code, because run-time translation and interpretation of high-level model expressions require additional time.

2.6.2 Model Replicability and Reproducibility

Another application domain for MDE is model replicability and reproducibility. Recent years have seen a proliferation of the use of simulation models in computational science. Most of these models have never been independently replicated by anyone but the original developer. Furthermore, there is a growing credibility gap due to widespread, relaxed attitudes in communication of experiments, models and validation of simulations used in computational research. Model-driven simulation engineering principles and model transformation concepts are adopted as solution strategies to improve replicability of models and reproducibility of experiments.

Reproducible research is a fundamental principle of the scientific method (Morin et al. 2012). It refers to the ability to reproduce the experiments, and, if needed, independently replicate computational artifacts associated with published work. Emergence of reproducibility as a critical issue is based on growing credibility gap due to widespread presence of relaxed attitudes in communication of the context, experiments and models used in computational science (Mesirov 2010). Replicability involves the implementation of a conceptual model in a simulation study that is already implemented by a scientist or a group of scientists. Unlike reproducibility of results by (re)using the original author's implementation via executable papers, workflow systems and repositories (Freire et al. 2011), or provenance-based infra-structures, replications creating a new implementation differ in some way (e.g., platform, modeling formalism, language) from the original. Yet the original and replicate are sufficiently similar so that experiments conducted on both generate results that achieve pre-specified similarity criteria: they cross-validate. The prem-ise of independent replication is based on the following observation. Although eventual exposure to the original model and its source code is important, if done too early, it may result in "groupthink" whereby the replicater, possibly unintentionally, adopts some of the original developer's practices: features of the original model are essentially "copied". In so doing, the replicater has failed to maintain scientific independence. In other situations, replicaters may have different implementation tools and infrastructure, or may be unfamiliar with the original model's platform.

Therefore, providing the ability to implement a conceptual model under specific experimental conditions and analysis constraints across multiple platforms and for-malisms is critical to lowering the barrier to – and enabling broader adoption of – the practice of reproducibility. Furthermore, by replicating a model and ignoring the biases of the original model, differences between the conceptual and implemented models may be easier to observe. To facilitate replicability, it is critical to provide the larger community with an extensible and platform neutral interchange language for specification, distribution and transformation of model, simulator and experi-mental frame elements. Support for – and a lowered technical barrier to – indepen-dent replication will enable computational experimentation to become more scientific. Cross-validation will demonstrate (or not) that the original findings and observed results are not exceptional.

2.6.3   *Model Composability and Simulation Interoperability*

In distributed simulation, interoperability refers to the ability of system models or components to exchange and interpret information in a consistent and meaningful manner. This requires both syntactic and semantic congruence between systems either through standardization or mediators that can bridge the syntactic and seman-tic gap between peer components. Such mediator or connector components should ensure both data-level interoperability (i.e., metadata/data interchange) and operational-level interoperability (i.e., behavioral specification). Common strate-gies for developing adapters involve the provision of standard APIs and connecting components through published interfaces that explicitly specify the required and provided services. This low-level connectors are often limited and do not achieve full data interoperability .

The use of MDE can provide a sound and comprehensive framework for defining connectors. By making the internal schema (i.e., meta-model) of each system explicit and then aligning them by matching or weaving concepts, we can leverage model-to-model transformations exploiting the matching information to export data conforming to the meta-model of the target system or component. While internal schema, structural specifications and behavioral models may be available along with the implementation of the simulation system, in their absence MDE methodology can also be supportive in deducing such models for transformation. By extracting the abstract syntax of the PSM of a system and then transforming it into a set of PSMs using MDE tools would be a first step to automate the derivation of high-level specifications. Such specifications could then be used to generate bridge models in terms of model transformation language, which serves as the meta-model for the translation rules that map the source data/behavioral specification to the target specification. Such mapping rules can be used as connector implementations in terms of mediator software components.

The implementation of a connector is achieved in terms of two components: syntactic mapping and semantic mapping. Syntactic mapping aims to cross from the technical space of Simulation A to the technical space of the homogeneous modeling domain within which semantic mapping takes place. Two types of projectors are used to inject and extract content to and from the modeling world. An *importer* translates a concrete message that conforms to the specific format used by a simulation component/system into a model that conforms to the meta-model of the simulation. An *exporter* works in the other direction, translating a message model to a message that conforms the format used by the target simulation component. Once a message is imported into the modeling domain, tools and methods of MDE can be applied. Within the MDE domain, semantic mapping aligns the concepts by using model-to-model transformation. The objective of this transformation is to express the concepts in the source domain by a set of equivalent domain concepts that can be interpreted by the target system. Meta-models for A and B can be manually generated from the message formats (XML schemas in the case of Service-Oriented Access Protocol (SOAP) where XML documents are used for message exchange). Also, for instance, if a generic bridge model from XML schemas to MDE metamodels that conform to a standard meta-metamodel is available, then transformations of XML-formatted documents to formats that conform to target meta-models can be automated.

2.6.4 Model Longevity and Modernization of Legacy Simulations

Many organizations are facing challenges in maintaining, managing and modernizing or replacing simulation systems and infrastructures that have been actively used for a long period of time. These simulation systems may continue to play critical roles in training, education, or decision-making, but they are often based on obsolete technology that makes them difficult to port and interoperate with applications developed using emergent advanced technologies. Modernization of such legacy simulation applications can take advantage of Model-Driven Reverse Engineering (MDRE) (Brambilla et al. 2012) to generate useful high-level representations and model-based views of systems. Provenance information is particularly important during the modernization of legacy simulation systems. Consider, for instance, the parallelization of legacy simulations in the presence of increasingly powerful multi-core systems.

Parallelization through model and code refactoring (transformation) generates efficient simulation software, while increasing complexity. However, increased complexity impacts understandability and results in simulation software that is hard to maintain. Therefore, provenance becomes critical when automated transformations are applied to abstract or concrete syntax of legacy systems. Provenance of a simulation system includes information about the process and transformations used to derive the new version of the software. It provides important documentation that is key to understanding, preserving and reproducing the transformation. Provenance-enabled model transformation strategies and simulation software evolution provenance can be leveraged to explain differences in multiple versions of the same simulation model. Among the critical challenges involved in capturing, modeling, storing and querying such provenance information for MDRE are the need for reduction of provenance overload and making the provenance information fine-grained.

The provenance management solution requires a capture mechanism, a representational model and an infrastructure for storage, access and queries.

- *Capture mechanism*: A major advantage of using the abstract syntax notation is that that it includes control and data dependencies depicted by reverse-engineered model views and therefore is tightly coupled to the source code. This enables development of a capture mechanism based on dependency graphs that are critical in identifying potential for concurrency.
- *Representation model*: The provision and formalization of the abstract syntax models and interface controls can present to the user a tree, where each edge between two nodes correspond to changes performed on the parent's abstract syntax representation. This change-based provenance representation model can record modification to control and data flow structures, similar to a database transaction log. For abstract syntax of the source code, such changes include an expression's or a statement's addition, deletion or addition of connection (i.e.,

data or control flow) between model constructs. The benefit of this approach is that it is concise and uses substantially small space, as compared to the alternative that requires storage of multiple versions of abstract syntax trees. This strategy can also be more convenient for presenting an abstract syntax model's evolution history as a tree, allowing maintenance engineers to return to previous versions in an intuitive manner for system understanding.

• *Storing, accessing and querying provenance data*: The ability to analyze simulation model and code refactorings and transformations allows querying transformed simulation system's provenance to compare and understand differences. Furthermore, alternative refactoring strategies can be defined and stored for analysis in one single model

2.7   Summary

In this chapter we presented a summary of concepts and principles of MDE, spanning from meta-models, model-transformation, types of models and modeling languages. Selected uses of MDE are overviewed to emphasize the role of MDE practices throughout the lifecycle of a simulation study. Besides the common use of MDE in code generation, potential roles of MDE in model replicability and reproducibility, as well as interoperability, reverse engineering and simulation system modernization, are highlighted.

References

Atkinson, C., & Kuhne, T. (2003). Model-driven development: A metamodeling foundation. *IEEE Software, 20*(5), 36–41.

Brambilla, M., Cabot, J., & Wimmer, M. (2012). *Model-driven software engineering in practice* (Synthesis lectures on software engineering). Morgan & Claypool Publishers.

Dahmann, J. S., Fujimoto, R. M., & Weatherly, R. M. (1997). The department of defense high level architecture. In *Proceedings of the winter simulation conference* (pp. 142–149). Atlanta: ACM.

Davis, P. K., & Anderson, R. H. (2004). Improving the composability of DoD models and simulations. *The Journal of Defense Modeling and Simulation: Applications, Methodology, Technology, 1*(1), 5–17.

Freire, J., Bonnet, P., & Shasha, D. (2011). Exploring the coming repositories of reproducible experiments: Challenges and opportunities. *Proceedings of the VLDB Endowment*, pp. 9–27.

Gaševic, D., Djuric, D., & Devedžic, V. (2009). Model driven engineering. In *Model driven engineering and ontology development*. Springer Berlin Heidelberg.

Gonzalez-Perez, C., & Henderson-Sellers, B. (2008). *Metamodelling for software engineering*. Wiley.

Jouault, F., & Kurtev, I. (2006). *Transforming models with ATL* (pp. 128–138). Springer Berlin Heidelberg.

Mellor, S. J., & Balcer, M. J. (2002). *Executable UML: A foundation for model-driven architecture*. Addison-Wesley Professional.

Mellor, S. J., Scott, K., Uhl, A., & Weise, D. (2002). Model-driven architecture. In *Advances in object-oriented information systems* (pp. 290–297). Springer Berlin Heidelberg.

Mesirov, J. P. (2010). Accessible reproducible research. *Science, 327*, 415–416.

Morin, A., et al. (2012). Shining light into black shining light into black boxes. *Science, 336*, 159–160.

Pilone, D., & Pitman, N. (2009). *UML 2.0 in a Nutshell*. O'Reilly Media.

Salay, R., et al. (2007). An eclipse-based tool framework for software model management. In *Proceedings of the OOPSLA workshop on eclipse technology eXchange* (pp. 55–59). New York: ACM.

Schmidt, D. C. (2006). Guest editor's introduction: Model-driven engineering. *Computer, 39*(2), 25–31.

Sendall, S., & Kozaczynski, W. (2003). Model transformation: The heart and soul of model-driven software development. *Software, 20*(5), 42045.

Steinberg, D., Budinsky, F., Merks, E., & Paternostro, M. (2008). *EMF: Eclipse modeling framework*. Pearson Education.

Van Deursen, A., Klint, P., & Visser, J. (2000). Domain-specific languages: An annotated bibliography. *Sigplan Notices, 35*(6), 26–36.

Weilkiens, T. (2011). *Systems engineering with SysML/UML: Modeling, analysis, design*. Morgan Kaufmann.

Chapter 3
High Level Architecture

The objective of this chapter is to provide a gentle introduction to High Level Architecture (HLA). HLA is a standard architectural framework for distributed simulation. It is an enabler for simulation reuse, interoperability and composability. In this chapter, various aspects of the standard will be reviewed to furnish user with a comprehensive introduction. Furthermore, a case study that demonstrates how to develop an object model for an HLA federation will be presented.

3.1 Introduction

As the historical perspective of distributed simulation is presented in Chap. 1, HLA is an IEEE standard and the latest version, called HLA Evolved, was published in 2010 as IEEE 1516.2010 series (IEEE 2010a, b, c). The major enhancements to IEEE 1516.2000 series was summarized as modular Federation Object Models (FOMs), web service support, fault tolerance support, smart update rate reduction and dynamic link compatibility (DLC) (Möller et al. 2008).

3.1.1 What Is HLA?

Its standard defines HLA as a simulation systems architecture that facilitates the reuse, interoperability and composability of simulations (IEEE 2010a). Interoperability and composability are the enablers of reuse. While interoperability can be defined as the capability of simulations to exchange information in a useful and meaningful way (Yilmaz 2007), composability is defined as the capability that enables selecting and assembling components in various combinations to achieve the system's objective (Davis and Anderson 2004).

© Springer International Publishing Switzerland 2016
O. Topçu et al., *Distributed Simulation*, Simulation Foundations, Methods and Applications, DOI 10.1007/978-3-319-03050-0_3

Cost effectiveness, quality and timeliness concerns have always promoted reuse of assets not only in simulation domain but also in all software intensive domains. Reuse, on the other hand, can only be achieved by assets that are designed for reuse. Interoperability and composability have long been addressed as the technical challenges of reuse. It can be noted that only interoperable assets can be composed together to build a system and reuse is nothing but using available assets as much as possible while composing or interoperating the systems.

As naively presented in Fig. 3.1, interoperability requires a means of communication between the interoperating entities; on the other hand, composability requires a specification of the interfaces to be composed. As well as the others, like Deutsches Institut für Normung (DIN) norms for screws and bolts or Morse code, simulation community required a shared specification that enables their products to interoperate and to be composed.

The motivation of HLA can be introduced as providing an enabling common architecture for distributed simulation (Kuhl et al. 1999). Thus the simulations, support utilities and live entities can be composed on a single infrastructure to achieve the federation objectives, which can be simulating a phenomena or training a pilot in an engagement scenario. Figure 3.2 pictures the common ways to integrate entities in a system. One is via pair-wise connections and the other one is over a shared bus that entities collectively use to communicate. Referring to the discussion in the HLA Tutorial (Pitch 2012), in pairwise connections, interoperating systems are tightly coupled to each other. Composability is pair specific. On the contrary, in a shared bus, interoperating systems are loosely coupled and composability is enabled over the services provided by the shared bus. HLA proposes standardization in shared bus by specifying the interfaces with the interconnected entities and the shared bus.

This shared simulation bus is called Runtime Infrastructure (RTI) and its task is to provide services for management of distributed simulation, entities and the data communication.

Standard introduces the architecture as "major functional elements, interfaces, and design rules, pertaining as feasible to all simulation applications and providing

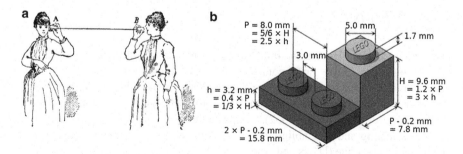

Fig. 3.1 (**a**) Interoperability and (**b**) Composability. © CMG Lee / http://commons.wikimedia. org/wiki/file:Lego_dimensions.svg / CC-BY-SA-3.0

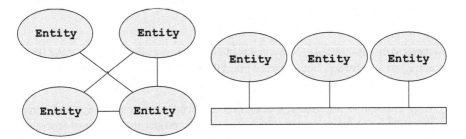

Fig. 3.2 Integration topologies (Pitch 2012)

a common framework within which specific systems architecture can be defined"
(IEEE 2010a). While functional elements specify the feature set that will be provided, interfaces define the way that user will consume them. Design rules introduce
the practices to be employed to use these functions over the described interfaces to
build up a system. This trio, namely functions, interfaces and rules, is described as
a common framework for developing simulations.

To wrap up, in a broad sense, the standard defines an architectural framework
whose aim is to enable component-based simulation development. The basic
assumptions and motivations underneath this effort are summarized as follows
(Dahmann et al. 1997).

- Diverse user requirements of today's simulation systems cannot be fulfilled by a
  single or monolithic structure. So HLA supports decomposing large simulation
  problems into smaller parts.
- Today's simulations sweep wide range of domains so no single set of developers
  possesses all required knowledge to develop the whole simulation. So HLA supports composing smaller parts to a big simulation system.
- Simulations can be used for more than one application some of which cannot be
  foreseen during development. So HLA supports reusable simulations that can be
  composed to various simulation systems that have different requirements.
- Simulations have long life spans so that the technology that uses them always
  changes. Thus, HLA provides an interface between the simulations and their
  users that insulates their use from the changing technology such as network protocols and operating systems.

No harm to stress it again that HLA was originated from the requirements of the
defense modeling and simulation community. Early requirements for distributed
simulations for collective training with later requirements for aggregate simulations
to make analysis resulted with a worldwide accepted simulation standard, HLA; but
the user community of the standard spread far beyond defense applications. Since
the standard was first published, there have been a number of distributed simulation
applications in homeland security, space, aeronautics, disaster recovery, air traffic
management, transportation systems, production and medical domains that make
use of it.

3.2   Basic Components

We need to discuss the basic components of HLA before going any further. As HLA is not a just a software, but a framework, HLA has a set of specifications, which mainly comprised of three major components:

- *HLA Framework and Rules*: specifies the elements of systems design and introduces "a set of ten rules that together ensure the proper interaction of federates in a federation and define the responsibilities of federates and federations" (IEEE 2010a).
- *Interface Specification*: The HLA Interface Specification defines "the standard services of and interfaces to the HLA runtime infrastructure (RTI). These services are used by the interacting simulations to achieve a coordinated exchange of information when they participate in a distributed federation" (IEEE 2010b). Thus this volume specifies the capabilities of the *RTI*.
- *Object Model Template (OMT)*: presents the mechanism to specify the data model – the information produced and consumed by the elements of the distributed simulation. More formally, the OMT describes "the format and syntax (but not content) of HLA object models" (IEEE 2010c).

Before presenting each major components in detail in the following sections, first, we will start with introducing some basic components such as federate and federations, runtime infrastructure and HLA rules in this section.

3.2.1   Federate and Federation

A *Federate (Application)* can be defined as an application that implements or conforms to the HLA standard. Federates consume and support the interfaces that are specified in the HLA Federate Interface Specification, thus can participate in a distributed simulation execution. When a federate participates in a federation execution, then it is called as *Joined Federate*. A federate application may join the same execution multiple times or may join into multiple executions, creating a new joined federate each time.

HLA does not mention how a federate is structured; rather it is interested only in the interface of the federate. Simulations of systems or phenomenon, simulation loggers, monitoring applications, gateways and live entities all can be a Federate. Federate technically can be defined as a single connection to the RTI. So we can pronounce it as a unit of reuse (IEEE 2010c) and a member of a federation. It can be a single process or, on contrary, can contain several processes running on more than one computer. It can be a data consumer, producer or both. Best practices advocate designing reusable set of simulation features as a federate. It can represent one platform such as an aircraft that simulates any type of aircraft in an aggregate level simulation or an F-16 flight dynamics model can be a federate in a full mission training simulator. In addition, legacy simulation application can be wrapped as a federate; thus, can participate in a federation execution.

Federation is the set of federates that share a common specification of data communication which is captured in Federation Object Model (FOM). As presented above in Fig. 3.3, federates, whose data communication requirements are documented in their Simulation Object Models (SOMs), are composed and interoperate over the Runtime Infrastructure throughout the Federation execution.

Federation Execution is a runtime instantiation of a federation; that is an actual simulation execution.

3.2.2 Runtime Infrastructure

Most architectures require infrastructures to enable their promises. HLA also comes with an infrastructure to enable inter-federate communication. RTI can be introduced as the HLA's underlying software infrastructure. It is the enabling software; the middleware. Federates interact with RTI through the standard services and interfaces to participate in the distributed simulation and exchange data. It supports the HLA rules with the services it provides over the interfaces specified in the Interface Specification.

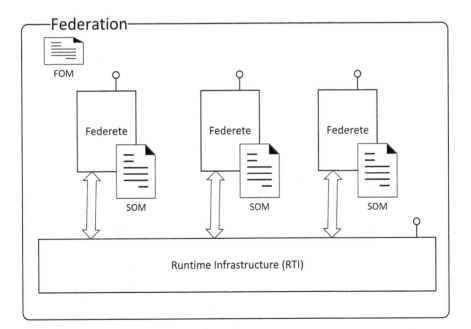

Fig. 3.3 Federation and federates

The first RTI, which was known as 0.X series, has been developed or prototyped by The MITRE Corporation, MIT Lincoln Laboratory, SAIC and Virtual Technology Corporation. In 1997, RTI 1.0 was released with C++ bindings. Then RTI 1.3 that implements the HLA version 1.3 was released in 1998 and made publicly available (Kuhl et al. 1999). Since then there have been more than 20 RTIs developed, half of which are open source. Some of the major commercial ones are MÄK RTI (MÄK 2015) from VT MÄK and pRTI™ from Pitch Technologies (Pitch 2012). And well maintained open source RTIs are CERTI (Noulard et al. 2009), Portico (2013), and Open HLA (Newcomb 2013).

3.2.3   HLA Rules

The principles that a distributed simulation system must adhere to be considered HLA compliant are specified in the standard (IEEE 2010a). They are categorized under two headings, namely federation rules and federate rules.

3.2.3.1   Federation Rules

- Federation shall have an HLA FOM, documented in accordance with the HLA OMT.

  The formalization of information exchange is one of the key points of HLA, thus it enables a domain independent interoperability. FOM is a major part of any federation agreement. So any federation shall have a FOM, in which all the data (object and interaction) exchange that can happen during a federation execution is specified.

- In a federation, all simulation-associated object instance representation shall be in the federates, not in the RTI.

  HLA aims to separate federate-specific (domain specific) functionality from the support for general purpose (simulation) capabilities. So it is the federates' responsibility to keep the copies of the object instance attribute values they are interested in. RTI does not provide a storage medium for shared data; rather it provides a medium of transmission.

- During a federation execution, all exchange of FOM data among joined federates shall occur via the RTI.

  To permit coherency in data exchange among the participants is an important challenge in a distributed simulation. To tackle it, federates shall utilize RTI for data exchange that is defined in the FOM. Then RTI can manage the execution and data exchange of the federation. Allowing a back door for communication would create hidden dependencies among federates.

- During a federation execution, joined federates shall interact with the RTI in accordance with the HLA Interface Specification.

  Federate – RTI interaction shall conform the Federate Interface Specification. It is a programming interface to enable developing federates independent from RTI implementation, and porting them to different RTIs.

- During a federation execution, an instance attribute shall be owned by at most one joined federate at any given time

  To keep data coherency, only one federate can own instance of an object attribute at a time. Initially the creator of an object is the owner of all its attributes. The ownership of an attribute confers the owner the right to update it. Transfer of ownership from one federate to another during execution is mediated by the RTI. Notice that ownership is at the attribute level; the attributes of the same object instance can be shared between different owners.

3.2.3.2   Federate Rules

- Federates shall have an HLA SOM, documented in accordance with the HLA OMT.

  Interoperability and reuse is only possible with an explicit specification of the capabilities and needs of the federates. This is the advertisement part. The object classes, class attributes and interaction classes with their parameters shall be specified for every federate in its SOM.

- Federates shall be able to update and/or reflect any instance attributes and send and/or receive interactions, as specified in their SOMs.

  Federates can interact with others over updating or reflecting object instance attributes and sending or receiving interactions as specified in their SOM. So the reuse is enabled. This and the next two rules simply say "No false advertisement!"

- Federates shall be able to transfer and/or accept ownership of instance attributes dynamically during a federation execution, as specified in their SOMs.

  As specified in the SOM, federates shall support transferring or accepting the ownership of object instance attributes during execution. This provides flexibility for federation designers in terms of the allocation of responsibility.

- Federates shall be able to vary the conditions (e.g., thresholds) under which they provide updates of instance attributes, as specified in their SOMs.

  In order to take part in various federations, or adapt to different phases of the same federation execution, a federate must be able to vary its object attribute update rates or interaction send rates, within the limits set forth in its SOM.

- Federates shall be able to manage local time in a way that will allow them to coordinate data exchange with other members of a federation.

  Being a simulation on its own, a federate shall be able to manage its own time. Moreover, it shall cooperate with the federation so that the RTI can maintain a notion of federation time. HLA supports federates with different time advancement mechanisms, such as time-driven or event-driven, using time management. So federates can keep their local time, but are capable to ensure that it is coherent with federation time.

3.3   Object Exchange and HLA Object Models

First, we briefly introduce the HLA data communication, the object exchange model. And, we will answer what an HLA class is and then explain all related concepts, HLA OMT and HLA object models, namely Federation Object Model, Simulation Object Model and Management Object Model (MOM).

We demonstrate how to develop HLA object models using an Object Modeling Editor, named SimGe, which accompanies this book.

3.3.1   HLA Data Communication

In a communication model, it is important to specify the policy of how data is exchanged among components. Here, there are two important aspects of this specification. First, it is important to know what to exchange and second, how to exchange.

In the HLA world, the answer for what to exchange is that HLA communication model is based on object exchange technology. In other words, HLA compliant federates communicate with each other by exchanging objects. Therefore, the technology differs from classical Distributed Interactive Simulation (DIS) protocols, in which data is exchanged through well-defined messages using pre-defined PDUs. The structure of the exchanged data is embedded in DIS protocol. This causes the DIS protocol to be inflexible. For instance, to exchange an entity state, DIS protocol specifies an entity state PDU. Therefore, the simulation engineer can only use those predefined PDUs. He/she cannot create or define new data structures as all is specified with the standard. In contrast, HLA separates the data and the architecture. In this regard, HLA does not define the structure of the data that will be exchanged but do enable to specify the structure of what to exchange. This is done by employing the HLA Object Model Template. The simulation engineer can model new data structures, in terms of *HLA classes*, using the HLA OMT specification. The collection of those specified data structures is called an *HLA object model*. In the following sub-sections, we will open up both OMT and object models.

Now we can ask how HLA exchanges objects among federates. Here, RTI plays a central role and routes the objects to the related federates. HLA uses a middleware architecture approach instead of end-to-end communication model. In end-to-end communication, which is adopted by DIS protocol, the sender must know the receiver. For instance, the sender must know the physical IP address of the receiver. But the middleware architecture model, which HLA adopts, uses a middleware software to route the data among federates.

In HLA, RTI does this duty using a *Publish/Subscribe Pattern*. In this pattern, the sender and receiver components (i.e. federates) do not know each other. They just declare (to RTI) what they need and what they can provide to the federation execution. In federation execution, it is essential to express the relationship between a federate and particular federation objects. Therefore, the most important federation design activity is to define the *Publish and Subscribe (P/S)* interests of federates with the objects of conceptual model at hand. The Publish/Subscribe pattern forms the basis of the model of communication used by HLA between federates in terms of objects and interactions. At runtime, software components can specify to the RTI, which plays the role of an object request broker, a set of data types they can provide, and a set of data types they are ready to receive according to the *Federation Execution Details (FED)* for HLA 1.3 federations or *FOM Document Data (FDD)* for IEEE federations, which both is derived from the FOM (Federation Object Model). *Publishing* means declaring willingness (and ability) to provide data, which is composed of object classes and attributes, and interaction classes that the federate is able to update or send. *Subscribing* means declaring interest and the needs in receiving certain data. RTI dynamically routes the data among publishers (producers) and subscribers (consumers). In the following sections, we will explain the pattern and give examples.

3.3.2   Objects and Interactions

The *objects* can be pronounced as the primary means of communication in HLA. They can be introduced as the abstractions of simulated entities. A simulated entity may have a lifetime as a long as the simulation life span. And for sure, more than one federate can share an interest over that simulated entity. While some controls the entity – one at a time, some may only observe it. Good examples of HLA objects can be platforms or sensors in combat simulations or airplanes in air traffic simulations.

Object modelers identify the objects to facilitate an organizational scheme. There are *attributes* that are associated with an object. These attributes can be pronounced as the portion of the object state. So the state of an object instance is defined by the values of all its attributes. The owner federate provides the attribute values by updating them and others (that are subscribed to those attributes) receive the values by reflecting those attributes. Position and velocity of a platform object can be good examples of attributes.

HLA objects are mostly compared and sometimes confused with class objects of object-oriented programming. The HLA standard also mentions this topic. It says, while class objects are data encapsulations for data and the operations, HLA Objects are defined by the data that is exchanged between federates during federation execution (IEEE 2010a).

Interactions, on the other hand, represent an occurrence or an event. So conceptually they are not entities of interest but contrarily events or occurrences of interest. Like a detonation of an entity or landing of an aircraft. An interaction possesses a collection of data that is related to the occurrence or the event. The members of this data collection are called parameters. So federates that have an interest in an interaction gets all the *parameters* of it as it is fired.

3.3.3 Object Model Template

Object Model Template (OMT) constitutes a metamodel for object models SOM and FOM, and it describes the structure of object models via specifying the syntax and the format. The motivation behind developing a metamodel for object models is presented in the standard as proving an established mechanism for defining capabilities of the participants of the federation over their data exchange specifications, thus facilitate the development of common tools sets for object model development (IEEE 2010c).

OMT is basically represented in tabular format and in OMT data interchange format (DIF). It consists of a number of components, which can be listed as Object Model Identification Table, Object Class Structure Table, Interaction Class Structure Table, Attribute Table, Parameter Table, Dimension Table, Time Representation Table, User Supplied Tag Table, Synchronization Table, Transportation Type Table, Update Rate Table, Switches Table, Datatypes Table, Notes Table, Interface Specification Services Usage Table and FOM/SOM Lexicon. These tables are created for all federations and individual federates. While some require specifications from the designer, certain tables can be left empty depending on the situation.

While the reader is gently advised to go through the standard for the details of the tables, authors would like to introduce some of the important ones. First to mention is the Object Model Identification Table. The purpose of this table is to annotate the object model with the information about how the federate or the federation has been developed. The information provided in this table includes version, modification date, purpose of the object model, its limitations, point of contact and references. An example object model identification table is given in Table 3.1.

In Object Class Structure Table, the hierarchical relation of the classes is specified. Which one is a super class and which one is child class and which object class inherits from which one, questions are answered with this table. Table also captures if federate can publish, subscribe or publish and subscribe these objects. A sample object class is depicted Table 3.2. In this example table, we can easily see the object class hierarchy. The ship object class, which can be thought as an abstract class for the derived classes: `CargoShip`, `RoRo` and `Tanker`.

Table 3.1 Object model identification table example for strait traffic monitoring simulation (STMS) federation

Category	Information
Name	STMS Object Model
Type	FOM
Version	1.0.2
Modification Data	5/24/2014 12:00 AM
Security Classification	Unclassified
Release Restriction	NA
Purpose	A sample federation object model for SimGe 2.3 and up
Application Domain	HLA General, Sea Traffic Management
Description	This object model is provided as a sample project in SimGe object modeling tool
Use Limitations	NA
Use History	(Topçu et al. 2008)
Keyword	
Taxonomy	Simulation, Sea Traffic Rules
Keyword	HLA, Strait Traffic Management, Navigation Management
POC	
POC Type	Sponsor
POC Name	SimGe Tool
POC Organization	oToT
POC Telephone	1-111-111-1111
POC Email	otot.support@outlook.com
References	
Type	Standalone
Identification	NA
Other	Created by SimGe at 12/24/2013.
Glyph	**STMS**

Table 3.2 Object class structure table example for STMS federation

HLA object Root (N)	Ship (N)	CargoShip (PS)	
		RoRo(PS)	ConRo (PS)
			RoLo (PS)
		Tanker (N)	GeneralPurposeTanker (PS)
			MediumRangeTanker (PS)
			LongRangeTanker (PS)
			VeryLargeCrudeTanker (PS)

Interaction Class Structure Table, likewise, consists of class-subclass relations of interaction classes as well as their publish/subscribe capabilities. Attribute Table is used to specify the characteristics of object classes that are subject to change through the simulation. They are updated by RTI and made available to related members of the federation. The table provides the necessary information to enable effective communication among federates in a federation. It includes data type, update type like periodical or conditional, if it is conditional, the update condition, ownership policy, publish/subscribe status, its dimensions, its transport method and its order of delivery. Parameter Table, on the other hand, specifies the parameters that character-ize the interaction classes (see Table 3.3 for an example). One must note that while the attributes can be published and subscribed individual bases, interaction param-eters cannot be. So while the Parameter Table looks like Attribute Table, it has some important differences. It only possesses Data Type at the parameter level, while having dimensions, transportation and order at the interaction class level.

3.3.4 HLA Object Models

HLA framework describes three types of object models. These are Simulation Object Model (SOM), Federation Object Model (FOM) and Management Object Model (MOM).

3.3.4.1 Federation Object Model

The participants of distributed simulation require a common understanding about the communication among themselves. FOM provides a standard way of defining this communication. FOM mainly describes the format and the structure of data (i.e. objects) and events (i.e. interactions) that can be exchanged among federates in a federation execution in form of object and interaction classes with their attributes and parameters, respectively. Using FOM, designers can specify the data exchange in their federation in a standard format. There is a FOM per Federation. So FOM can be regarded as an "information contract" that enables the interoperability among federates. FOM takes the form of a file, called FDD/FED file, which is supplied to RTI in the simulation execution. A new FOM can be developed from scratch for each federation as well as an existing reference FOM can be used. The reference FOMs

Table 3.3 Parameter table example for STMS federation

Interaction	Parameter	Data type	Avilable dimension	Transportation	Order
RadioMessage	CallSign	String	VHF	HLA best Effort	Time Stamp
	Message	String			

are developed for increasing the interoperability by the simulation communities in order to agree on a common data model. For instance, Real-time Platform-level Reference FOM (RPR FOM) is developed to provide a pre-ready reference FOM for real-time platform-level simulations targeting in general the pre-HLA simulations that use the DIS protocol (SISO 2015); it is still being used widely today.

3.3.4.2 Simulation Object Model

With SOM, federates specify their capabilities and data interfaces. Thus, it serves as the specification for the composition of federates. RTI has nothing to do with SOM, but FOM is used by RTI to identify inter-federate interactions of the Federation.

3.3.4.3 Management Object Model

MOM is used to define the constructs for controlling and monitoring of a federation. Federates require insight about the federation execution as well as controlling the execution of individual federates, federation execution or the RTI. MOM utilizes the object model template format and syntax to define the information to be monitored and the control parameters. Its inclusion is compulsory for all FOMs. This inclusion can be accomplished by consolidating MOM data by an Initialization Module (MIM). MIM can be defined as a subset of FOM that contains the tables that describes the MOM. Normally, all FOMs have a MIM that is specified by the standard as default, but this can be overridden by a user supplied MIM.

3.3.5 Modularity

The latest HLA standard (i.e. HLA Evolved) prescribes SOM to be composed of one or more SOM modules and FOM to be composed of one or more FOM modules and one MIM. Modules are introduced as the partial object models that lay out a modular component. As a design pattern, one may have a module for all base classes or super classes. Then application specific object models include this module and inherit all object classes from these base classes.

3.4 Interface Specification

Each federate must interact with RTI by making method calls. The methods, which are provided to user federates, constitute the federate interface. The interface specification is standardized by IEEE 1556.1-2010 High Level Architecture (HLA) – Federate Interface Specification (IEEE 2010b). Thus, this specification provides a basis for interfacing between a federate and RTI component. Methods are grouped as (i) federate-initiated and (ii) RTI-initiated methods, in order to stress the direction of the communication. RTI-initiated methods are also called callback methods. Typically, we make method calls when we want to instruct RTI to do something. For example, the AFd federate, in Fig. 3.4, calls the method "Request Federation Save" in order to make RTI to initiate a federate save. In response, RTI initiates a federate save by informing each federate with a callback method "Initiate Federate Save". Federate-initiated methods are called via a module, generally known as RTI Ambassador and the callbacks are received by Federate Ambassador. Figure 3.4 depicts the federate interface and two-way communication. Here, all the object exchange is done by using this federate interface (i.e. using the methods and callbacks).

In some specific RTI distributions (e.g. DMSO RTI 1.3 NG v6), a central process (e.g. RtiExec) is required to run RTI software. *RtiExec* (RTI Executive) is a global process, where each federate communicates with RtiExec to initialize its RTI components. The RtiExec's primary purpose is to manage the creation and destruction of FedExecs (Federation Executive). RtiExec also provides a naming service for federation executives and ensures that each FedExec has a unique name. Each *FedExec* manages a federation execution. It allows federates to join and to resign, and facilitates data exchange between participating federates. FedExec assigns a unique handle to each federate joining the federation.

3.4.1 Content of an Interface Specification

Interface specification can be introduced as the language independent specification of services that are provided by RTI for distributed simulation. It is an Application Programming Interface (API) for inter-federate communication.

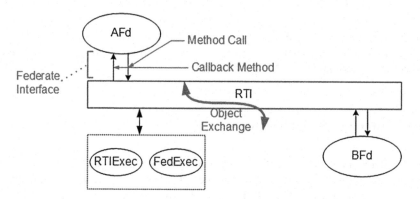

Fig. 3.4 The federate interface

The services provided by this API to its users are structured in seven groups as follows:

- *Federation Management* provides services to create, control and end a federation execution.
- *Declaration Management* provides services for federates to declare their intentions on publishing or subscribing object classes and sending and receiving interactions.
- *Object Management* provides services to register, modify and delete object instances and to send and receive interactions.
- *Ownership Management* provides services to transfer ownership of instance attributes among the federates of the federation.
- *Time Management* provides services and mechanisms to enable delivering messages in a consistent order.
- *Data Distribution Management* provides services to refine data requirements at the instance attribute level, thus enables reducing unnecessary data traffic.
- *Support Services* include utilities for federates like name-to-handle, handle to name transformations and getting update rate values.

The interface specification provides a description of the functionality of each service and required arguments and pre-conditions necessary for use of the service. Post-conditions specify any changes in the state of the federation execution resulting from the call. Exceptions give all possible exceptions thrown by the service routine. Requests for services should be included in try-catch blocks so that appropriate action may be taken for error processing. The parts of interface specification are:

- Interface name and brief description of service
- Supplied arguments
- Returned arguments
- Pre-conditions
- Post-conditions
- Exceptions
- Related services

As an example, authors would like to introduce *Join Federation Execution* service provided under Federation Management service group. This service is used to affiliate a federate to a federation execution or in other words indicate the intention of a federate to participate in a specific federation. Its supplied arguments are federate name if it exists, the federate type, federation execution name and optional set of additional FOM module designators. The returned argument is the designator of the joined federate. As the precondition, the federate need to be connected to the RTI and there needs to exist the federation execution specified. And the federate name need to be not used, federate save and restore not in progress and the federate has not been connected to the federation execution. At the post condition, the joined federate is a member of the federation execution. And standard specifies eleven exceptions for this service two of which are "federate name already exists" and "federate save in progress". Below you can find a C++ and a Java implementation of this service specification from two well-known open source RTIs, CERTI (Noulard et al. 2009) and Portico (Tu et al. 2011) respectively.

```
FederateHandle joinFederationExecution
          (const std::string& Federate,
          const std::string& Federation,
          RootObject* rootObject,
          TypeException &e);
FederateHandle joinFederationExecution
          (String federateType,
          String federationExecutionName,
          FederateAmbassador federateReference,
          MobileFederateServices serviceReferences)
          throws FederateAlreadyExecutionMember,
              FederationExecutionDoesNotExist,
              SaveInProgress,
              RestoreInProgress,
              RTIinternalError
```

3.4.2   Simulation Flow

A typical federation execution lifecycle starts with the connection to RTI as depicted in Fig. 3.5, and then:

- Federate application connects to RTI in order to interact with RTI.
- Federate first tries to create the federation execution if not created and then joins the federation execution. After joining the federation execution, a joined federate instance in RTI is created that represents the federate in the federation execution.
- Federate should inform the RTI about its capabilities and interests by publishing and subscribing the object classes and interaction classes. Thus, it establishes its initial data requirements.
- Federate creates (registers) objects that it will provide to other federates.
- Federate may create new objects or update the attributes of the objects that it created; may discover new objects, that are created by other federates; may receive updates for the subscribed attributes; may send and receive interactions.
- Federate deletes objects that are created by itself before leaving.
- Federate manages its time according using RTI time management services (e.g. time advance request), if it specifies a time management policy (e.g. time regulating federate).
- Federate manages ownership of attributes, if necessary.

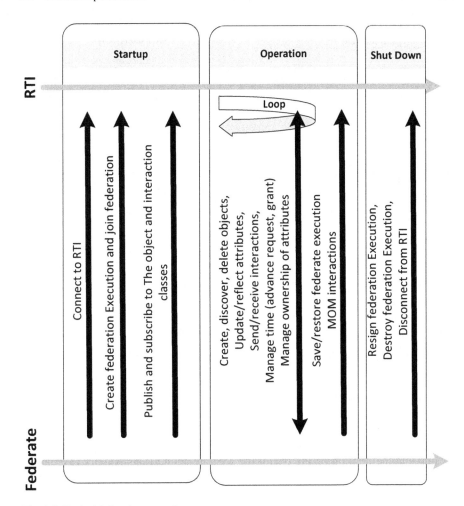

Fig. 3.5 Typical federation execution

- Federate resigns and tries to destroy the federation execution, and succeeds if it happens to be the last federate.
- Federate disconnects from RTI.

This typical federation execution lifecycle affect the design of federates. With no surprise, the basic program flow of a federate (see Fig. 3.6) is divided into three phases: system initialization (startup), main application loop (operation) and system termination (shut down).

System initialization and termination phases include RTI initialization and termination phases, which involve federation wide principles. Generally, there are two federation management models: centralized and non-centralized models. In centralized model, a specific federate is responsible for the initialization and termination of

Fig. 3.6 Basic program
flow of a typical federate

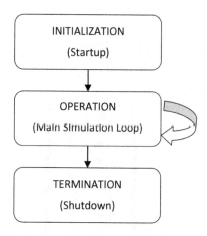

the federation execution. In non-centralized models, each federate has the equal responsibility for initialization and termination.

Initialization and termination phases also include the scenario play initialization and termination activities respectively. See Chap. 8 for handling of the scenario specific details.

3.4.2.1 Initialization

HLA does not mandate the creation of a federation execution to the privilege of a particular federate. This policy provides flexibility and non-centralization. One may design that the first job of any one of the federate applications is to try to create a federation execution. The first federate succeeds to create the federation execution if the specified federation execution does not exist, while subsequent federates receive an exception, which indicates that the federation execution does already exist and then they directly join the federation instead of creating it.

In many RTI releases, if joining to the federation execution is attempted immediately after the creation of the federation execution, the federation execution may not yet be initialized to communicate with the federate (e.g. the Fedexec process is not forked and initialized in case of HLA 1.3). Beforehand, we cannot assume which federate is the first, so the join logic will loop until the join is successful or until some predetermined number of join attempts is exhausted.

The creation of a federation execution requires a federation name. It designates a unique federation execution, and the participating federates use it to join the specified federation execution. All member federates should agree on the unique federation execution name. Therefore, the federation execution name either should be distributed by hand to all participants at start up or the federation execution name should be hard coded in federates.

3.4.2.2   Operation

Operation phase generally includes the main simulation loop and an alternative behavior path. The main simulation loop specifies the behavior of the federate for the normal federate execution, which includes the object management, time management and the ownership management services, while the alternative behavior path is used for abnormal situations such as when save and restore is requested in the federation execution or when MOM interactions are required.

The main simulation loop may also include the integrated activities with scene drawing in case of a graphics intensive federate application. A typical HLA-based interactive graphical simulation repeatedly calls the pre-frame, frame and post-frame stages, as it is presented in Fig. 3.7. A frame is the scene to be drawn.

Let's review and explain the pre-frame stage:

- First thing we do is to broadcast our own state to network. In HLA terms, we update the attributes of objects that we create and own.
- Ticking means reading the callbacks and the incoming events sent by RTI, so that we can discover new objects or reflect the attribute updates done by other federates.
- Lastly, if the simulation has a graphical user interface (GUI), we update the scene graph (e.g. the transformation and rotation nodes). The scene graph is the geometry tree drawn to the screen.

After all the necessary calculations are done in pre-frame, we draw (i.e. render) the scene graph on the screen (e.g. a view of the virtual environment in 3D).

At the post-frame stage, the snapshot of user input queues, both from keyboard and mouse, are captured and handled. The GUI is being updated based upon the user inputs. We also send interactions, where trigger mechanism based on the user inputs (e.g. sending a message when a user presses send button).

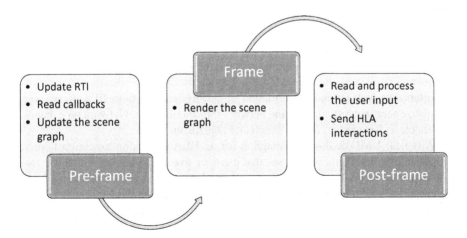

Fig. 3.7 Main simulation loop for a typical graphics-intensive simulation

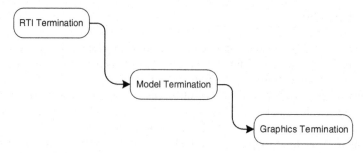

Fig. 3.8 Termination

3.4.2.3 Termination

The shutdown/termination of a federation execution is accomplished by the federate, which resigns from the federation execution last. In a non-centralized simulation, the same rule applies here; all federates, while resigning, attempt to terminate the federation execution. The last one succeeds while others receive an exception because the federation still has members and resigns from the federation without terminating it.

The termination phase consists of three stages (Fig. 3.8): RTI termination, local model termination and Graphics termination. At RTI shut down stage, the created RTI objects and interactions are deleted and other federates are informed, and then the federate resigns and tries to destroy the federation. At model termination stage, the local objects that represent the simulation entities are deleted to free up the application memory and lastly the graphics subsystem is shut down.

3.5 Typical Federation Deployment

UML deployment diagrams are used to plan and design the execution environment in software intensive systems. In this context, the specialized and extended form of deployment diagrams can be employed to capture the execution details of federation requirements such as node information (e.g., Physical location, IP address, port number, operating system, etc.) and network information (e.g., Network type, bandwidth, etc.) (Topçu et al. 2003) (Topçu and Oğuztüzün 2005).

A typical UML deployment diagram for an HLA federation execution is presented in Fig. 3.9. Here, we can see that there are five hosts, four of which are distributed in a TCP/IP network and one (Node 4) is a web client connecting from Internet. The diagram shows us which federate is executed on which host and gives some information (e.g. the host's operating system) about the host.

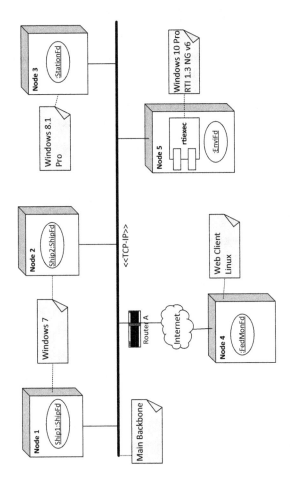

Fig. 3.9 Typical federation execution deployment

3.6   Federation and Federate States

During a federation run, federates and the federation execution can be found in specific states from the viewpoint of RTI. Those states are useful to define the context of federates and federation execution during simulation run.

3.6.1   Federation Execution States

Federation execution states are depicted in Fig. 3.10. A federation execution can be in either FEDERATION EXECUTION DOES NOT EXIST state or FEDERATION EXECUTION EXISTS state. The directed links show the events (denoted as 1 and 2) that trigger the transition from one event to another event.

Tables 3.4 and 3.5 explain the states and the events respectively.

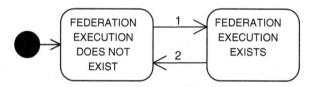

Fig. 3.10 Federation execution state diagram

Table 3.4 Federation execution states

States	Description
FEDERATION EXECUTION DOES NOT EXIST	No federation execution exists (either it is destroyed or not created yet)
FEDERATION EXECUTION EXISTS	Federation execution is created and running. This state also encapsulates two sub-states: No joined federates and supporting joined federates. See (IEEE 2010b) for details

Table 3.5 Events for federation execution states

Events	Description
1	Federation execution is created
2	Federation execution is destroyed

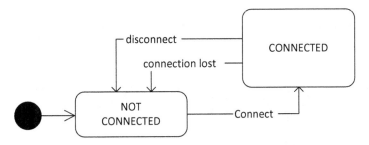

Fig. 3.11 Federate states

3.6.2   Federate States

A federate is either connected or not connected according to its connection with RTI. Figure 3.11 depicts the basic state diagram from a federation management perspective. The Connected state is a combined state including the states that show a federate is joined to the federation execution or not. The joined federate state also includes some sub-states such as active federate state, federate save in progress state and federate restore in progress state (IEEE 2010b).

Most distributed interactive simulations use scenarios to drive the simulation execution. A federation wide scenario slightly changes the lifetime of federate introducing new states for scenario-dependent run. See Chap. 8 for scenario-related federate states.

3.7   Case Study: Object Model Construction

In order to develop an object model, it is convenient to use an HLA object model editor. In this section, we will use a tool called Simulation Generator (SimGe) (2015).

3.7.1   SimGe

SimGe is a fully dressed HLA object model editor, simulation design and development environment, and a federation prototyping tool with its code generation capability. SimGe object model editor (OME) allows the user to manage the object model and enables the creation and modification of HLA object model template and object models and the import and export of the HLA related files (i.e. FED and FDD), which contains configuration data for the federation execution.

SimGe organizes all the simulation generation efforts using simulation projects. A *Simulation Project* is the main container and organizer for the simulation design

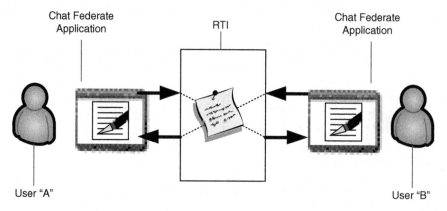

Fig. 3.12 Chat application conceptual view

and code generation. SimGe OME supports to work with multiple federation object models at the same time. SimGe provides three options to begin construction of an object model (i.e. FOM and SOM) for the simulation project. The user can opt to construct an object model by:

- Developing from scratch
- Loading a previously saved SimGe object model
- Importing either an existing FED file or FDD file (for example, importing a generic FOM – RPR FOM FED file).

3.7.2   Example: Chat Federation

Chat is an HLA-based distributed interactive application that provides basic chatting functionalities such as selecting a nickname, entering a chat room and so on. By using the chat federate application (ChatFdApp), one can exchange messages with his/her friends in chat rooms. Before entering a chat room, he/she has to pick up a unique nickname. The ChatFdApp provides a graphical user interface for the user interaction and deals with the RTI communication. The conceptual view of the application is presented in Fig. 3.12.

3.7.3   Object Model

SimGe OME provides all the HLA OMT tables. The simulation engineer may fill in those tables from scratch or may import an existing model. Figure 3.13 depicts a screenshot presenting the identification table for the object model. Here, the type of the model (i.e. FOM or SOM) can be defined.

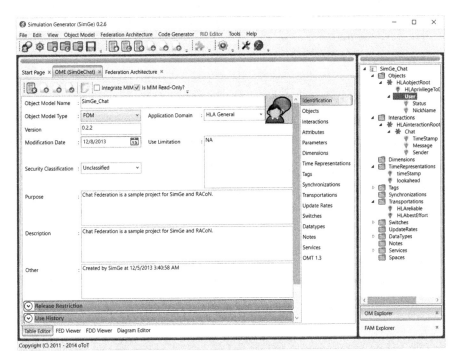

Fig. 3.13 Chat federation object model – SimGe screenshot

3.7.4   FDD/FED File

Once an object model is constructed in SimGe, the files that are used at runtime by RTI is generated automatically. Federation Execution Details (FED) file "is used to supply RTI with all necessary federation execution details during the creation of a new federation" (DMSO 1998). It is a text file with a syntax that conforms to OMT Data Interchange Format. FED file is used by RTIs that conform to the HLA 1.3 specification. Figure 3.14 depicts a piece of FED file for Chat federation.

FOM Document Data (FDD) file is the newer format than FED and is used by RTIs that conform to the IEEE 1516 specification. Its syntax is based on widely used XML. Figure 3.15 depicts a screenshot of part of FDD file for Chat federation. Please note that the model identification part seen in the screenshot corresponds to Table 3.1.

3.8   Summary

In this chapter, we presented a complete introduction to the concepts and principles of High Level Architecture. Various aspects of the standard, including its historical roots, concepts and rules with how it works, have been covered.

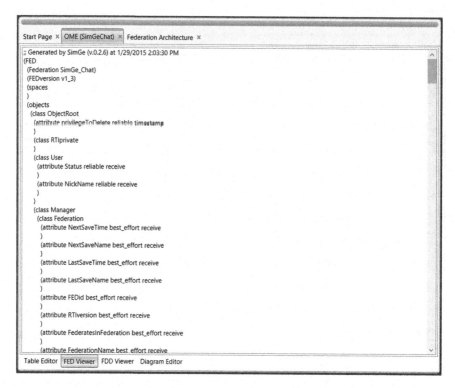

Fig. 3.14 Chat federation FED file

High Level Architecture provides a framework for distributed simulations with special emphasis on interoperability and reusability of simulation components (IEEE 2010a, b, c). More formally: "HLA provides a common framework and approach for distributed simulations and virtual worlds to share information and capabilities, to expand interoperability, and to promote reuse and extensibility" (Dahmann et al. 1997) (Dahmann et al. December 1998). HLA is a set of specifications which include the HLA Rules, Interface Specification and the Object Model Template. HLA was developed under leadership of the U.S. Defense Modeling and Simulation Office (DMSO). The HLA was approved as an open standard through the Institute of Electrical and Electronic Engineers (IEEE), namely IEEE Standard 1516, in September 2000 and then revised in August 2010 (a.k.a. HLA Evolved).

It became a widely accepted standard in the area of distributed modeling and simulation over the last decade, and it is not surprising to see that many new distributed simulations in both the civilian and, to a larger extent military domains are being built to be HLA compliant while HLA itself evolves. Although much effort has been spent on developing HLA federations, the state-of-the-art in federation design representation and documentation still has room for improvement specifically for full automation of the federation development process with user guidance (Stytz and Banks 2001).

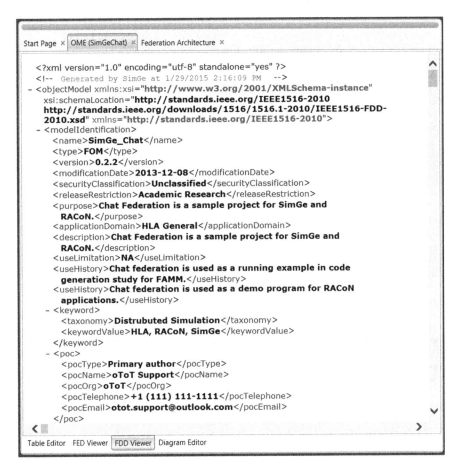

Fig. 3.15 Chat federation FDD file

References

Dahmann, J. S., Fujimoto, R. M., & Weatherly, R. M. (1997). *The department of defense high level architecture.* In *Proceedings of the 1997 Winter Simulation Conference* (pp. 142–149). Atlanta: IEEE.

Dahmann, J., Kuhl, F., & Weatherly, R. (1998). Standards for simulation: As simple as possible but not simpler the high level architecture for simulation. *Simulation, 71*(6), 378–387.

Davis, P. K., & Anderson, R. H. (2004). *Improving the composability of department of defense models and simulations.* [Online] Available at: http://www.rand.org/pubs/monographs/MG101.html. Accessed 24 Nov 2013.

DMSO. (1998). *High level architecture federation execution details (FED) file specification.* Alexandria: DMSO.

IEEE. (2010a). *IEEE standard for modeling and simulation high level architecture (HLA) – Framework and rules.* IEEE Std 1516-2010. New York: IEEE.

IEEE. (2010b). *IEEE standard for modeling and simulation (M&S) high level architecture (HLA) – Federate interface specification.* IEEE Std 1516.1-2010. New York: IEEE.

IEEE. (2010c). *IEEE standard for modeling and simulation (M&S) high level architecture (HLA)-object model template (OMT) specification*. IEEE Std 1516.2-2010. New York: IEEE.

Kuhl, F., Weatherly, R., & Dahmann, J. (1999). *Creating computer simulations: An introduction to the high level architecture*. Upper Saddle River: Prentice Hall PTR.

MÄK. (2015). *HLA RTI – Run time infrastructure: MÄK RTI*. [Online] Available at: http://www.mak.com/products/link/mak-rti. Accessed 13 Dec 2015.

Möller, B., et al. (2008). HLA evolved – A summary of major technical improvements. In *Proceedings of the 2008 Spring Simulation Interoperability Workshop*. Providence: SISO.

Newcomb, M. (2013). *Open HLA*. [Online] Available at: http://sourceforge.net/projects/ohla/. Accessed 13 Dec 2015.

Noulard, E., Rousselot, J. Y., & Siron, P. (2009). CERTI, an open source RTI, why and how. In *Proceedings of the 2009 Fall Simulation Interoperability Workshop*. Orlando: SISO.

Pitch. (2012). *The HLA tutorial: A practical guide for developing distributed simulations* [Online]. Available at: http://www.pitch.se/images/files/tutorial/TheHLAtutorial.pdf. Accessed 13 Dec 2015.

Portico. (2013). *The portico project*. [Online] Available at: http://www.porticoproject.org/. Accessed 30 Aug 2015.

SimGe. (2015). *SimGe web site*. [Online] Available at: https://sites.google.com/site/okantopcu/simge. Accessed 15 Aug 2015.

SISO. (2015). *Standard for real-time platform reference federation object model v2.0*. Orlando: Simulation Interoperability Standards Organization (SISO).

Stytz, M., & Banks, S. (2001). Enhancing the design and documentation of high level architecture simulations using the unified modeling language. In *Proceedings of the 2001 Spring Simulation Interoperability Workshop (SIW)*. Orlando: SISO.

Topçu, O., & Oğuztüzün, H. (2005). Developing an HLA based naval maneuvering simulation. Naval Engineers Journal, 117(1), 23–40.

Topçu, O., Oğuztüzün, H., & Hazen, M. (2003). Towards a UML profile for HLA federation design, Part II. In *Proceedings of the summer computer and simulation conference* (pp. 874–879). Montreal: SCS.

Topçu, O., Adak, M., & Oğuztüzün, H. (2008, July). A metamodel for federation architectures. *Transactions on Modeling and Computer Simulation (TOMACS)*, 18(3), 10:1–10:29.

Tu, Z., Zacharewicz, G., & Chen, D. (2011). Developing a web-enabled HLA federate based on poRTIco RTI. In *Proceedings of the 2011 Winter Simulation Conference* (pp. 2289–2301). Phoenix: IEEE.

Yilmaz, L. (2007). Using meta-level ontology relations to measure conceptual alignment and interoperability of simulation models. In *Proceedings of the 2007 Winter Simulation Conference* (pp. 1090–1099). Washington, DC: IEEE.

Part II
Development Process

Chapter 4
Process Models

This chapter presents road maps for how to build and execute a distributed simulation in a model-driven way. In this respect, we introduce process models for distributed simulation development and execution. First, we introduce the standards FEDEP and DSEEP and then we present a process model enhanced with a model driven engineering (MDE) approach. Current distributed simulation development and execution process models generally focus on the processes and data that flow among them. They picture the simulation development and execution in terms of activities, information flow, and products that answer what needs to be done by prescribing which workproducts to produce. In general terms, they follow a well-known waterfall software engineering paradigm, where one activity follows another. Although those process models are well suited for guidance for the simulation development and execution, they generally fall short of supporting engineering processes in terms of automation, tool development, and code generation. On the other hand, MDE presents new opportunities for distributed simulation development and execution. First of all, an MDE-based process model sees the models and transformations among them as primary workproducts in the system development lifecycle. So, the focus is on designing and developing models and specifying transformations. Second, well-defined transformations facilitate automation. So, ideally, a model can be transformed into another model, at least semi-automatically with user intervention. Definition of transformation is similar to programming; it requires setting the aim and design for that end. As all artifacts, save for the executable codes and supporting files, are models, they can be reused in many ways. For instance, a federation architecture model can be transformed into source code in a preferred programming language, where the transformation is the code generation. Reusing the same model, we can generate code in another language by crafting another transformation.

© Springer International Publishing Switzerland 2016
O. Topçu et al., *Distributed Simulation*, Simulation Foundations,
Methods and Applications, DOI 10.1007/978-3-319-03050-0_4

4.1   Distributed Simulation Engineering and Execution Process (DSEEP)

Simulations have been developed since the very first computing machines. ENIAC was built to simulate the trajectories of artillery shells (MacCartney 1999). Since then, there have been various approaches to develop simulations. As architectures for distributed simulation, process models or development approaches have also been subject to standardization efforts although they depend on various constraints and requirements of the developed system. The community managed to develop domain independent process models that embody the recommended practices.

In 2003, IEEE 1516.3 Recommended Practice for High level Architecture (HLA) Development and Execution Process (FEDEP) provided a generic systems engineering methodology for HLA federations (IEEE Std 1516.3-2003 2003). It was introduced and well accepted as a starting framework for tailoring an end-to-end process for the development and execution of HLA federations. The top level steps of FEDEP were introduced as:

Step 1: Defining federation objectives
Step 2: Performing conceptual analysis
Step 3: Designing federation
Step 4: Developing federation
Step 5: Planning, integrating and testing of the federation
Step 6: Executing federation and preparing outputs
Step 7: Analyzing data and evaluating the results

The standard specifies the details of these seven major steps in terms of lower level activities and supporting information resources.

In 2007, Simulation Interoperability Standards Organization (SISO) FEDEP Product Development Group (PDG) decided to extend the standard to support not only HLA but also other distributed simulation approaches independently of the distributed simulation architecture. It was 2010, when IEEE Std 1730-2010 Recommended Practice for Distributed Simulation Engineering and Execution Process (DSEEP) was published (IEEE Std 1730-2010 2010). DSEEP specifies a higher level framework for processes and procedures recommended to develop and execute distributed simulations.

DSEEP revised the seven steps of FEDEP. The recommended process starts with defining simulation environment objectives. At this step, objectives of the simulation experiment are set forth by the consensus among stakeholders, such as users, sponsors, and developers. The second step is characterized by the requirements engineering study. The development team conducts scenario development, conceptual modeling, and requirements definition study. At the third step, simulation environment is designed. Development team selects members or the participants of the distributed simulation. Team identifies the members to be reused as well as ones to be newly developed. Required functions or requirements are allocated to the members. Then third step of the process is completed with a development and implementation plan for the simulation environment. In the fourth step, the standard endorses development of data exchange model and the simulation environment agreement. Later, new members as well as the modifications to the existing members are implemented accordingly. Fifth step is named as integration and test of simulation environment, at which interoperability requirements are verified via integration and testing. Execution of the distributed simulation is introduced as the sixth step. And finally, the standard prescribes data analysis and evaluation step.

For each step, recommended activities are introduced by the standard. Activities are defined by their inputs, suggested outputs, and tasks. DSEEP has been a standardization attempt for a generic framework to allow specification of detailed process models for particular communities or domains. DSEEP for sure inherits all the heritage from FEDEP and manages to present a more comprehensive standard. But one needs to note that this generic framework requires a considerable amount of effort to be adapted to a specific DS architecture. DSEEP should be supplemented with overlays to customize it for a particular distributed simulation approach, such as HLA, Test and Training Enabling Architecture (TENA) (Powell and Noseworthy 2012), or DIS (IEEE Std 1278). Overlays exist for HLA, TENA, and DIS. When needed, one may develop an overlay, say for DEVS (Zeigler 1984) for example. As DSEEP is independent of the simulation environment architecture, it allows simulation environments, which are composed of more than one simulation architecture such as DIS and HLA. In case of multi-architecture simulation environments, a DSEEP Multi-Architecture Overlay is published in 2013 (IEEE Std 1730.1-2013 2013) to overcome the limitations of a single architecture for a simulation environment.

HLA process overlay to the DSEEP is provided in (IEEE Std 1730-2010 2010) as annex-A. Table 4.1 presents a correspondence of DSEEP terminology to HLA.

4.2   MDE-Based Process Overlay to DSEEP

The FEDEP and DSEEP are basically seen as activity driven paradigms presented as data flow diagrams. From the view point of the Model Driven Engineering, MDE naturally supports a generic process model like DSEEP and reimagines it in a model driven way with its emphasis on models and transformations. The biggest advantage of MDE approach is the possibility of automation of transformations from one model to another. Thus, the MDE-based process model supports tool automation and code generation by design. In the following sections, we present an MDE interpretation of DSEEP and we will show how an MDE-based process model, based on DSEEP, supports code generation and enables tool support (e.g. model checkers for verification and document generators).

First, we present a generic process model for MDE-based simulation development. Although it is designed specifically for HLA simulations, it helps us to see the essence of an MDE-based process model in the context of distributed simulation engineering. The process model is explained by forming a methodological view and

Table 4.1 DSEEP to HLA terminology mapping

DSEEP	HLA
Simulation environment	Federation
Simulation member, member, member application	Federate, federate application
Simulation data exchange model (SDEM)	FOM, SOM
Simulation environment agreements	The federation agreements such as the synchronization points, save/restore, ownership management data, and publish/subscribe responsibilities in FDD file.
	The Federation Engineering Agreements Template (FEAT) (SISO 2015)
Simulation environment design	Federation design
Conceptual model	Federation conceptual model
Simulation environment infrastructure	RTI initialization data (RID) file, UML deployment diagram, etc.
Execution environment description	Federation Execution Planner's Workbook (FEPW) for HLA 1.3

tool-support view, and then the activities are aligned with DSEEP lifecycle view. The methodological side of the process model emphasizes the workproducts (models) and the transformations, and then the tool-support view presents the tools that can be used to develop these models.

4.2.1   Methodological View

The generic model is put forth by articulating a methodological view emphasizing models and transformations. Adopting the model-driven engineering approach (Bezivin 2005) (Schmidt 2006), development steps can be seen as a series of model transformations. HLA-based distributed simulation development results in workproducts (models) such as a conceptual model, federation architecture model, detailed design model, and federation (consisting of federates in executable form). Figure 4.1 sketches the roles of the models. Each model layer corresponds to a distinct level of abstraction, for example, the conceptual model layer pertains to the problem domain entities, while the detailed design model layer pertains to the software objects.

Conceptual Model (CM) is a platform independent model (PIM) of the reality with which the simulation is concerned. A CM can also address simulation capabilities and limitations, then, it is called as a simulation conceptual model. It serves as

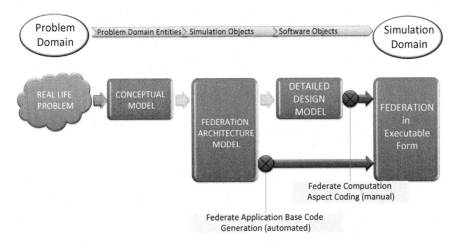

Fig. 4.1 Development methodology for HLA-based distributed simulations (Topçu et al. 2008)

an agreement among project stakeholders about what is to be developed and represents how developers understand the problem domain.

The Detailed Design Model (DDM), also called *federate architecture*, outlines
the internal structure (e.g. computational model) of the federate components. It
helps generate the software skeleton for the computational part.

Federation Architecture Model (FAM), also called federation architecture[1] in
short, is a major portion of the federation design documentation, and it is a platform-
specific model (PSM) where, in our case, the platform is the RTI, and it comprises
the federation model (federation structure, federation object model, and HLA services) and the behavioral models for each participating federate. The model of a
particular federation architecture conforms to Federation Architecture Metamodel
(FAMM) (refer to Chap. 6 for the details of FAMM).

Federation in executable form is the source code for each member federate in the
target language (e.g. C++). The source code can be generated using the FAM and
the related federate architectures.

Figure 4.2 details the generic process and depicts the basic models incorporated
with verification and validation (V&V). Each layer represents a different abstraction level. Going bottom-up, abstraction level increases. Each abstraction level
includes one (or more) models. One model in one layer can be transformed into
another model in the other level. Following the top-down path in the process model,
the transformations are generally done from the platform independent models (generalized models) to obtain the platform-specific models (specialized models),
although the reverse is also quite possible. Two major transformations are defined in
the process model. The first one is a model-to-model transformation from a formal
conceptual model to the federation architecture model, and the next one is the code

---

[1] "Federation Architecture" is used as replaceable with "Federation Architecture Model".

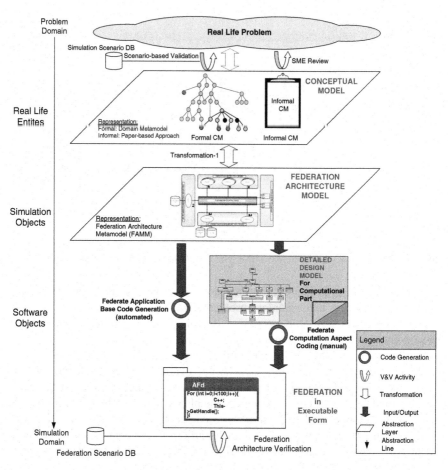

Fig. 4.2 V&V oriented development methodology for HLA-based distributed simulations (Topçu 2007)

generation from the federation architecture model to a specified programming language. The following subsections explain the process model in detail.

4.2.2   Workproducts (Models)

4.2.2.1   Conceptual Model

When we talk about a conceptual model, in general, it is meant to be a domain model and it may not give any simulation-related clues. However, a simulation conceptual model (SCM), being simulation-oriented, is normally expected to have computational aspects, such as entity representation, algorithms for entity behaviors, and mathematical models. A SCM, being platform independent, is not normally expected to have platform-specific properties, for instance HLA-specific or DEVS-specific. Therefore, the simulation conceptual model is a platform independent model of the reality with which the simulation is concerned (Pace 2000). Simulation conceptual models serve a variety of purposes. From the users' perspective, conceptual model provides a documentation to understand the simulation capabilities and limitations. From the developers' perspective, it serves as an agreement among project stakeholders about what is to be developed and represents how developers understand the problem domain. From a communication perspective, conceptual model serves as a communications mean between users and developers.

The methodology suggests two representations of conceptual model, namely: informal conceptual model and formal conceptual model. *Informal CM* will be used especially by the sponsor and the user group, which we can call CM users. Informal CM will help CM users to assess the capabilities and the intended focus of the simulation without requiring any background in modeling technology. Informal CM can be validated by a domain expert (called subject matter expert (SME) in V&V terminology), who typically has limited technical background of the simulations and software. We can accept this as the main technique for informal conceptual model validation. Meanwhile, being informal does not imply being unformatted. A scientific paper-based approach (Pace 1999, 2000) can be used for the representation of an informal CM. On the contrary, *formal CM* representation will be directly used by the CM developers, who may modify or re-develop the conceptual model. At the same time, the formal CM can be consulted to solve disputes when there is an uncertainty or a disagreement in the informal CM (e.g., two people can infer different things by reading the same sentence in an informal CM). Another main objective of the formal CM is to transform a conceptual model into machine-processable form. In this respect, it will be possible for all kinds of software tools (e.g., V&V tools, HLA federates) and software agents (e.g. web robots) to employ the conceptual model. Note that it may not always be practical to formalize the entire conceptual model (e.g., CM may include some photos, charts, etc.). A formal CM can be represented using an implementation specific language such as Unified Modeling Language (UML) (OMG 2015) or a domain specific language specified as a metamodel for a specific domain, such as field artillery conceptual metamodel (Özhan et al. 2008). Moreover, it is possible to utilize the ontologies for CM representation.

The conceptual modeling and conceptual models, in the view of the presented methodology, are elucidated in Chap. 5 as well as providing two case studies for the ontology representation and metamodeling approaches of the CM representation.

CM Validation

An error in the conceptual model affects all the simulation models and the output data resulting from simulation runs at the end. Sometimes, it is not possible to trace down the source of the error from the results. Therefore, conceptual model validation is required before transforming the CM to the other models. Generally, conceptual models are validated using domain SMEs. The quality of this validation process depends on the subjective assessment of the expert. This process can be lengthy and dependent on the individual SMEs involved (Pace 2004).

There is a need to support and to formalize the conceptual model validation process. For instance, scenarios can be used as a supporting validation technique for formal CM validation. Simulation requirements are captured as use cases by using use case requirements analysis techniques (Jacobson et al. 1993). These use cases (a.k.a. use case scenarios) provide the main part of the simulation scenarios. Then, CM will be meaningful according to its level of support for scenarios. The meaning of support should be defined operationally within the overall problem domain. At minimum, the entities, actions, relationships, states, and parameters implied by scenarios should be explicit in the CM representation.

4.2.2.2   Federation Architecture Model

It has become more important to design the information flow and interactions between components (specifically federates in HLA federation) in a simulation as the simulations have become more distributed. This points to the simulation environment design activity in DSEEP. In this respect, the federation architecture model is the main portion of the federation design documentation and it includes the structural and the object model of a federation and action models for each participating federate.

Federation design for HLA-based distributed simulations includes, but is not limited to the following activities:

- Forming a federation object model and possibly simulation object models:

  - Designing relatively static information interests of federates (related to declaration management interface)
  - Designing dynamic information interests of federates (related to object management interface)
  - Designing dynamic object flows (related to data distribution and ownership management interfaces)
  - Designing synchronization scheme (related to time management interface)

- Specifying the behaviors of participating federates (so that they can fulfill their responsibilities within the federation)

The Federation Architecture model is a PSM, where, in HLA case, the platform is the RTI, and it comprises the federation model (federation structure, federation object model, and HLA services) and the behavioral models for each participating federate. The FAM will serve as a transformation between the formal conceptual model and the detailed software design. The federation architecture can be formally represented by using a metamodel. In this regard, a set of metamodel, called Federation Architecture Metamodel (FAMM) (Topçu et al. 2008), is prepared to support a more formalized and standardized description of the federation design and documentation. FAMM lays the groundwork for implementing model interpreters in order to generate useful artifacts, such as FED/FDD file and to extract interesting views, such as publish/subscribe diagrams. FAMM is discussed at length in Chap. 6 with a case study.

Federation Architecture Verification

Federation architecture verification is to check that FAM does what it promises and whether it is consistent within itself. First check is whether it really conforms to its metamodel, FAMM. Fortunately, this tedious task is undertaken by the modeling tool, such as Generic Modeling Environment (GME) or Eclipse Modeling Framework (EMF).

If the FAM is developed using CM, it must be verified that whether or not it is developed via a reliable transformation from formal CM to FAM. A transformation should preserve meaning between the source and the target model. Moreover, it should add information pertaining to the target environment. A FAM includes more detailed information than the conceptual model. The focus of CM is in the mission/problem space, while the focus of a FAM is in simulation/application space.

Federation architecture verification is one of the areas that can be supported with automation. As the federation architecture has a formal representation, some syntactic and semantic verification rules can be defined. For instance, a federate cannot register an object before publishing it. So, an interpreter can check the federation architecture whether the model ensures this constraint or not. A study about RTI-related behavior verification of HLA federates using pre- and postconditions of federate interface (Kızılay et al. 2009) is summarized in Chap. 6.

4.2.2.3 Federate Architecture (Detailed Design Model)

The federate architecture outlines the internal structure of the simulation member applications (i.e. federate applications) in detail and it is the critical design effort before the implementation. It helps generate the software skeleton for the computational part.

The design of member applications follows the simulation environment design activity according to DSEEP. If the components, which compose the distributed simulation, are ready at hand, then there is no need for a detailed member design. However, if federation design model implies a requirement to develop a new member application or to modify an existing one, then a detailed analysis and design that

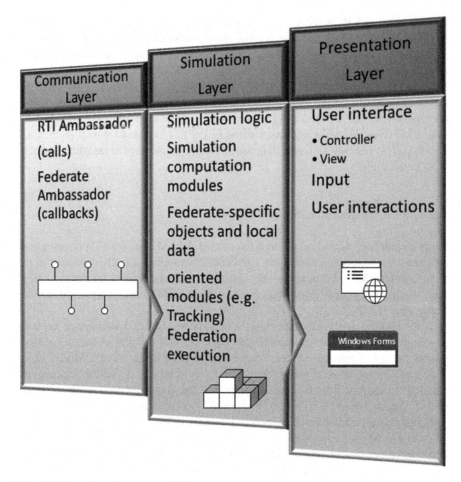

Fig. 4.3 Layered architecture of a federate

is focused on the member application must be conducted. In this case, it will be a complementary approach to use object-oriented analysis and design techniques and UML in designing each application's internal structure. A typical internal structure of a federate is recommended in Fig. 4.3 using a layered federate architecture, and this internal architecture has been applied successfully in the development of some federates for naval federations (Topçu and Oğuztüzün 2005) (Savaşan and Oğuztüzün 2002).

Presentation layer is related to the simulation capabilities of a federate. These modules have nothing to do with the distributed simulation concepts or HLA/RTI interface; they merely model the user interface view. *Simulation layer* is one that deals with the other participants in the common virtual environment and they satisfy the federation-wide needs of the federate. *Communication layer* is responsible communicating with simulation architecture infrastructure (e.g. RTI middleware) and receiving callbacks.

For HLA based simulation architectures, if the federates at hand can be reused for a new federation, then the following rules-of-thumb can be followed to select federates in a complex project:

- Check that the simulation object model (SOM) of the candidate federate satisfies the published classes and interactions from the FAM.
- Check that the needs (in terms of objects and interactions) of the candidate federate are satisfied by other federates.

The details and advantages of a layered federate architecture are discussed in Chap. 7. In this respect, RACoN is a sample of the concrete implementation of the communication layer (RACoN 2015).

4.2.3 Transformations and Code Generation

"A transformation is the automatic generation of a target model from a source model, according to a transformation definition, which is a set of transformation rules that together describe how a model in the source language can be transformed into a model in the target language" (Kleppe et al. 2003).

The transformations (including code generations) defined in this framework are summarized in Table 4.2. DSEEP suggests utilizing the conceptual models as a major mean to appropriately translate the user domain-specific requirements into the simulation environment design. In this respect, a formal transformation (T_1) ensures a verifiable translation from a domain model (i.e. conceptual model) to a federation architecture. The evaluation criteria for choosing the best among the candidate model transformations is listed in (Çetinkaya 2013). An example for T_1 is provided in Chap. 5 using a Field Artillery Conceptual Metamodel (Özhan and Oğuztüzün 2015).

Table 4.2 Transformations

Transformation	Source model	Target model
Transformation – 1 (T_1)	Domain Model (e.g., a model conforming to the field artillery conceptual metamodel)	Federation architecture model (FAM)
Transformation – 2 (T_2) Federation architecture base code generation for HLA	FAM (conforming to FAMM)	Executable code (Java base code by the generator)
Transformation – 3 (T_3) Code generation for computational model	FAM and Detailed Design Model (federate architecture)	Executable code (Java aspect code by the user woven by the AspectJ compiler onto the Java base code)

The use of FAMM provides functionality helping the developer in prototyping federates and federations at a higher level of abstraction than that offered by a state-based representation, such as statecharts. The code generation, a form of model-to-text transformation, comes to scene in two roles in the presented process model. First, it is used to generate the RTI related code using a federation architecture as the source model (T_2 in Table 4.2). Second, it is used to generate the computational related code (T_3 in Table 4.2). Here, the detailed design model is the major source model that helps generate the software skeleton for federate's computational part (Adak et al. 2009).

Bringing the convenience of aspect-oriented programming (AOP) (Kiczales et al. 1997) to bear on the code generation and integration is helpful in realizing functional HLA federate applications from formal specifications. In our use of AOP, computation (which takes place internally to the federate) and communication (which enables the federate to interact with other federates, by receiving the inputs required for the computation and sending the computed outputs) are treated as separate concerns. While the generated base code handles communication, it leaves the computation to be woven as an aspect. As an example, if we think about a gun fire event, the base code will cover the generation of an HLA interaction class for fire event, while the computational aspect will be the implementation the body of fire method. For the computational parts, standard programming techniques can be used.

Another approach is to use text templating techniques for code generation such as Microsoft T4 text templates (Microsoft 2015). SimGe uses this technique. It allows the designer to construct a federation architecture model and then using this model it generates code for the target platform, RACoN. The architecture of the generated code by SimGe conforms to the layered simulation architecture as specified in Chap. 7 (Topçu and Oğuztüzün 2013). The development and code generation is expounded in Chap. 9.

4.2.4 Tools

Despite the fact that the presented methodology is independent from the presented tools in Table 3, the support of each phase of the methodology with a tool is important as the tools increase the applicability of the presented methodology. Table 3 only presents a set of sample tools for each phase. The existence of tools helps to automate many activities and eases the development activities for M&S developers. Therefore, the following table summarizes the categorization of some current sample tools that may be employed. Please note that a generic categorization of tools is presented in (IEEE Std 1730-2010 2010).

Table 4.3 Categorization of tools (Adapted from (Topçu 2004))

Phase	Sub-phase	Explanation	Sample tools
Conceptual model	Scenario development tools	Scenario development tools are used to support the activities of the development, editing, and classification of the simulation scenarios	For military simulations, MSDL (SISO 2008) enabled scenario editors
	Conceptual model development tools	They are used in developing and in modeling the CMs, which comprises the formal conceptual model. They are also employed in the formalization of the simulation scenarios	Generic (meta)modeling tools. For instance, GME (ISIS 2015)
	Conceptual model validation tools	They are used to validate the formal conceptual model (by SMEs)	Custom tools
Federation design	Federation architecture modeling tools	They generally include the object modeling tools	SimGe (SimGe 2015), Federation Architecture Modeling Environment (FAME) (Topçu 2007), MAK FE[a]
	Architecture verification tool	They are used to check structural consistency of the federation architecture	OCL tools, Promela Code Generator, which employs Promela/SPIN for the verification of proper use of federate interface (Kızılay et al. 2009)
Detailed design	UML modeler	General UML CASE tool	Many commercial and open source tools (e.g. Enterprise Architect,[b] StarUML[c])
	Graphical modeling tools	Causal graphical modeling tools	Many commercial and open source tools (e.g. Matlab/Simulink,[d] Scilab/Xcos,[e] Open Modelica[f])
	Design verification tool	They are used to check structural consistency of the UML and simulation models	OCL tools and static model checking tools (e.g. Matlab/Simulink Model Advisor,[g] MES Model Examiner[h])

(continued)

Table 4.3 (continued)

Phase	Sub-phase	Explanation	Sample tools
Execution model	Development environment	They are integrated development environments for specific platforms	SimGe, Pitch Developer Studio,[i] MAK VR-Link[j]
	Manual implementation (languages)	Selection of an implementation language is dependent to an RTI API or RTI binding support	RTI API (e.g. C++, Java) RTI Abstraction Layers (e.g. RACoN)
	Code generators	Selection of code generators is dependent to the target platform, the HLA specification, and RTI	SimGe, AOP based Code Generator for FAMM (Adak et al. 2009), Simulink Coder,[k] X2C[l]
	Results validation	Validation of simulation execution results vs. referent results	Statistical analysis tools, such as R, can be employed according to the application, data, and analysis requirements

[a]http://mak.com/Fe/, last accessed at August 30, 2015
[b]http://www.sparxsystems.com/, last accessed at August 6, 2015
[c]http://staruml.io/, last accessed at August 6, 2015
[d]http://www.mathworks.com/products/simulink, last accessed at August 6, 2015
[e]http://www.scilab.org/, last accessed at August 6, 2015
[f]https://www.openmodelica.org/, last accessed at August 6, 2015
[g]www.mathworks.com/products/simverification/, last accessed at August 6, 2015
[h]http://www.model-engineers.com/en/model-examiner.html, last accessed at August 6, 2015
[i]http://www.pitch.se/products/developer-studio, last accessed at August 6, 2015
[j]http://www.mak.com/, last accessed at August 6, 2015
[k]http://www.mathworks.com/products/simulink-coder/, last accessed at Aug 6, 2015
[l]http://www.mechatronic-simulation.org/features/, last accessed at August 6, 2015

4.2.5   DSEEP Alignment

The development lifecycle consists of a series of activities necessary to develop an HLA-based distributed interactive simulation. As DSEEP is a high level process framework, all the activities coincide with DSEEP top level process flow, specifically with the HLA process overlay.

MDE does not enforce a new workflow, but it views the workproducts as models and the activities as transformations among them. Thus, it enhances DSEEP with additional representation and transformation techniques to put MDE principles into practice. For instance, DSEEP suggests the activity of preparation of federation design, but neither does it say how to represent and develop such a design nor does it explain what a federation design is in detail. Here, the MDE point of view brings clarity to the picture.

4.3 Summary

This chapter has presented a technical framework for developing MDE-based HLA-compliant distributed simulations with verification and validation support. This technical framework includes a methodological view and presents the tool support and aligns the lifecycle activities with DSEEP. In summary, the typical activity steps in the federation development are as follows:

1. Capture and standardize requirements using use case analysis techniques.
2. Develop the simulation scenarios (these are scenarios at the conceptual level).
3. Develop informal conceptual model and validate the informal CM using a SME review technique.
4. Develop formal conceptual model and validate the formal CM using scenarios.
5. Design federation architecture using a formal language such as FAMM.
6. Verify federation architecture.
7. Use the code generator to generate HLA specific base code and the HLA-related documents, especially the FOM document data (FDD), which is required by the RTI to execute the federation.
8. For the internal computation aspect of federates, develop code using object oriented programming techniques. At this point we are doing the coding. Important note: The algorithms we are coding should be found in the simulation conceptual model (developed in steps 3 and 4 above).
9. Build each federate application.
10. Run the federation execution (multiple times as necessary).
11. Validate the results with real life data if available.

References

Adak, M., Topçu, O., & Oğuztüzün, H. (2009, February). Model-based code generation for HLA federates. *Software: Practice and Experience, 40*(2), 149–175.

Bezivin, J. (2005). On the unification power of models. *Journal of Software and Systems Modeling, 4*(2), 171–188.

Çetinkaya, D. (2013). *Model driven development of simulation models defining and transforming conceptual models into simulation models by using metamodels and model transformations.* Delft: Delft University of Technology.

IEEE Std 1516.3-2003. (2003). *Standard for IEEE recommended practice for high level architecture (HLA) federation development and execution process (FEDEP).* New York: IEEE.

IEEE Std 1730.1-2013. (2013). *IEEE recommended practice for distributed simulation engineering and execution process multi-architecture overlay (DMAO).* New York: IEEE.

IEEE Std 1730-2010. (2010). *IEEE recommended practice for distributed simulation engineering and execution process (DSEEP).* New York: IEEE.

ISIS. (2015). *GME manual and user guide* (GME 15 ed.). Institute for Software Integrated Systems Vanderbilt University.

Jacobson, I., Christerson, M., Jonsson, M., & Overgaard, G. (1993). *Object-oriented software engineering: A use case driven approach.* Addison-Wesley.

Kiczales, G., et al. (1997). *Aspect-oriented programming* (pp. 220–242). Berlin/Heidelberg/New York: Springer.

Kızılay, V., Topçu, O., Oğuztüzün, H., & Buzluca, F. (2009). *RTI-related behavior verification of HLA federates using pre- and postconditions.* Orlando: SISO.

Kleppe, A., Warmer, S., & Bast, W. (2003). *MDA explained: The model driven architecture, practice and promise.* Addison-Wesley.

MacCartney, S. (1999). *ENIAC: The triumphs and tragedies of the world's first computer.* New York: Walker and Company.

Microsoft. (2015). *Code generation and T4 text templates.* [Online] Available at: https://msdn.microsoft.com/en-us/library/bb126445.aspx. Accessed 09 July 2015.

OMG. (2015). *OMG unified modeling language (OMG UML) version 2.5.* Object Management Group.

Özhan, G., & Oğuztüzün, H. (2015). Transformation of conceptual models to executable high level architecture federation models. In L. Yılmaz (Ed.), *A tribute to Tuncer Ören* (pp. 135–173). Switzerland: Springer International Publishing.

Özhan, G., Oğuztüzün, H., & Evrensel, P. (2008). Modeling of field artillery tasks with live sequence charts. *The Journal of Defense Modeling and Simulation: Applications, Methodology, Technology, 5*(4), 219–252.

Pace, D. K. (1999). Conceptual model descriptions. In *Simulation Interoperability Workshop Spring.* Orlando: SISO.

Pace, D. K. (2000). Ideas about simulation conceptual model development. *Johns Hopkins APL Technical Digest, 21*(3), 327–336.

Pace, D. K. (2004). Modeling and simulation verification and validation challenges. *Johns Hopkins APL Technical Digest, 25*(2), 163–172.

Powell, E., & Noseworthy, J. (2012). The test and training enabling architecture (TENA). In A. Tok (Ed.), *Engineering principles of combat modeling and distributed simulation* (pp. 449–478). Hoboken: Wiley.

RACoN. (2015). *RACoN Web Site.* [Online] Available at: http://www.ceng.metu.edu.tr/~otopcu/racon/. Accessed 19 Dec 2015.

Savaşan, H., & Oğuztüzün, H. (2002). Distributed simulation of helicopter recovery operations at sea. In *Proceedings of Military, Government, and Aerospace Simulation (MGA02), Advanced simulation technologies conference simulation series* (pp. 120–125). San Diego: The Society for Modeling & Simulation International (SCS).

Schmidt, D. (2006). Model-driven engineering. *IEEE Computer, 39*(2), 25–32.

SimGe. (2015). *SimGe Web Site.* [Online] Available at: http://www.ceng.metu.edu.tr/~otopcu/simge/. Accessed 19 Dec 2015.

SISO. (2008). *Standard for military scenario definition language (MSDL).* Simulation Interoperability Standards Organization (SISO).

SISO. (2015). *Federation engineering agreements template (FEAT) programmer's reference guide.* [Online] Available at: https://www.sisostds.org/featprogrammersreference/index.htm. Accessed 30 Aug 2015.

Topçu, O. (2004). *Development, representation, and validation of conceptual models in distributed simulation.* Halifax: Defence R&D Canada – Atlantic (DRDC Atlantic).

Topçu, O. (2007). *Metamodeling for the HLA federation architectures.* Ankara, Turkey: The Computer Engineering Department, The Graduate School of Natural and Applied Sciences, Middle East Technical University (METU).

Topçu, O., & Oğuztüzün, H. (2005, Winter). Developing an HLA based naval maneuvering simulation. *Naval Engineers Journal, 117*(1), 23–40.

Topçu, O., & Oğuztüzün, H. (2013, March). Layered simulation architecture: A practical approach. *Simulation Modelling Practice and Theory, 32*, 1–14.

Topçu, O., Adak, M., & Oğuztüzün, H. (2008, July). A metamodel for federation architectures. *Transactions on Modeling and Computer Simulation (TOMACS), 18*(3), 10:1–10:29.

Zeigler, B. (1984). *Multifaceted modeling and discrete event simulation.* Orlando: Academic Press, Inc.

Part III
Modeling and Design

Chapter 5
Conceptual Modeling

This chapter elaborates on the notion of conceptual modeling. First, we answer in detail what a conceptual model (CM) is and then present the two forms of a conceptual model from the representation point of view. Afterwards, two approaches for the formalization of a conceptual model are presented. The first approach is based on using ontologies and the second is based on metamodeling. Both approaches are presented with a case study. All simulations simulate a system in the context of an abstract world or CM, documented or not. Conceptual models, simulation conceptual models, in particular, are widely used in modeling and simulation (M&S) and are becoming one of the main building blocks of the distributed simulation development. The creation of a CM is one of the main steps in simulation development and facilitates the transition between simulation requirements and the simulation high-level design by helping simulation engineers understand the requirements clearly. CMs are also used as a means of communication between simulation stakeholders, including users, developers, and sponsors. From a user's perspective, the CM is the most important document about the simulation capabilities because it includes assumptions, limitations, algorithms, objects, and relations among these objects related to the real world. From a developer's perspective, the conceptual model prepares the basis for simulation development. From the verification and validation (V&V) agent's perspective it is a vital element in simulation V&V.

5.1 What Is a Conceptual Model?

A concept is defined as "(i) something conceived in the mind, (ii) an abstract or generic idea generalized from particular instances" in Merriam-Webster (online) dictionary (Merriam-Webster 2015). Thus, conceptual is defined as "of, relating to, or consisting of concepts" (Merriam-Webster 2015). We find the meaning (ii) closer to our understanding of a conceptual model as we expect an analyst to study some

© Springer International Publishing Switzerland 2016
O. Topçu et al., *Distributed Simulation*, Simulation Foundations,
Methods and Applications, DOI 10.1007/978-3-319-03050-0_5

domain of application and come up with concepts that will help all stakeholders arrive at a common understanding of the domain that they can rely upon to achieve their objectives. The analyst could be generalizing from particular instances (Borah 2002), making use of existing concepts found in related literature or reusing bits and pieces from existing conceptual models.

The idea of conceptual model can be related to Zeigler's modeling and simulation (M&S) theory (Zeigler 1976). Zeigler stated that "the informal model should help both users and colleagues to grasp the basic outlines of the model and to visualize it within the framework of their prior conceptions about how things work". This is (one of) the fundamental purpose(s) of a conceptual model.

Chapter 1 defined the notion of a model briefly as a representation of reality and went on to elaborate on it. When we use the term conceptual model, the reality we are referring to is a domain of application, a field of study, an area of interest, or, using military terminology, a mission space (Lozano and Mojtahed 2005). Hence, the coverage of a conceptual model is typically larger; a conceptual model often involves multiple specialized models. For example, the conceptual model of rescue operations at sea can involve functional models of military and civilian vessels, rule-bases that prescribe courses-of-action, standard models of sea and weather conditions, and so on.

Although "conceptual model" is a frequently used term in M&S, it is used in many different meanings. Sometimes the term conceptual model is used interchangeably with terms, such as logical model, logical view, domain model, or high-level design. A conceptual model, in its most general sense, does not have to address any computational issues. It can be an abstraction of some application domain, identifying the key concepts and their relationships, but without paying any attention to how they can be simulated. A simulation conceptual model delves into the matter of how the domain concepts and relationships can be represented on a computer and gives the associated algorithms at a level of detail so that a capable engineer can implement them in the form of simulation software.

For the sake of brevity and generality, we talk about a CM, but, for practical reasons, what we usually have in mind is a SCM (Simulation Conceptual Model). In the view of MDA terminology of Chap. 2, CM is conceptually aligned with CIM (computation-independent model) whereas SCM is aligned with PIM (platform-independent model).

From a developer's perspective, a conceptual model is the developer's way of translating the requirements into a detailed software design from which the simulation software will be built (Pace 2000). In High Level Architecture (HLA) based distributed simulations, the Federation Development and Execution Process (FEDEP) (IEEE Std 1516.3-2003 2003) describes a conceptual model so that "The federation conceptual model provides an implementation-independent representation that serves as a vehicle for transforming objectives into functional and behavioral capabilities; the model also provides a crucial traceability link between the federation objectives and the design implementation. This model can be used as the structural basis for many federation design and development activities (including scenario development) and can highlight correctable problems early in the federation development process when properly validated."

Conceptual models can be viewed from different perspectives. CM is the result of an effort to understand, to reason about, and to obtain consensus about the real world domain as related to the simulation objectives at hand. Therefore, it is important to state explicitly the purpose, objectives, and the intended uses of any conceptual model.

The objective of the descriptive format for the conceptual model (system representation) is to provide a coherent set of information that fully, and correctly, describes the system representation so that its capabilities, limitations, and characteristics can be readily understood by subject matter experts (SMEs) and simulation development personnel (Pace 2000). An important point is that a simulation conceptual model is the document where the issue of fidelity is resolved to the satisfaction of all stakeholders.

The following excerpt from (Fırat 2000) states the use of conceptual modeling:

"System developers must have a clear understanding of the domain, for which the system is developed, to produce the system [that is] is valid and sufficient for the intended use. Since development of an information system starts with the definition of informal requirements specification (usually in natural language) defined by the users, these informal specifications are formalized in to the conceptual models so that the system design has a more structured and clarified base. The main motivation behind this activity is that the structure of natural language statements may cause different interpretation, while the formal representation of these statements have inherently one valid interpretation."

Conceptual models serve several purposes:

- A conceptual model helps the developers understand the problem domain.
- A conceptual model provides criteria for the verification and validation of the simulation and simulation results.
- A conceptual model provides a structured and precise document for the communication between system developers and application domain specialists.
- A conceptual model serves a basis for high-level reuse (Balci et al. 2008).

From our description of the term the connection between a conceptual model and an ontology, in the sense of "explicit specification of a conceptualization" (Gruber 1995), should become visible. From our perspective, an ontology is a conceptual model expressed in an ontology language. The trajectory simulation ontology TSONT, discussed in below in Sect. 5.3.1, is a case in point. It is a simulation conceptual model for the domain of trajectory simulation, expressed in the language OWL (Web Ontology Language). Expressing conceptual models as ontologies is becoming commonplace given the wide-spread adoption of ontology-related techniques and tools.

When we bring together the conceptual model with other M&S concepts, the general modeling and simulation approach will follow the diagram in Fig. 5.1, which represents the relationships between models, simulations, and reality. Here, the simulation is regarded as software application or more generally as computer-based system including hardware/software mix as in training simulators. But, in this book, we generally tend to have a software outlook.

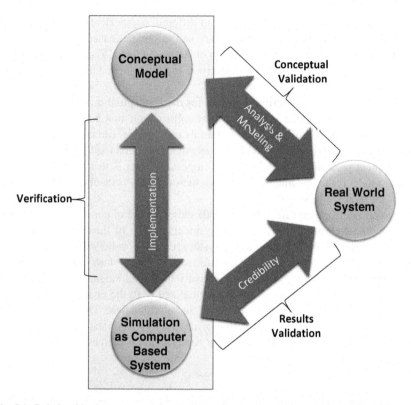

Fig. 5.1 Relationships between models, simulations, and reality (Adapted from (Topçu 2004))

Conceptual model validation is the evaluation of a conceptual model with respect to the system or real life, where the objective is primarily to evaluate the realism of the conceptual model with respect to the objectives of the study (Birta and Nur 1996). Results validation is the evaluation of the simulation output. Verification is the process of checking that the implementation of the conceptual model as a simulation system is correct. Thus, the conceptual model plays the role of the specification in the verification of simulation software. For an extensive treatment of V&V topics, the readers may refer to Sargent (2015).

Conceptual models have gained more importance due to the rapid growth of distributed simulations. In a distributed simulation, generally, the components are developed independently or reused from another simulation. Therefore, it is important to define the intersection of intended domains of each component (also called federate), which is a part of the distributed simulation (federation), in order to determine the combined interest of the whole simulation.

HLA (IEEE Std 1516-2010 2010) (IEEE Std 1516.1-2010 2010) (IEEE Std 1516.2-2010 2010), generally speaking, distributed simulation slightly changes the view of a simulation as a single, centralized, though not necessarily monolithic, application, by introducing a new step: Simulation Environment (Federation) Design. In HLA terms, a federation is a group of distributed simulation components. Federation design defines the data flow and interactions between distributed components (see Chap. 6 for more on simulation environment design). The revised picture is depicted in the Fig. 5.2. In classical waterfall software engineering processes, design precedes before coding.

The MDE-based process model, which is introduced in Chap. 4, for distributed simulation development is based on this model.

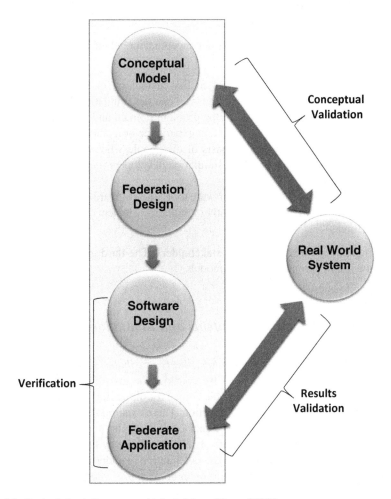

Fig. 5.2 Revised simulation process (Adapted from (Topçu 2004))

5.2   Conceptual Model Representation

This section presents two forms of conceptual model (CM) representation: informal and formal, and also describes how these relate to each other. Before presenting the details of conceptual model representation, we will briefly overview the potential users and the potential content of the conceptual model.

5.2.1   User Profiles

In general, we can categorize the users of conceptual model into three groups (Topçu 2004). These groups are:

- CM Customers: This group refers to the customers (or sponsors in defense domain) and the users, who need and who use the simulation respectively. This group is generally experienced in the problem domain and does not necessarily have software/simulation development experience or technical background.
- CM Developers: This group consists of the people who will develop, modify, adapt and re-use the CM, and the simulation developers (i.e., software designers and programmers).
- Non-Human Users: All kind of software tools and software agents. For example, V&V tools, HLA federates, and other simulation elements (e.g., computer generated forces).

The first two groups are obvious stakeholders. The third group may come into play in the use of formal conceptual models.

5.2.2   Conceptual Model Contents and Limitations

The domain elements include *entities*, *entity attributes/descriptive variables*, *functions/actions*. As an example, if we consider the maritime domain, a surface vessel is an entity in that domain and the course (of the vessel) is an entity attribute. Changing the course or docking is a function. There exist *relationships/interactions* between domain entities. A frigate is a surface vessel (inheritance relation) and air-defense radar is part of a frigate (part-of relation). We may have *assumptions*, for instance an assumption stating that signal attenuation in underwater acoustics is due to spherical spreading only, and the problem domain *pre- and post-conditions* that are related with actions and interactions. In the problem domain, we may have also *constraints/bounds/limitations* (e.g., operational area is 50×50 km) and *domain-specific algorithms* (e.g., target motion analysis algorithms in target localization or line-of-sight algorithms). Additionally, the problem domain includes the *processes*. A process is a sequence of discrete actions or events, continuous developments, or a mixture of the two. Functions/actions can be regarded as being instantaneous while processes as time consuming.

The following documents can be considered as parts of a conceptual model. They are mainly used to capture the items presented above by use of verbal sentence analysis and use case methodology techniques (Jacobson et al. 1993). The level of fidelity should be regarded as a cross-cutting concern of the CM; therefore, all these items should comply with the same fidelity requirements.

- Scenarios
- The aim of simulation, Objectives, Requirements, Research Questions
- Experimentation or Usage Plan for Simulation
- Any authoritative information explaining the intended problem domain (e.g., military operation concepts)

The extent of the content and limits of the conceptual model is an open research question. Some researchers also include simulation domain elements, such as entity representations and algorithms, then it is called a *simulation conceptual model*, which makes the CM more simulation-oriented.

5.2.3   Informal Conceptual Model

Informal CM is especially used by the customer group. CM customers can easily understand the capabilities of the simulation without technical information by reviewing the informal CM. Note that being informal does not imply being unformatted.

As an example, we may consider the military domain, which is a well documented domain. The art of war is generally documented as military operational concepts. In many cases (if a military concept coincides with the objectives of the simulation), we can adopt a military operational concept as an informal conceptual model directly (but most likely not as a simulation conceptual model). If the content of the simulation limits the existent military concept or the objectives of the simulation do not coincide with the military concept, then military concepts may be used only as authoritative information source. The informal CM may be a subset of two or more military concepts (e.g. a mixture of surface warfare and anti-air warfare concepts).

In the literature, there are various methods used to document an informal conceptual model, such as use cases in software engineering (Jacobson et al. 1993), the scientific paper-based approach (Pace 1999), and using a general modeling language like UML and SysML (M&SCO 2011). All the common effort is to specify the domain concepts, entities, and the relations among them. The following techniques may facilitate this approach by explicitly stating the domain concepts, entities, and their relations in a predefined form.

Domain concepts can be captured by using a use case methodology used in object-oriented analysis (Jacobson et al. 1993) and noun-verb analysis in natural language. For example, a navy concept may state that:

"In a surface operation, the surface task group should operate in formations. The surface task group is composed of frigates and commanded by the Officer in Tactical Command (OTC) to accomplish a specific task. OTC gives an order to form one of the formations in accordance to operation phase, and the Officer of the Watch (OOW) of each frigate must adjust their ship's course and speed to take the appropriate position and form the ordered formation as well as keeping their positions in a formation. Officer Scheduling the Exercise (OSE) will give the task and the operation details to OTC..."

The simulation developer can perform a grammatical parse on the given text and can select the nouns (and noun phrases) and *verbs (and verb phrases)*. Then he (or she) can select the important domain concepts and entities by interviewing the domain experts. Nouns are generally domain entities (e.g., frigate) or attributes of entities (e.g., ship's course and ship's speed) while verbs tend to be operations (e.g., to give an order) or relations (e.g., is composed of) among those entities.

"In a surface operation, the surface task group should *operate* in formations. The surface task group *is composed of* frigates and *commanded by* the Officer in Tactical Command (OTC) to *accomplish* a specific task. OTC *gives* an order to form one of the formations in accordance to operation phase, and the Officer of the Watches (OOWs) of frigates must *adjust* their ship's course and speed to *take* the appropriate position and form the ordered formation as well as keeping their positions in a formation. Officer Scheduling the Exercise (OSE) will *give* the task and the operation details to OTC..."

Table 5.1 can be used to document the domain concepts and entities. Entity is the term for things in the problem domain; it is characterized by a description, its attributes, its functions, and its relationships with other entities in the problem space. Attributes are defined by a name, a type, and limit information if applicable. Operations (a.k.a. member functions) related to entity are expressed in terms of a name, input variables, and output variables. Relations or interactions between entities can be expressed as text descriptions. These tables will also ease the development of the formal conceptual model.

An example table for a sea vessel domain entity is presented in Table 5.2.

Table 5.1 Table format for domain entities (Topçu 2004)

Entity name				
Description				
Attributes	Name	Type	Limits	Description
Operations (Member Functions)	Name	Input variables	Output variables	Description
Relationships interactions				
Constraints				
Examples of instances				

Informal CM can be validated by domain expert (SME) reviews. It is important to use expert intuition because the real world does not have a formal presence. Therefore, SME review technique is accepted as the main validation technique. Here, we use SME term for domain expert who is qualified to validate the conceptual model. This implies that an SME must have a basic understanding of the M&S field.

5.2.4   Formal Conceptual Model

Simulation informal conceptual models may contain contradictions, ambiguities, vagueness, incomplete statements, and mixed levels of details. To overcome these, formal methods are employed. Unfortunately, formal methods are not a panacea. Although they can help with these issues, they are difficult to apply. To apply formal methods to CMs, the CM must be formalized in the first place. Thus, the first recommendation is to practice CM validation rigorously. One step further, we attempt a formalization of the CM. Domain-specific modeling is a remarkable way to formalize a CM as a metamodel. Finally, we can formally check properties of the CM using automated tools, such as model checkers.

A formal conceptual model is directly used by the CM developers and non-human users. One of the main rationales for the formal CM is to transform the conceptual model (or domain knowledge) into a machine-readable and machine-

Table 5.2 Example for documentation of a domain entity (Topçu 2004)

Sea vessel				
Description	The word "vessel" includes every description of watercraft, used or capable of being used as a means of transportation on water. "Sea vessel" and "vessel" is used interchangeably			
Attributes	Name	Type	Limits	Description
	Course	Degrees	0–359	N/A
	Speed	Knots	0–70	N/A
	Position (Lat, Long)	True in degrees	Lat: 0–90 Long:0–180	N/A
	Draft	Meters	0–20	N/A
	Class	String	N/A	N/A
	Source Level (SL)	dB	−30 – N/A	N/A
Operations	Name	Input variables	Output variables	Description
	Change Speed	Speed	New Speed	N/A
	Change Course	Course	New Course	N/A
	Change Source Level	Source Level	New Source Level	N/A

(continued)

Table 5.2 (continued)

Sea vessel	
Relationships Interactions	Sea vessel moves in and injects acoustic energy into the environment
	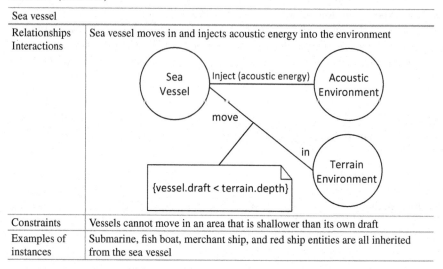
Constraints	Vessels cannot move in an area that is shallower than its own draft
Examples of instances	Submarine, fish boat, merchant ship, and red ship entities are all inherited from the sea vessel

understandable form. This makes possible for all kinds of software tools and agents to read and understand the conceptual model. Some possible formalization techniques are presented in the following sections.

5.3 Representation by Ontologies

Referring to Pace who describes simulation conceptual model as the collection of information about the developer's concept of the simulation and its pieces (Pace 2000), there have been some efforts to utilize ontologies as simulation conceptual models. Miller and his coworkers argued that M&S could benefit from ontologies just like other fields and introduced DeMo (Discrete Event Modeling and Simulation Ontology) (Silver et al. 2011). In 2011, Durak and his colleagues introduced Trajectory Simulation Ontology (TSONT) as a simulation conceptual model.

The term ontology is borrowed from philosophy, where it means a systematic account of "what there is" (Quine 1980). In our quest, though, we are interested in specialized ontologies targeted to our domain of application, and also upper ontologies that support them in terms of more fundamental concepts. We recall Gruber's (1995) influential definition of ontology as an "explicit specification of conceptualization". As noted by Guarino and his colleagues (Guarino et al. 2009), this definition evolved to "formal, explicit specification of a shared conceptualization" on the account of its being formal and representing a common view (rather than a personal view) of the domain.

Knowledge in ontologies can be formalized using five kinds of components: concepts, relations, functions, axioms, and instances. Concepts can be anything about which something is said. They can be a description of a task, function, action, strategy, etc. Taxonomies are widely employed to organize the ontological knowledge in domain using generalization/specialization relationship. Relationships declare a type of interaction among the concepts of the domain. Finally, axioms are statements which are always true. Instances are the terms that are used to represent the elements of the domain (Corcho and Perez 2000).

The basic idea of utilizing ontologies as a bases for specifications is to author an ontology which models the application domain and provides a vocabulary for specifying the requirement for one or more target applications. Then, the software is developed based on the ontology (Fablo et al. 2002). This approach is well aligned with requirements of conceptual modeling.

Research on knowledge representation produced several logic-based languages. Thanks to the attraction of the Semantic Web vision, ontology research produced a series of web ontology languages and frameworks, culminating in OWL (Corcho and Perez 2000). Web Ontology Language (OWL) became a standard in 2004 as the broadly accepted ontology language of the Semantic Web by World Wide Web Consortium (W3C) Web Ontology Working Group (Dean et al. 2004). Later OWL is extended to OWL 2 with various new features such as richer data types and data ranges (Motik et al. 2012).

The PhysSys, the ontology of physical systems, is one of the first efforts to employ ontologies in modeling and simulation (Borst and Akkermans 1997). It was developed as based on systems dynamics theory and captures multiple conceptual viewpoints upon a physical system which include system layout, physical processes, and mathematical relations. It was proposed as the conceptual foundation for the structure of Open Library for Models of mEchatronic Components (OLMECO). The aim of the OLMECO project was to develop a modeling and simulation environment for industrial applications. The use of ontologies for mission space modeling is proposed in (Mojtahed et al. 2005). The next section will present TSONT as an example that employs ontologies for conceptual modeling.

5.3.1 Case Study: Trajectory Simulation Ontology

Trajectory Simulation Ontology, abbreviated as TSONT, is being developed in order to establish a common vocabulary that is agreed by people working on trajectory simulations and to create a backbone for systematization of knowledge on how to build a trajectory simulation.

Trajectory simulation, in the present context, means computing the flight path and other parameters, such as orientation and angular rates, of a munition from the start to the end of its motion (US DoD 1995). There is a wide variety in types of trajectory simulations with respect to their performance and fidelity characteristics, from simple point-mass simulations to 6–7 degrees of freedom hardware-in-the-loop missile simulations. They involve the mathematical models for the behavior of a munition and its subsystems during its operation. The equations of motion can be given as an example mathematical model that determine the acceleration, velocity, position, and attitude of the munition resulting from forces and moments due to gravity, thrust, and aerodynamics.

TSONT presents the major concepts of trajectory simulation. The following paragraph will introduce an excerpt from TSONT in order to exemplify the employment of an ontology as a simulation conceptual model. Trajectory simulation classes as presented in Fig. 5.3 are the entities of a trajectory simulation domain that are used to compute a trajectory. The first level entities include coordinate system, model, parameter, solver, trajectory simulation and trajectory simulation phase. A phase is described as the segment of a munition flight whose simulation can be performed by using a particular set of models. A trajectory simulation can be composed of multiple phases. TSONT captures also the hierarchy of phases and excerpt of which is depicted in Fig. 5.4.

For example, computing the trajectory during the guided phase requires a different set of models than those required for free flight. A trajectory simulation model refers to the logical or mathematical models of the actors that have an effect on the flight of the munition. Aerodynamics model, atmosphere model, autopilot model, dynamics model, earth model, gravity model, and guidance model are some of the models covered in TSONT.

As an example, the equations of motion which characterize the relationships between the forces and moments acting on the munition and the resulting motion constitute the Dynamics Model. It uses forces and moments to compute the dynamic model's state derivatives, namely, the velocity and acceleration of the munition. TSONT captures a large hierarchy for Dynamic Models. Excerpted from this hierarchy, Fig. 5.5 provides a specification of Body Fixed6DOF Dynamics Model.

The Dynamics Models serves a functionality called Update Dynamics Model State and Derivatives to compute the angular and translational accelerations using the instantaneous forces and moments. TSONT captures the mathematical formulations of the algorithms to compute the functions with utilizing Dynamic Aerospace Vehicle Exchange Markup Language (DAVE-ML) (AIAA 2011). The mathematical model, the equation and the DAVE-ML excerpt, from Update Body Fixed Dynamics Model State and Derivatives for one of the translational accelerations in body coordinate system is given below in Fig. 5.6 as an example

5.4 Formalization by Metamodeling

Domain-specific modeling is another powerful approach to build formalized conceptual models (Kelly and Tolvanen 2008). A domain-specific model is a metamodel specifically defined to capture the domain concepts. The case study presented in this section comes from a branch of military domain, namely, field artillery. Some field artillery missions, which can be regarded as conceptual scenarios, are modelled using live sequence charts (LSCs). In fact, the LSC is the basis for the behavioral part of the metamodel, whereas the data part is based on a UML-like language.

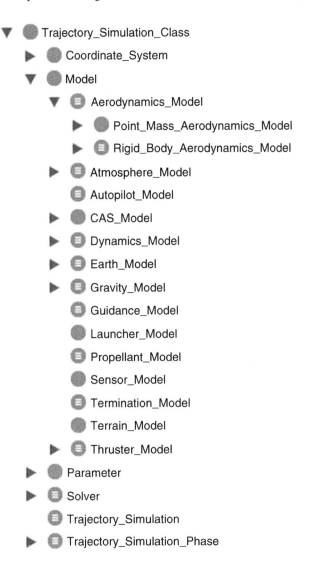

Fig. 5.3 Trajectory simulation classes

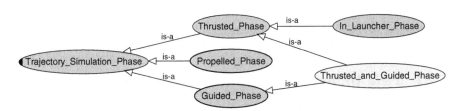

Fig. 5.4 Hierarchy of trajectory simulation phases

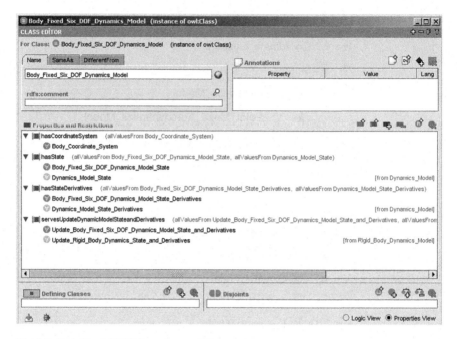

Fig. 5.5 Body fixed 6DOF dynamics model

Constructing a metamodel requires that we have a meta-metamodel that serves as the language of definition for the metamodel. In our example, the meta-metamodel is provided by the tool being used, namely GME; and it is called metaGME. By a series of transformations, the mission models can be mapped to executable simulation code.

5.4.1 Case Study: Field Artillery (Indirect Fire)

This case study presents a formal conceptual model for a portion of the field artillery (FA) domain (Özhan et al. 2008). The structural part of the model identifies the entities in the FA domain along with their properties and associations. The behavioral part of the model describes the FA missions in the language of live sequence charts (LSCs). Formalization of the CM is achieved by devising a metamodel. The metamodel is developed using the GME tool. First, we present background domain information and then give the technical details.

5.4.2 Field Artillery Observed Fire – Background

The overall mission of field artillery is to destroy, neutralize, or suppress the enemy by cannon, rocket, and missile fire and to help integrate all fire support assets into combined arms operations. Observed fire is carried out by the coordinated efforts of

```
<variableDef name="udot" varID="udot" units="m/s2">
    <description> Body fixed tranlational acceleration in X </description>
    <calculation>
        <math xmlns='http://www.w3.org/1998/Math/MathML'>
            <apply>
                <eq/>
                <ci>udot</ci>
                <apply>
                    <plus/>
                    <apply>
                        <times/>
                        <ci>FX</ci>
                        <apply>
                            <power/>
                            <ci>mass</ci>
                            <cn type='integer'>-1</cn>
                        </apply>
                    </apply>
                    <apply>
                        <times/>
                        <ci>r</ci>
                        <ci>v</ci>
                    </apply>
                    <apply>
                        <times/>
                        <cn type='integer'>-1</cn>
                        <apply>
                            <times/>
                            <ci>q</ci>
                            <ci>w</ci>
                        </apply>
                    </apply>
                </apply>
            </apply>
        </math>
    </calculation>
    <isOutput/>
</variableDef>
```

$$\dot{u} = \frac{F_x}{m} - qw + vr$$

Fig. 5.6 DAVE-ML example

the field artillery team, which is composed of the forward observer, the Fire Direction Center (FDC), and several firing sections of the firing unit. The basic duty of the forward observer, considered the eyes of the team, is to detect and locate suitable indirect fire targets within his zone of observation. In order to start an attack on a target, the forward observer issues a Call For Fire (CFF) request to the FDC. It contains the information needed by the FDC to determine the method of attack (Özhan and Oğuztüzün 2015). As it is quite possible to miss the target in the first round of fire, the common practice is first to conduct adjustment on the target. Usually the central gun is selected as the adjusting weapon. The observer provides correction information to the FDC after each shot based on his spotting of the detonation.

Once a target hit is achieved, the observer initiates the Fire For Effect (FFE) phase by noting this in his correction message. FFE is carried out by the cannons of a firing unit firing all together with the same fire parameters as the last adjustment shot. After the designated number of rounds is fired, the observer sends a final correction including surveillance information. If the desired effect on the target is achieved, based on the surveillance, the mission ends. Otherwise, the observer may request repetitions or restart the adjustment phase if deemed necessary.

5.4.3   Field Artillery Metamodel

ACMM, the metamodel of ACM (field Artillery Conceptual Model), serves as a conceptual model for the field artillery observed fire domain. It is developed using the GME tool. Once registered as a "paradigm" in GME, ACMM yields a domain-specific language for the formal definition of an observed fire mission (i.e., an ACM), such as fire for effect. An ACM is the input source model for a transformation.

ACMM consists of a behavior component and a data component. The data model addresses certain aspects of tactical, rather than technical, fire direction. Technical fire direction, which involves ballistic calculations, is beyond the scope of ACMM. Every top-level entity in the data model is specialized from NATO's Joint C3 Information Exchange Data Model (JC3IEDM) (NATO 2011) by means of the inheritance mechanism. In that sense, JC3IEDM serves as an upper ontology related to fundamental military domain knowledge.

The ACMM's data portion consists of a set of domain entities called actors, which are able to perform computations and send/receive messages (to/from other actors and the environment) on a one-to-one or multi-cast basis. The multi-cast communication media are called nets, which are represented simply as sets of references to actors. The communicated messages are collections of domain information, extracted from authoritative sources and composed in different granularities.

The upper level modeling hierarchy in metamodel is depicted in Fig. 5.7.

The behavior modeling capability of ACMM encompasses the military commands and structured messages exchanged between the participating actors in a field artillery observed fire mission. The behavioral part of ACMM is essentially the LSC metamodel (Topçu et al. 2008). As LSC (Brill et al. 2004) is extended from MSC (International Telecommunication Union (ITU-T) 2004), the metamodel covers the MSC metamodel in its core. MSC is a visual language for specifying the behavior of a concurrent system, focusing on the communication aspect. It is quite similar to UML 2.x sequence diagram notation. The LSC Metamodel (LMM) is developed as part of the Federation Architecture Metamodel (FAMM). FAMM serves as the distributed simulation architecture model for transformations. Both metamodels are introduced in Chap. 6.

Both parts are integrated by defining integration points in a separate GME paradigm sheet as seen in Fig. 5.8.

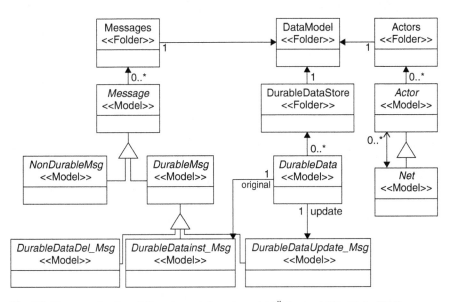

Fig. 5.7 The upper level modeling elements in metamodel (Özhan and Oğuztüzün 2015)

5.4.4 Modeling Environment

Once the FA metamodel is loaded, GME automatically provides a customized environment to model particular FA missions. The intended application is to use the FA metamodel as the source for defining model transformations targeting FA federation architectures. The FA mission modeled in LSC serves as the federation scenario.

5.4.5 Transformations

The ACM is a PIM of the reality (field artillery domain) with which the simulation is concerned. The FAM is a PSM, where the platform is the HLA-RTI in our case. A FAM constitutes a major portion of the federation design documentation (Topçu et al. 2008). The model transformer produces a FAM from an ACM by executing the ACM2FAM transformation rules, and the AspectJ/Java-based code generator produces executable code from that FAM.

The ACM-to-FAM transformation is carried out with the Graph Rewriting and Transformation (GReAT) tool and partly hand-coded for reasons of efficiency.

Code generation from FAM is accomplished by employing a model interpreter (a plug-in to GME) that produces source code for each member federate. The code for a federate application becomes ready for execution on an HLA Runtime Infrastructure (RTI) after weaving the computational aspect provided by the user with the AspectJ compiler.

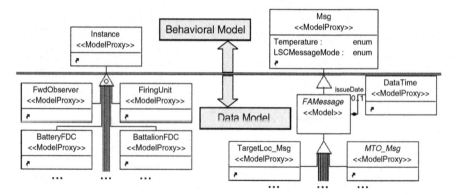

Fig. 5.8 Data and behavioral model integration (partial view) (Özhan et al. 2008)

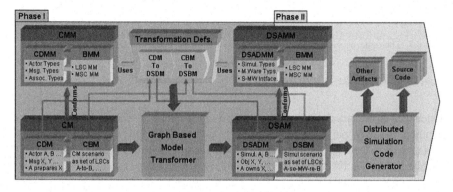

Fig. 5.9 ACM to FAM and executable code (Özhan and Oğuztüzün 2015)

The overall model transformation process is depicted in Fig. 5.9.

As shown in Fig. 5.10, the development environment is GME, which is tailored towards defining model transformations using the GReAT paradigm. The figure has the start rule block in the center area and shows a top-level view of the entire transformation configuration folder, meta-models, transformation rule definitions folder, and other utilities for providing easy global access and cross-domain associations on the right panel. Cross-links establish cross-model associations between the source and target metamodels. They can be defined not only between different domains but can also be used to extend a domain temporarily to provide extra functionality required by the transformation.

As seen in case study, when a formal CM is created using a metamodel, then many simulation artifacts such as code can be generated afterwards.

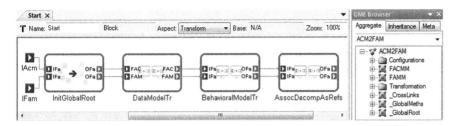

Fig. 5.10 The start rule block of ACM2FAM transformation in GME/GReAT (Özhan and Oguztuzun 2013)

5.5 Summary

It may seem expensive to develop a conceptual model first, especially for large-scale simulations. However, due to the reusability characteristics of ontologies and metamodels, following the initial effort, the others will be developed more quickly.

Two representation techniques for formalization of conceptual model have been presented. One is by building and using ontologies, and the other one is employing metamodeling.

A variation on the metamodeling approach, not discussed here, is the use of a standard modeling language, such as UML, possibly taking advantage of its extension facilities, such as profiling.

Faced with the task of constructing a domain-specific model, should we use an existing language such as an ontology language, or should we define our own modeling language, in the form of a metamodel? The logical complexity of the language is a good criterion. We do not want our modeling language to be burdened with unused features. Being domain-specific, a custom-built metamodel is in general likely to be a much simpler artifact than a fully fledged ontology language like OWL, or an existing modeling language like UML. However, the cost and difficulty of maintaining the modeling language should be weighed against the simplicity argument. Also, tool availability is a practical consideration which can nudge the decision either way.

Formalization generally introduces additional cost and complexity to the development efforts. To develop a formal conceptual model, experts who have the knowledge about software engineering (modeling techniques and tools), knowledge engineering (knowledge acquisition, knowledge representation), and ontology engineering are necessary to guide the process.

In our treatment of conceptual modeling, enabling the application of MDE principles and techniques is an overriding concern. For a varied coverage of the field, the reader is referred to the collection of articles in (Robinson et al. 2010).

References

AIAA. (2011). *Standard: Flight dynamics model exchange standard*. Reston: AIAA.

Balci, O., Arthur, J. D., & Nance, R. E. (2008). Accomplishing reuse with a simulation conceptual model. In S. J. Mason et al. (Eds.), *Winter simulation conference* (pp. 959–965). Piscataway: IEEE.

Birta, G. L., & Nur, F. (1996). A knowledge-based approach for the validation of simulation models: The foundation. *ACM Transactions on Modeling and Computer Simulation, 6*(1), 76–98.

Borah, J. (2002). Conceptual modeling – The missing link of simulation development. In *Spring Simulation Interoperability Workshop*. Orlando: SISO.

Borst, W., & Akkermans, J. (1997). Engineering ontologies. *International Journal of Human-Computer Studies, 46*(2/3), 365–406.

Brill, M., et al. (2004). Live sequence charts: An introduction to lines, arrows, and strange boxes in the context of formal verification. In *Integration of software specification techniques for applications in engineering* (Lecture notes in computer science, Vol. 3147, pp. 374–399). Berlin: Springer.

Corcho, O., & Perez, A. (2000). Evaluating knowledge representation and reasoning capabilities of ontology specification languages. In *ECAI'00 workshop on applications of ontologies and problem solving methods*. Berlin: s.n.

Dean, M., et al. (2004). *OWL web ontology language*. W3C.

Fablo, R., Guizzardi, G., & Duarte, K. (2002). An ontological approach to domain engineering. In *Proceedings of the 14th international conference on software engineering and knowledge engineering*. Ischia: ACM.

Fırat, C. (2000). Conceptual modeling and conceptual analysis in HLA. In *Fall Simulation Interoperability Workshop*. Orlando: SISO.

Gruber, T. (1995). Toward principles for the design of ontologies used for knowledge sharing. *International Journal of Human-Computer Studies, 43*, 907–928.

Guarino, N., Oberle, D., & Staab, S. (2009). What is an ontology? In S. Staab & R. Studer (Eds.), *Handbook on ontologies* (2nd ed., pp. 1–20). Berlin: Springer.

IEEE Std 1516.3-2003. (2003). *Standard for IEEE recommended practice for high level architecture (HLA) federation development and execution process (FEDEP)*. s.l.: IEEE.

IEEE Std 1516-2010. (2010). *Standard for modeling and simulation (M&S) high level architecture (HLA) – Framework and rules*. New York: IEEE.

IEEE Std 1516.1-2010. (2010). *Standard for modeling and simulation (M&S) high level architecture (HLA) – Federate interface specification*. New York: IEEE.

IEEE Std 1516.2-2010. (2010). *Standard for modeling and simulation (M&S) high level architecture (HLA) – Object model template specification*. s.l.: IEEE.

International Telecommunication Union (ITU-T). (2004). *Formal description techniques (FDT) – Message sequence charts*. Telecommunication Standardization Sector of ITU-T.

Jacobson, I., Christerson, M., Jonsson, M., & Overgaard, G. (1993). *Object-oriented software engineering: A use case driven approach*. s.l.: Addison-Wesley.

Kelly, S., & Tolvanen, J.-P. (2008). *Domain-specific modeling: Enabling full code generation*. Hoboken: Wiley-Interscience: IEEE Computer Society.

Lozano, M. C., & Mojtahed, V. (2005). A process for developing conceptual models of the mission space (CMMS) – From knowledge acquisition to knowledge use (05F-SIW-038). *Fall Simulation Interoperability Workshop*. Orlando: SISO.

M&SCO. (2011). *Verification, validation, & accreditation (VV&A) recommended practices guide (VVA RPG)*. [Online] Available at: http://www.msco.mil/vva_rpg.html. Accessed 04 Sept 2015.

Merriam-Webster. (2015). *Merriam-Webster online dictionary*. [Online] Available at: http://www.m-w.com. Accessed 6 Sept 2015.

Mojtahed, V., et al. (2005). *DCMF – Defence conceptual modeling framework (FOI-R--1754-SE)*. Stockholm: Swedish Defence Research Agency.

Motik, B., et al. (2012). *OWL 2 web ontology language structural specification and functional-style syntax.* s.l.: W3C.

NATO. (2011). *Overview of the joint C3 information exchange data model (JC3IEDM Overview),* s.l.: NATO Multiliteral Interoperability Programme.

Özhan, G., & Oguztuzun, H. (2013). Data and behavior decomposition for the model-driven development of an executable simulation model. In G. Wainer & P. Mosterman (Eds.), *Theory of modeling and simulation (TMS/DEVS).* San Diego: SCS.

Özhan, G., & Oğuztüzün, H. (2015). Transformation of conceptual models to executable high level architecture federation models. In L. Yılmaz (Ed.), *A tribute to Tuncer Ören* (pp. 135–173). Switzerland: Springer International Publishing.

Özhan, G., Oğuztüzün, H., & Evrensel, P. (2008). Modeling of field artillery tasks with live sequence charts. *The Journal of Defense Modeling and Simulation: Applications, Methodology, Technology, 5*(218), 218–251.

Pace, D. K. (1999). Conceptual model descriptions. In *Simulation Interoperability Workshop (SIW) Spring.* Orlando: SISO.

Pace, D. K. (2000). Simulation conceptual model development. In *Simulation Interoperability Workshop (SIW) Spring.* Orlando: SISO

Quine, W. V. (1980). On what there is. In: *From a logical point of view: Nie Logico-philosophical essays* (2nd Rev. ed., pp. 20–46). Cambridge, MA: Harvard University Press.

Robinson, S., Brooks, R., Kotiadis, K., & van der Zee, D.-J. (2010). *Conceptual modeling for discrete-event simulation.* Boca Raton: Taylor & Francis.

Sargent, R. G. (2015). Model verification and validation. In M. L. Loper (Ed.), *Modeling and simulation in the systems engineering life cycle* (pp. 57–65). London: Springer.

Silver, G. A., et al. (2011). DeMO: An ontology for discrete-event modeling and simulation. *Simulation: Transactions of the Society for Modeling and Simulation International, 87*(9), 747–773.

Topçu, O. (2004). *Development, representation, and validation of conceptual models in distributed simulation.* Halifax: Defence R&D Canada – Atlantic (DRDC Atlantic).

Topçu, O., Adak, M., & Oğuztüzün, H. (2008, July). A metamodel for federation architectures. *ACM Transactions on Modeling and Computer Simulation (TOMACS), 18*(3), 10:1–10:29.

US DoD. (1995). *Missile flight simulation, Part One surface to air missiles.* s.l.: s.n.

Zeigler, P. B. (1976). *Theory of modeling and simulation.* New York: Wiley-Interscience Publication.

Chapter 6
Federation Architecture: Simulation Environment Design

This chapter introduces the concept of federation (simulation environment) architecture. For rigorous federation design, we need more than lollipop diagrams. In this regard, first, we outline what federation architecture means and then show how to formalize a federation architecture using metamodeling, so that a federation architecture can be put into a machine processable form, thereby enabling tool support for the code generation and the early verification of the federation architectures. To this end, we present a realized metamodel, called Federation Architecture Metamodel (FAMM), for describing the architecture of a HLA compliant federation. We also discuss the verification techniques for federation architectures. Chapter concludes with a case study detailing the federation architecture modeling.

6.1 Introduction

Formalization of a federation architecture is one of the main goals of federation design (simulation environment design in DSEEP jargon), so that a federation architecture can be put into a machine processable form, thereby enabling tool support for the code generation and the early verification of the federation architectures.

As stated in Chap. 3, HLA became a widely accepted standard in the area of distributed simulation over the last decade, and it is not surprising to see that the majority of new distributed simulations in both the civilian and military context are being built to be HLA compliant while HLA itself evolves. Although much effort has been spent on developing HLA federations, the state-of-the-art in simulation environment design representation and documentation still does not provide adequate support for automation of the simulation environment development process (Stytz and Banks 2001).

© Springer International Publishing Switzerland 2016
O. Topçu et al., *Distributed Simulation*, Simulation Foundations,
Methods and Applications, DOI 10.1007/978-3-319-03050-0_6

HLA process overlay to the Distributed Simulation Engineering and Execution Process (DSEEP) (IEEE Std 1730-2010 2011), and Federation Development and Execution Process (FEDEP) (IEEE Std 1516.3-2003 2003) assists and guides the activities of developing an HLA federation. Although DSEEP has defined some design activities, it has left design representation and documentation methods to the designers. With respect to the HLA object model, the Object Model Template (OMT) standard (IEEE Std 1516.2-2010 2010) is adequate for representing the mostly static view of a federation such as the publish/subscribe of object class attributes. OMT, however, does not attempt to capture the dynamic view of a federation or member federates.

As presented in Chap. 2, Model Driven Engineering (MDE) is a promising approach in software industry and academia, which views the system development as a series of models and transformations among the models (Bezivin 2005) (Schmidt 2006). Therefore, it is well suited to specify a federation architecture. A known MDE initiative is the Model Driven Architecture (MDA) of Object Management Group (OMG). MDA advocates separating the specification and implementation of a software-intensive system, in terms of Platform-Independent Model (PIM) and Platform-Specific Model (PSM), respectively. Most prominently, MDA promotes automated transformations between models. In particular, the PIM of a system to be constructed is to be transformed into a PSM. Automated tools, then, could carry out code generation from a PSM to the target execution platform. An earlier manifestation of MDE is Model Integrated Computing (MIC). MIC relies on metamodeling to define domain-specific modeling languages and model integrity constraints (Ledezci et al. 2001). The domain-specific language is then used to automatically compose a domain-specific model-building environment for creating, analyzing, and evolving the system through modeling and generation (Özhan and Oğuztüzün 2006).

The main objective of metamodeling is to formalize the federation architectures, so that a federation architecture can be put into a machine processable form, thereby enabling tool support for the code generation and the early verification of the federation architectures. One of the anticipated benefits is to eliminate the limitations of OMT and DSEEP and thus to bring dynamism into the architectural descriptions. A metamodel for HLA federation architectures provides a domain-specific language (DSL) for the formal representation of the federation architecture. To put differently, such a metamodel is essentially an architecture description language specialized for a particular architectural framework, namely HLA. Serving both as a source and a target, the metamodel supports the definitions of transformations. A metamodel for describing the architecture of a High Level Architecture compliant federation is developed and called as Federation Architecture Metamodel (FAMM) (Topçu et al. 2008).

FAMM formalizes the standard HLA Object Model (IEEE Std 1516.2-2010 2010) and Federate Interface Specification (IEEE Std 1516.1-2010 2010). FAMM supports processing through automated tools and in particular through code generation (Fig. 6.1). It is formulated in metaGME, the metamodel for the Generic Modeling Environment (GME) (ISIS 2015). FAMM is developed by adopting the

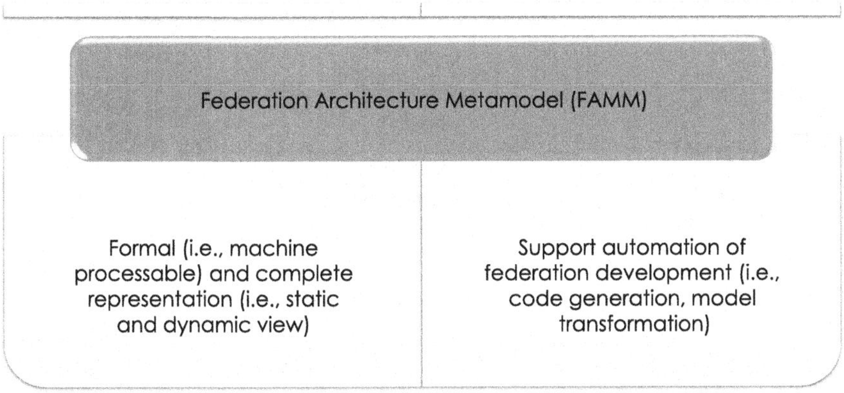

Fig. 6.1 Major properties of FAMM

Domain-Specific (Meta-)Modeling approach to facilitate tool support for federation development. A salient feature of FAMM is the behavioral description of federates based on live sequence charts (LSCs) (Brill et al. 2004). The metamodel treats the structural and dynamic views of a federation on equal footing. The dynamic view of a federate is tantamount to its interactions with the HLA Runtime Infrastructure (RTI), the middleware implementing the HLA Interface Specification. The dynamic view of the federation emerges as the joined federates interact with each other over the RTI as the federation execution unfolds. Specifically, FAMM supports federate base code generation from a described federate behavior and transformations from a simulation conceptual model (which could be regarded as a PIM).

6.2   What Is Federation Architecture?

First let's clarify the development context where this metamodel fits by articulating a methodological view emphasizing models and transformations to elucidate the purpose and the use of the metamodel. Using the MDE-based process model presented in Chap. 4, HLA-based distributed simulation development basically is comprised of a conceptual model, federation architecture model, detailed design model, and federation (in some executable form). All the models are explained in Chap. 4, here we only expound the federation architecture model (FAM), which conforms to FAMM. Figure 6.2 presents the FAM and the related models and transformations.

The Federation Architecture Model is a PSM where, in HLA, the platform is the RTI, and it comprises the Federation Model (Federation Structure, Federation Object Model, and HLA Services) and the Behavioral Models for each participating federate, corresponding to data and action models in Fig. 6.2, respectively. The FAM will serve as an intermediate model acting as a target and source model for model transformations. As a source model, it can be used for generating executable federation skeleton code and the federation artifacts such as FDD file, while as a

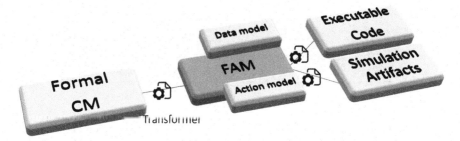

Fig. 6.2 Federation architecture model at the heart of transformations

target model, it serves as an intermediate model for transformations from the formal conceptual model (CM).

The model of a particular federation architecture conforms to the FAMM. FAMM is a typical example of how to integrate the domain-specific data model (i.e. HLA Federation Metamodel) and action model (i.e. LSC Metamodel)

Both tasks, metamodeling and modeling, are accomplished using the Generic Modeling Environment, developed and maintained by Institute for Software Integrated Systems at Vanderbilt University, as a tool to put the MIC vision into practice. GME is an open source, meta-programmable modeling tool that supports domain-specific modeling, where, in our case, the domain is HLA (Ledezci et al. 2001) (ISIS 2015). GME initially serves as a metamodel development environment for domain analysts, and then, based on the metamodel, it provides a domain-specific, graphical model-building environment for the developers. GME also provides support for model interpreter development in terms of an Application Programming Interface (API). A model interpreter, in GME parlance, is a plug-in software component to traverse a domain-specific model and produce some artifact, such as code.

In MDE-based simulation approach, domain-specific (meta-)modeling (DSM) is used as the glue between models. "Domain specific (meta)modeling is an approach to modeling that emphasizes the terminology and concepts specific to the domain (Gray et al. 2001), where data types and logic are abstracted beyond programming" (Çetinkaya 2005).

6.3   Federation Architecture Representation

FAMM can be regarded as a domain-specific architecture description language for HLA federations. A federation architecture model conforming to FAMM is in a machine-processable form, thus enabling tool support.

Here, we present the benefits of FAMM to federation developers expecting to show, in general, how many benefits a metamodel may offer.

- FAMM serves both as a basis for source models for code generation (cf. (Adak et al. 2009)) and as a basis for target models for transformation from the domain-related models (e.g., conceptual models of mission space) (cf. (Özhan et al.

2008)). A model interpreter,[1] called Code Generator, takes a model (i.e., a FAM) including a federate behavior specification as input and produces the federate application base code as output (Adak, et al. 2009).

- FAMM brings forth the expressive power to represent not only the static view of the federation but also the behavior of the federates. It relates behavior with the structure. This power comes from the Behavioral Metamodel, which is integrated with the HLA Object Model and HLA Services Metamodel.
- FAMM lays the groundwork for implementing model interpreters in order to generate useful artifacts such as FED/FDD file and to extract interesting views such as publish/subscribe diagrams.
- FAMM provides support for the verification and validation activities due to the increased precision in the description of the federation.

  - Constraints support early verification (in the sense of consistency checking) in the architectural design phase. Cardinality constraints are supported by design. Further constraints that cannot be enforced by metamodel structure can be formulated using Object Constraint Language (OCL) (OMG 2014).
  - Generating codes for member federate applications and executing the federation serve as a preliminary test for integration of the federation architecture. Thus, it supports a dynamic verification of the federation design.

- FAMM enables static analysis of the federation architecture. This can be helpful, for example, in collecting metrics for assessing the complexity of federation architectures. For instance, an interpreter, called Model Metrics Collector, is used for collecting several metrics over FAM.
- FAMM can help improve the communication among simulation engineers, software engineers, and programmers, again due to increased precision.

The metamodel, along with the libraries, the interpreters, and documentation for sample case studies, including the federation architecture and the automatically generated code of the Strait Traffic Monitoring Simulation, and other sample models are available from the FAMM website (FAMM 2011).

6.3.1   FAMM Structure

The Federation Architecture Metamodel is comprised of two main sub-metamodels: the Behavioral Metamodel (BMM) for specifying the observable behaviors of the federates and the HLA Federation Metamodel (HFMM) for defining both the HLA Federation Object Model (FOM) and the service interface. These two metamodels, included as GME libraries, are connected through a GME paradigm, named Model Integration Metamodel. The structure of FAMM is depicted in Fig. 6.3. BMM is a

---

[1]Do not confuse the model interpreter with a normal interpreter, which is a kind of language processor.

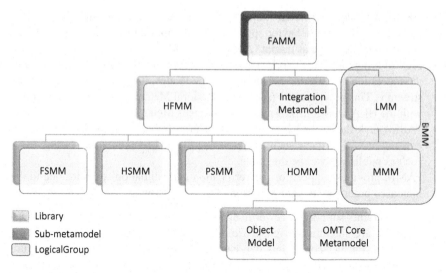

Fig. 6.3 FAMM hierarchy

logical container for the Live Sequence Charts Metamodel (LMM), which is extended from the Message Sequence Charts (MSC) Metamodel (MMM). HFMM is composed of the HLA Object Metamodel (HOMM), Federation Structure Metamodel (FSMM), and HLA Services Metamodel (HSMM). Lastly, the Publish/ Subscribe (P/S) Metamodel (PSMM) is included as a derivative metamodel in order to illustrate the extraction of utility metamodels from the core FAMM. Once the federation architecture is modeled conforming to FAMM, a model interpreter can traverse this model to extract the federation publish and subscribe view and then display it as P/S diagrams (Topçu and Oğuztüzün 2000; Topçu et al. 2003).

Metamodels support each other in a way that an element defined in one model can be used in other models. For example, any method parameter that occurs in HSMM is accounted for by HOMM. Nevertheless, each sub-metamodel can be used independently. This was a main concern in devising the structure of FAMM. In particular, the Metamodel for Message Sequence Charts (ITU-T 2004) as well as Live Sequence Charts can be used to model the MSCs/LSCs for any system of communicating components, not only for distributed simulation components. In the same vein, the HOMM (Çetinkaya 2005) stands on its own and can be used to generate useful artifacts, such as the FOM Document Data (FDD).

The implementation of FAMM in GME is depicted in Fig. 6.4. HFMM, LMM, and HOMM are included as GME libraries.

One may visualize a (meta)model as a graph, whose nodes correspond to concepts and edges to relationships. Thus, the following table should give a rough idea about the size of FAMM. Concepts include the GME stereotypes: atom (models, atoms, FCOs,[2] attributes, references, and inheritances), model (paradigm sheet),

---

[2] First Class Object in GME Jargon.

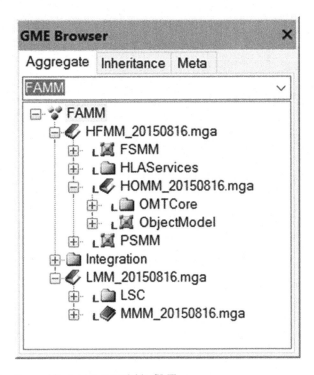

Fig. 6.4 Federation architecture metamodel in GME

Table 6.1 Size of FAMM and its sub-metamodels (for FAMM version 20080817)	Sub-metamodel	Number of concepts	Number of relationships
	BMM	284	400
	HFMM	418	368
	Model integration	18	35
	Total	**720**	**803**

and folder. The stereotypes set (aspects) and reference (proxies) are excluded. Relationships include GME connections (Table 6.1).

Figure 6.5 depicts the "conforms to" relationship between the FAM and FAMM. A Federation Architecture encompasses a federation model and a behavioral model (see Fig. 6.6).

The MSC documents of a federate manifest its interaction with the RTI and possibly with other entities (e.g., users and live entities), and so they describe the federate's observable behavior. FAMM provides the underlying language to describe the federation architectures. Each participating federate's behavior is modeled conforming to BMM and HSMM. The FOM is constructed in conformance with the HLA Object Metamodel and the Federation Structure Metamodel.

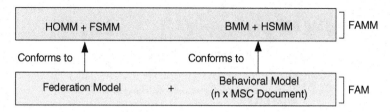

Fig. 6.5 Relationship between a federation architecture and the metamodel

FAM = Federation Model + Behavioral Model

Where:

Federation Model = Federation Structure + HLA Object Model
HLA Object Model = FOM + MOM + SOMs (for each federate) + Other OMT related data (e.g. Dimensions)
Behavioral Model = One or more MSC Documents for each federate
MSC Document = LSCs or MSCs or HMSCs (High Level MSCs)

Fig. 6.6 Formulization of a FAM

6.3.2 User Perspective

A modeling environment, which we can call it as the Federation Architecture Modeling Environment (FAME) for users, is made available by GME once FAMM is invoked as the base paradigm. The screen shot in Fig. 6.7 shows an example-modeling environment, for FAMM users, who are federation designers. GME allows creation of a project for developing a new federation architecture. Figure 6.7 presents a screen shot of the project for the case study: Strait Traffic Monitoring Simulation (STMS) federation architecture (see Sect. 6.7). The root folder (StraitTrafficMonitoringSimulation) serves as a project container for the federation architecture. It includes three major sub-folders, namely, federation structure, behavioral models, and the HLA object models. The federation structure folder contains information about the federation, such as the location of the FDD/ FED file, the link for the related FOM, and the structure of the federation, where the participating federate applications and their corresponding Simulation Object Models are linked. The folder for behavioral models includes an MSC document for each participating federate. The HLA object models folder includes the FOM, SOMs, and the other Object Model Template related information (e.g., data types, dimensions, etc.). In the example, SOMs for ship and station applications and a FOM for the STMS federation are provided.

There are auxiliary libraries that can be readily attached to a project. Three libraries are currently provided: IEEE 1516.1 Methods Library, IEEE 1516.1 Management Object Model (MOM) Library, and IEEE1516.2 HLA Defaults Library. In the example, the methods library (designated with a book icon) is attached to the project.

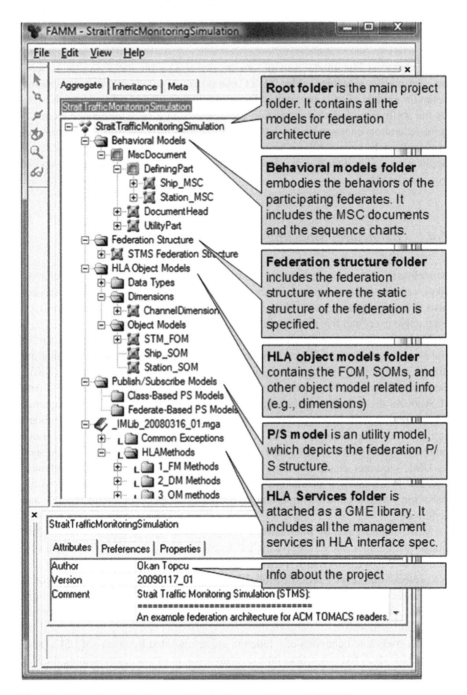

Fig. 6.7 Federation architecture modeling environment (Topçu et al. 2008)

6.4   Behavioral Metamodel

The Behavioral Metamodel provides an abstract syntax for specifying the observable (primarily, as witnessed by the RTI) behaviors of a federate. Forming precise behavior models of the participating federates along with their object models gives us the ability to exercise a federation architecture. In a fully automated exercise, intra-federation communication will follow the specified patterns; the communicated values, however, will not be correct. Taking a step towards complete federate application generation, the developer can weave the computation logic onto the generated code.

6.4.1   Behavioral Modeling

Modeling the behavior of a federate can involve not only the HLA-specific behavior (e.g., creating regions in runtime, exchanging ownership of the objects, etc.) but also the interactions between the components of the federate and the actors (e.g., interactive users and live entities) in the environment.

Modeling the observable behavior of a system is considered an important part of the system specification. There is a variety of visual modeling languages that are aimed at behavior specification, such as Unified Modeling Language (UML) Sequence Diagrams, Message Sequence Charts (MSCs), and Live Sequence Charts (LSCs). As the basis for the behavioral modeling of the federates, Live Sequence Charts, and in turn, Message Sequence Charts are adopted. For behavioral modeling, it is possible to employ UML behavior diagrams such as sequence diagrams and activity diagrams (OMG 2015). LSCs are chosen among the alternatives, such as UML sequence charts and activity diagrams, to model the federate's behavior because LSCs allow a distinction to be made between mandatory and possible behavior, which is believed important for the behavior specification for federate and federation.

MSC, standardized by International Telecommunication Union, is a formal language that enables one to specify the interactions among the components of a system (ITU-T 1998, 2004). MSCs are commonly used in the telecommunications area for protocol and service specification. LSCs (Brill et al. 2004) have been proposed as an extension to MSCs primarily to allow distinguishing between the mandatory and the possible behaviors of a system. The sequence diagrams of UML 2.x are quite similar to MSCs.

The observable behaviors of a federate are represented by means of LSCs, specialized for HLA federates. Specialization involves, in essence, formulating the RTI methods as MSC/LSC messages and integrating the HLA Object Model as the data language of MSC/LSC. Initially, MSC is formalized as the basis of the behavioral metamodel, and then LSC extensions are added on top of the MSC metamodel. Note that BMM covers all the standard MSC features (ITU-T 2004) and the pro-

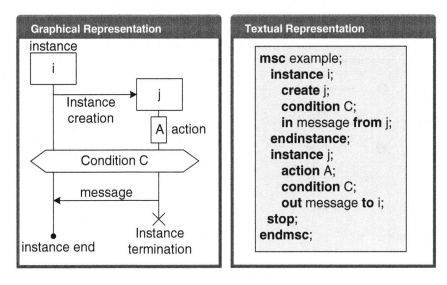

Fig. 6.8 Graphical and textual representation of an MSC diagram (Topçu et al. 2008)

posed LSC extensions (Brill et al. 2004) as long as they do not conflict with the MSC standard (e.g., an MSC loop is used instead of LSC iteration).

As an example, consider the graphical and textual representation of an MSC diagram presented in Fig. 6.8, where the basic MSC elements such as instance, message, action, and condition are depicted. Here, instance i creates the instance j. Afterwards, j performs some initialization action and then if condition C is true, j sends a message to i and terminates.

6.4.2 Modeling Process

The overall process and the workflow is presented in Fig. 6.9 as well as the necessary input and the output in this context including the languages and tools involved.

The metamodeling study is conducted by taking textual language for MSCs as a starting point. A behavioral modeling case study is presented in (Topçu et al. 2009).

6.5 Federation Architecture Verification

Federation architecture verification is to check that whether it is consistent within itself (e.g. well integrated or not) and FAM does what it promises. Once the FAM has been developed, it must be verified that whether or not it is developed via a reliable transformation from formal CM to FAM. A transformation should preserve

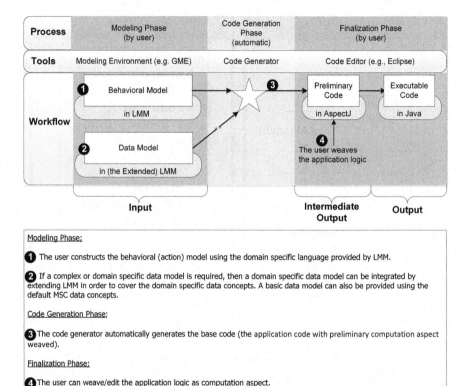

Fig. 6.9 The overall process and workflow, the tools, the languages, and the input and output (Topçu et al. 2009)

meaning between the source and the target model. Moreover, it should add target-specific information, otherwise we would not be making progress. A FAM includes more detailed information than conceptual model (while the focus of CM is in the mission/problem space, the focus of a FAM is in simulation/application space).

Some potential objectives/issues to be addressed are as follows:

- The static analysis of a federate to determine the observed state of the federate from RTI's viewpoint.
- Automatic-check whether that the RTI-related behavior is correctly modeled prior to any transformation. Thus, the RTI-related verification of a federate behavioral model can be achieved using the pre- and postconditions related to each method in the federate interface.
- The transformation rules for RTI methods.
- The determination of the correct position for the generated elements in the model.

6.5.1   Static Analysis and Verification

The federation scenarios can be used to verify the federation architecture. The main idea is that if the federation scenarios can be "played" with the current federation architecture, then it can be asserted that the FAM is a reliable model up to the available set of scenarios. Playing the scenario in the design phase means static model checking (decomposition of Federation Scenario LSC into the corresponding federate HLA-specific LSCs).

Both Federation scenario(s) and FAM can be represented using LSCs. Therefore, the static model checking can be performed using the model interpretation over both LSCs, where the Federate LSCs must include the Federation Scenario LSCs.

As seen in Fig. 6.10, the FAMM in the representation layer is used to model federation model and the federate behaviors, the domain scenarios in the conceptual layer are used to instantiate the federation scenarios.

The static analysis and verification of federation architectures can be seen as a research direction in this field that needs attention. A current study is presented in the following section.

6.5.2   RTI-Related Behavior Verification of HLA Federates Using Pre- and Postconditions of Federate Interface

A federation architecture model consists of the object models and the behavioral models of participating federates. The communication behavior of each federate is to be modeled in the same level of detail as the HLA Federate Interface Specification

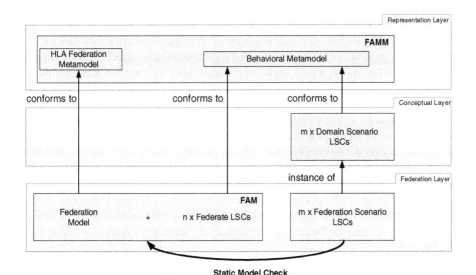

Fig. 6.10   Static federation architecture verification

so as to facilitate standard-compliant code generation. However, this level of detail increases the likelihood of the modelers making mistakes in following the standard. The deep level of modeling causes:

- To augment the modeling effort and time
- The modeler to focus to the more HLA-specific details
- The modeler to orient to programming than modeling

Moreover, the hand-crafted detailed behavioral models may contain impossible behavior for a federation execution according to the HLA Federate Interface Specification (IEEE Std 1516.1-2010 2010) and HLA Framework and Rules Specification (IEEE Std 1516-2010 2010). For example, a federate cannot update the value of an object class attribute before registering the object. If the modeler mistakenly models the behavior of updating an attribute before registering the related object, then the generated code will not run. Thus, beyond well-formedness, static checking of the well-behavedness of federate behavioral models is desirable. If it can be shown that all the preconditions of the RTI services used in a behavioral model are satisfiable then we have some assurance that the interface behavior can be compliant to the HLA Federate Interface Specification.

In order to successfully generate the code, a well-formed federation architecture model and a well-behaved interface behavior model are both necessary. Well-formedness, being a syntactical notion, is guaranteed by the conformance of a FAM to FAMM. In the context of this book, well-behavedness, a semantical notion, of the interface behavior means that the use of the RTI services in a FAM is in accordance with the HLA Federate Interface Specification in the sense that the preconditions of each invoked service are satisfiable when the federate runs.

In order to support the accordance with the HLA Federate Interface Specification, the interface behavior of federates must be checked during the modeling phase. A static analysis is performed to check that the preconditions of each RTI service invoked in the behavioral models (i.e. the behavioral part of a FAM) in a federation architecture are satisfiable or not. Relevant preconditions must be satisfied for an RTI service to fulfill its function. Note that a precondition of an RTI service can be equivalent to (or imply) a postcondition of some other RTI service. Relevant postconditions hold as a result of performing an RTI service successfully (i.e. with no exception).

In this section, we present a model checking based procedure to verify the interface behavior of an HLA federate modeled in FAMM. Verification is performed automatically by the help of (i) a model interpreter that takes a FAM as input and generates the PROMELA model of its behavioral part as output, (ii) the SPIN model checker (SPIN Web Site 2015) that performs model checking given the generated PROMELA process as input and then outputs the verification result in terms of the preconditions that will not hold at run-time. SPIN is a popular open-source software tool that can be used for the formal verification of distributed software systems. The tool, developed at Bell Labs, has been available since 1991. SPIN takes a PROMELA model as input. PROMELA (short form of "Process Metalanguage") is not meant to be an implementation language but a systems description language. To make this

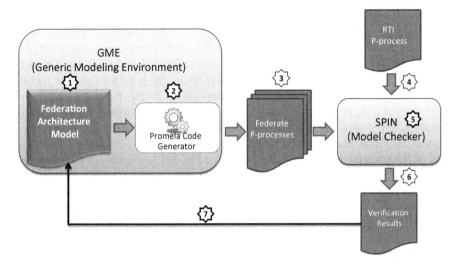

Fig. 6.11   Verification process (Kızılay et al. 2009)

possible, the emphasis in the language is on the modeling of process synchronization and coordination, rather than computation (Holzmann 2003).

6.5.2.1   The Approach

The verification approach consists of the steps illustrated in Fig. 6.11. (i) The federation designer constructs the FAM. (ii) The PROMELA code generator, which takes the FAM as input, is executed. (iii) The PROMELA code generator generates a Federate PROMELA process (P-process) for each federate. The Federate P-process is the PROMELA code of the interface behavior of each federate. (iv) The generated code and the HLA Federate Interface Specification in PROMELA, called RTI P-process, are supplied to SPIN as inputs. The RTI P-process was coded once. (v) In this step, the federation designer can configure the settings of SPIN. (vi) SPIN presents the verification results and then the modeler interprets the results. (vii) The modeler makes corrections on the model, if necessary.

The model checker may report that a precondition in a method call is not satisfiable. Considering the input behavior model, this result can only be due to a missing method call that would establish the precondition. The generated code, then, would certainly raise an exception in that method call at runtime. Thus, the corrective action of the modeler would be to supply the prior method call that was missing. The result that the precondition is satisfiable, though, does not guarantee that it will indeed be satisfied in every run of the federate. This is because model checking ignores the possible values that the method parameters can take at runtime.

The interface behavior of a federate specified in a FAM is represented as the message exchanges between the RTI P-process and the Federate P-processes. The RTI

P-process represents the RTI services specified in the HLA Federate Interface Specification, including the pre- and postconditions. It models the behavior of an RTI (e.g. keeping federation and federate states, sending messages to the federates, etc.). The RTI P-process is implemented once and for all for representing the interfaces of the RTI services. Further, for each federate, the interface behavior part of the FAM is automatically transformed into the Federate P-process using the PROMELA code generator. Processes are the basic execution unit of the PROMELA models. SPIN takes PROMELA model as input so the PROMELA code generator forms the PROMELA model (i.e. the Federate P-processes) of the interface behavior of federates by walking over the FAM. The PROMELA models of the federates, which are FAM-specific, are created for each federate model. Federates of a federation are transformed to P-processes. Federate P-processes run in parallel. The federate P-process consists of the main thread (federate main P-process) and callback thread (federate callback P-process) that run in parallel. The callback thread handles the RTI-initiated messages. The main thread is the main simulation loop and it sends the federate-initiated messages to the RTI. The PROMELA code generator, implemented as a model interpreter in GME parlance, is specifically developed to analyze the given FAM to extract the interface methods and then to generate the PROMELA code in accordance with the LSC constructs (e.g. the LSC parallel construct is mapped to an inner process). Figure 6.12 depicts a portion of the interaction of P-processes of the case study presented in Sect. 6.7. See (Kızılay et al. 2009) (Kızılay 2010) for further details.

State space is an important point in model checking. It is common to encounter with the state space explosion if the resources are not enough. There can be made some improvements to solve this problem, such as creating some sub-models to be verified distinctly and the verification results can be combined afterwards, so that much bigger federations can be verified with limited resources.

Modeling the behavior of a federate can involve not only the HLA-specific behavior but also the interactions between the components of the federate and the

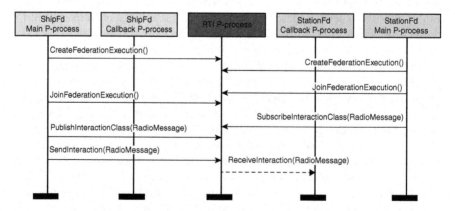

Fig. 6.12 Interaction of P-processes (partial view) (Kızılay 2010)

actors (e.g., interactive users and live entities) in the environment. So verification of behavior models, which are not HLA-specific, can be studied (Kızılay 2010).

6.5.3 Dynamic Verification (Runtime Verification, Monitoring)

Verification can be interpreted in the dynamic sense (federation execution). Dynamic verification is based on the automatic code generation. See Chap. 9 for code generation details.

The federation designer can monitor the emergent behavior of a federation by generating the code from a given federation architecture and then executing it as seen in Fig. 6.13. The execution of the generated code can facilitate the early validation of the behavioral specification expressed in an MSC or LSC. By observing the traces produced as the generated code runs, the modeler may detect unsafe behaviors, such as a request with no reply until the timer expires.

Model-based code generation for HLA federates from the given FAM, which conforms to FAMM, is discussed and explained in (Adak et al. 2009).

6.6 Metamodel/Model Assessment

Metamodel assessment can be carried out, in qualitative terms, based on the criteria of completeness, traceability, modularity, layering, partitioning, extensibility, reusability, and usability (partially adapted from (OMG 2015)). It is believed that all the

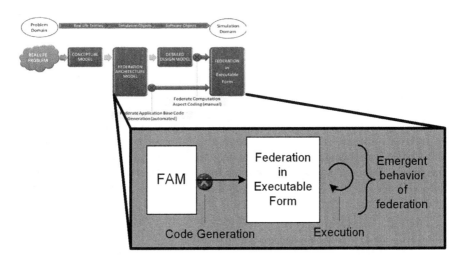

Fig. 6.13 Dynamic verification

criteria defined here determines the metamodel quality. In this respect, we explain each criteria by giving FAMM assessment as an example (Topçu 2007).

6.6.1   Completeness

Completeness criterion answers whether the metamodel includes all the relevant concepts and entities of the intended domain (Pace 2000) (Lindland et al. 1994). It determines the scope of the metamodel. The completeness of the metamodel can be checked using the specifications and standards of the intended domain. The completeness of a model (i.e. federation architecture) can be checked using the functional and non-functional requirements of the problem.

6.6.2   Traceability

Traceability between the domain-specific concepts and the metamodel/model elements is important. Because the modelers generally tend to expect to see the familiar concepts from the domain. For example, in MSC domain, the modelers would like to see the `coregion`[3] construct instead of a new devised construct doing the same work. This situation also alleviates the learning and adaptation period. Therefore, keeping traceability between the standardization documents and the metamodel elements straightforward is a (meta)modeling guideline. Another traceability issue is between the model and the generated code. Traceability via comments is significant because the application developer works over the generated code (e.g., he/she weaves the application logic code after automatic base code generation).

6.6.3   Modularity

The modularity principle addresses high coherence and low coupling between the modules. It should be evident from the FAMM presentation, as seen in Fig. 6.3, that modularity principle is adhered to so that each concern area is addressed by a self-functional (high coherence) sub-metamodel (e.g., LMM and HFMM) as these sub-metamodels are connected loosely through Integration Metamodel. Moreover, each sub-metamodel is also separated into sub-metamodels (e.g., LMM is separated to

---

[3] Coregion is the concurrent part of an instance axis in MSC.

MMM) to increase the modularity. In terms of GME, sub-metamodels are provided as GME libraries.

6.6.4 Layering

Layering is defined as (i) separating the core constructs from the higher-level constructs that use them, (ii) separating concerns by a four-layer metamodel architectural pattern (OMG 2015). The correlation of FAMM with OMG's four-layer metamodel hierarchy is presented in Table 6.2. Layers M1 and M2 each conform to the layer one above, and M0 is an instance of M1. For example, a particular federation architecture conforms to FAMM. FAMM structure separates the core constructs and higher level constructs by using the GME folder and the GME paradigm sheet structures. For example, the HOMM encompasses the OMT Core folder and the Object Model paradigm sheet, where the former includes the core OMT elements and the latter includes the elements, which use the core elements.

FAMM ensures three properties of relations to determine "meta-ness": FAMM is non-transitive, acyclic, and level-respecting (Kühne 2006). In a federation architecture, two levels become visible by separating the model specific (i.e., federation/federate specific) and non-specific (i.e., HLA specific) concerns. The base layer is the HLA-specific layer. The top layer is the federation/federate specific layer. The top layer uses the constructs found in the base layer. The layers are depicted in Fig. 6.14.

This layering is done via the GME libraries. The libraries, provided with FAMM, are all specific to HLA standard rather than to a specific model. These libraries pro-

Table 6.2 FAMM correlated with OMG's four-layer metamodel hierarchy (Topçu et al. 2008)

OMG's four-layer metamodel hierarchy	Related model
Meta-Metamodel (M3 Layer)	GME Metamodel (MetaGME)
Metamodel (M2 Layer)	Federation Architecture Metamodel (referred to as a "paradigm" in GME vernacular)
Model (M1 Layer)	Federation Architecture of a particular federation (e.g., Strait Traffic Monitoring Federation Architecture, see Sect. 6.7 for case study)
Run-time Instance (M0 Layer)	Federation Runtime Instance (e.g., a particular execution of the Strait Traffic Monitoring Federation. For instance, Bosporus Federation)

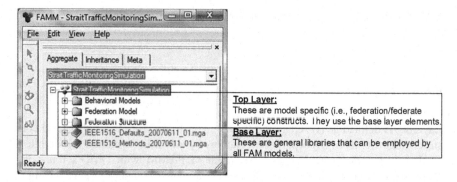

Fig. 6.14 Layers in a federation architecture model

vide the core constructs and form the base layer in a federation architecture project. The top layer, which is formed by the behavior models, the federation structure model, and the federation model in the project use the core constructs provided with the libraries.

6.6.5   Partitioning

Partitioning is used to organize the conceptual areas within the same layer as specified in (OMG 2015). In the case of FAMM, partitioning is provided by grouping constructs into folders for each sub-metamodel. For example, considering MMM (see Fig. 6.15), it organizes the MSC constructions in four folders, namely, auxiliaries, basic constituents, data concepts, and time concepts. In each folder, by using the GME paradigm sheets, the constructs are grouped. For instance, in Basic Constituents folder, there are actions, charts, comments, gates, etc. paradigm sheets and in Time Concepts folder, there is measurement, time interval, time offset, etc. paradigm sheets.

Partitioning can be conducted according to the specifications and standards of the intended domain (e.g., for MMM, the MSC specification is taken into consideration) to support the traceability between FAMM and the domain-specific concepts. Thus, the conceptual areas are organized according to the domain authoritative documentation.

6.6.6   Extensibility

In order to construct a new metamodel as an extension of an existing one (e.g. extending the MSC metamodel to the LSC metamodel), one could copy the existing metamodel and then make modifications and additions to it. Alternatively, one may attach the existing metamodel as a library and then build the new model on top of it

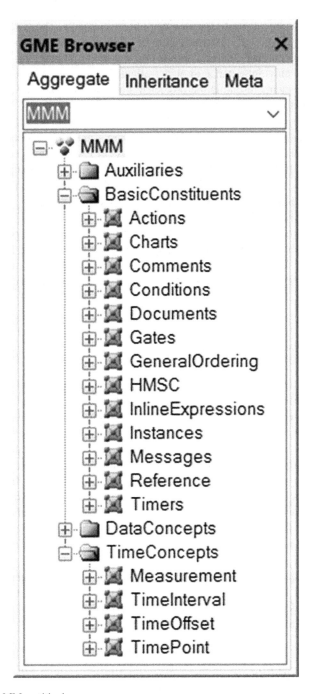

Fig. 6.15 FAMM partitioning

without any modifications to the attached library elements. The latter method, for instance using the nested libraries feature of GME, yields better model encapsulation. Attaching a metamodel into another metamodel as a library can be seen as an analogy to the class inheritance in object-oriented languages. Moreover, read-only metamodel elements resemble the protected attributes in a class where model elements to be extended resemble the public attributes.

Extensibility emphasizes modifiable models and metamodels. Extension to a metamodel is inevitable because the requirements and the expectations from a metamodel will change from time to time. In case of FAMM, for specific domains, it is essential to provide a domain-specific data model, which extends the basic MSC data model. The proposed metamodel's facility of integration with domain-specific data models plays a critical role to achieve code generation.

UML specification dictates two kinds of extension mechanism: (i) using profiling mechanism (i.e., profiles are used to customize the language for specific domains) and (ii) reusing part of the infrastructure package and augmenting it (OMG 2015). FAMM does not provide a profiling mechanism; instead, it has built-in explicit integration points for model extensions. Reusing infrastructure package strategy is also followed for instance, in extending MMM for LMM.

6.6.7 Usability

It determines how easily models are created conforming to the metamodel. In the matter of usability, the granularity of modeling matters. For instance, regarding to FAMM, the user must model all the RTI interactions in full detail. For example, the number of concepts (elements with a kind of model, atom, and folder stereotypes in GME parlance) and connections (association in GME parlance) that constitute the STMS model, given in case study in Sect. 6.7, is about 634 and 243, respectively.

One means of alleviating this situation is to reduce the size of the handcrafted model with the help of model transformation. The idea is that the designer (or an automated conceptual model transformer) will need to specify only the essential interactions in the behavior model, and then an auxiliary model transformer will fill in the implied message exchanges taking the method pre- and post-conditions into account. Static analysis of the behavior model is, of course, a prerequisite for such model manipulations. A complementary approach is to isolate the users as much as possible from the metamodel details. A graphical front-end that supports, for instance the LSC graphical syntax, would facilitate more intuitive behavior specification as well as prevent making mistakes in modeling easily.

6.6.8 Reusability

As doing a modeling work, it is always viable to think reusability of the model. In metamodel terms, reusability means that a sub-metamodel is reused in another metamodel. For instance, FAMM incorporates the LSC Metamodel. This metamodel is also reused in Field Artillery Mission Space Conceptual Metamodel, presented as a case study in Chap. 5, to model the message communication (Özhan et al. 2008).

6.6.9 Other Criteria

The criteria that are often applied as the quality criteria for the conceptual models can also be applied to assess the metamodels. Especially, two criteria among them: being *analyzable* and *executable* (Lindland et al. 1994), which is an expected effect of Model Integrated Computing, is important for models that conform to a metamodel. For instance, the code generation capability of FAMM proves that the federation architecture models are executable (Adak et al. 2009).

The quality of definitions of the documentation criterion leads us to give importance to the *documentation* for a metamodel.

The *correctness* criterion (OMG 2015) (Pace 2000) (Lindland et al. 1994), in terms of syntactic and semantic correctness, is an indispensable characteristic of a metamodel. Syntactic correctness is ensured by the conform relation between a model and a metamodel. Semantic correctness criterion must be evaluated by objective studies and it takes longer time to assess a metamodel.

Consistency (Pace 2000) (Lindland et al. 1994) criterion emphasizes that the metamodel constructs are not in conflict with any other constructs. Due to compound structure of FAMM, which integrates specifications from interdisciplinary domains (i.e., HLA, MSC, and LSC), consistency was a major design principle. Especially, while (i) extending the MSC metamodel to form the LSC metamodel and (ii) while integrating HLA and behavioral sub-metamodels, eliminating the conflicts was a design principle.

Comprehension criterion (Lindland et al. 1994) addresses the need for understandable models. It is clear that if a metamodel is not understandable, then no one will use it.

6.7 Case Study: Strait Traffic Monitoring Simulation

The case study Strait Traffic Monitoring Simulation (STMS) shows how to model a federation architecture using FAMM. On a larger scale, the reader may refer to the architectural modeling of Naval Surface Tactical Maneuvering Simulation System (NSTMSS) (Topçu and Oğuztüzün 2005), a distributed interactive simulation, presented in Molla et al. (2007).

A traffic monitoring station tracks the ships passing through the strait. Any ship entering the strait announces her name and then periodically reports her position to the station and to the other ships in the strait using the radio channels. Channel-1 is used for ship-to-ship and channel-2 is used for ship-to-shore communication. The traffic monitoring station tracks ships and ships track each other through these communication channels. All radio messages are time-stamped to preserve the transmis-

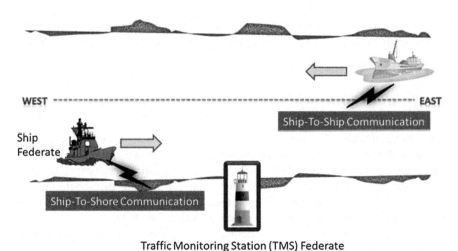

Traffic Monitoring Station (TMS) Federate

Fig. 6.16 Strait traffic monitoring simulation conceptual view (Topçu et al. 2008)

sion order. The traffic monitoring station and the ships are represented with two types of applications[4]; a station application and a ship application, respectively. The ship application is an interactive federate allowing the player to pick up a unique ship name, a direction (eastward or westward), and a constant speed by means of a textual interface. Joining a federation corresponds to entering the strait and resigning from the federation corresponds to leaving the strait. The station application is a monitoring federate, which merely displays the ships (in the strait) and their positions. The federation has a time management policy where each ship application is both time regulating and time constrained and station application is only time constrained. The conceptual view of the application is presented in Fig. 6.16.

While selecting this example, the following highlights were in mind:

- Evidently, the essence of this simple federation is an example of a set of objects tracking each other. It is a common scenario/interaction pattern for most distributed simulations.
- It is believed that this example has a simple conceptual model, which will make it easily understandable and capture the reader's attention immediately. Thus, it will force the user focus on the modeling part than the example itself.
- Moreover, the sample federation naturally includes time management, ownership management, and data distribution management services in addition to the base services (e.g., federation management services).
- The sample federation involves two distinct federate applications and it has a potential to support multiple federations.
- It is an interactive simulation. Thus, it presents how to model a federation that involves the user interactions.

---

[4] In this section, application is used as a short form for "federate application".

The following modeling activities is done using GME. The practitioner must download and install GME (ISIS 2015) first and then register FAMM as the base paradigm. The STMS FAM as well as the metamodels, along with other supporting material, can be downloaded from the FAMM website (FAMM 2011).

6.7.1 Federation Model

Federation Model is a GME folder that includes all the federation specific object models and related data (e.g., data types). The object model of STMS is also distributed as a sample application with SimGe tool and can be downloaded from (SimGe 2015).

6.7.1.1 Object Model

An appropriate FOM for the STMS federation is prepared conforming to the HOMM. The object class and interaction class hierarchies of the object model are presented in Fig. 6.17. The FOM involves two object classes `Ship` and `Station`, and one interaction class `RadioMessage`. The ship object has four attributes `CallSign`, `Course`, `Speed`, and `Position`; and the station object has two attributes, `StationName` and `Location` as the radio message interaction class has two parameters `CallSign` and `Message`, indicating the name of the entity that sent the message and the content of the message (i.e., the position data), respectively.

The federation model also includes the Dimensions, Transportations, Data Types, or Notes. A new folder is created for each. By right clicking on the new folder, you can select the related model elements. In addition, in the same way with object

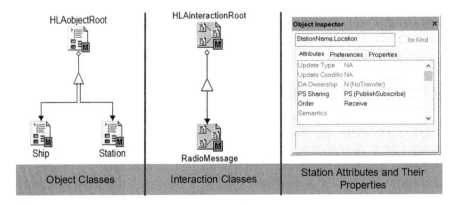

Fig. 6.17 A part of the STMS FOM (Topçu et al. 2008)

models and federation design model, you can define the model elements. For adding HLA notes, define notes under the Notes folder and give references to them; or directly add notes to the notes attribute of each model element. For adding design notes, use annotation facility of GME. If you want to check the validity of your model, you can use Check facility of GME, by selecting "File->Check" option.

6.7.2 Federation Structure Model

Right click on the root folder in the Browser window (the one usually positioned at the right side), and select the option "Federation Structure" within the "Insert Folder" option. Then create a new model named "Federation Structure" is created under the federation structure folder; you may change the name from Attributes browser. Double click on the model to open it. An empty window appears in the user-area.

The Part Browser, a small window in the lower left portion of the program, displays the model elements that can be inserted into the model in its current aspect. The elements in this browser are Federation, FederateApplication, FOMReference and SOMReference. You can use them by dragging from the Part Browser onto the main window. You can connect federation to federate applications to denote the members of the federation; federation to FOMReference; and FederateApplication to SOMReference. When using references, you drag the referred element over the reference and drop it when the mouse icon changes. But before referring elements you should first define FOM and SOM object models. Copy and paste operations on elements are supported by GME and all elements can be created, moved, or copied by drag and drop as usual.

In the federation structure model of STMS, the connection is made for the federation and federate applications with the FOM and SOMs, respectively. The model is depicted in Fig. 6.18. The federation is named "Traffic Monitoring Federation". The multiplicity information is also supplied while connecting the applications to the federation. The ship application (ShipFdApp) may join the federation multiple times while the station application (StationFdApp) is limited to two in this specific scenario. The connection lines show this multiplicity.

6.7.3 Behavioral Models

The folder for behavioral models defines the whole system of MSC documents and includes MSC documents for each participating federate. The behavior model folder includes a detailed structure; a screen shot for MSC/LSC building environment is presented in Fig. 6.19. A document consists of head, utility, and defining parts where defining and utility parts include the (MSC) charts. A chart includes an MSC

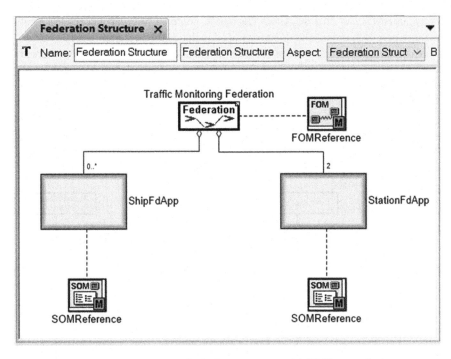

Fig. 6.18 The strait traffic monitoring federation structure model (GME screenshot)

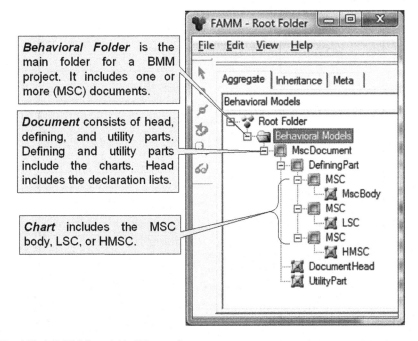

Fig. 6.19 MSC/LSC model building environment

body, an HMSC, or an LSC. Charts also have precedence order indexes to specify the interpretation order. The document head includes the declaration lists.

To illustrate the usage of MMM, referring back to the STMS federation, there are four actors that contribute to the overall behavior of the federation. These are the ship and station applications, the user, and the federation execution (with the RTI "behind the scene"). The ship application can join the federation execution multiple times as distinct federates. Hence, it will be the focal point for the code generation process. The behavior model of the ship application will be presented first in LSC graphical form (Fig. 6.20), and then in the FAM form (Fig. 6.21).

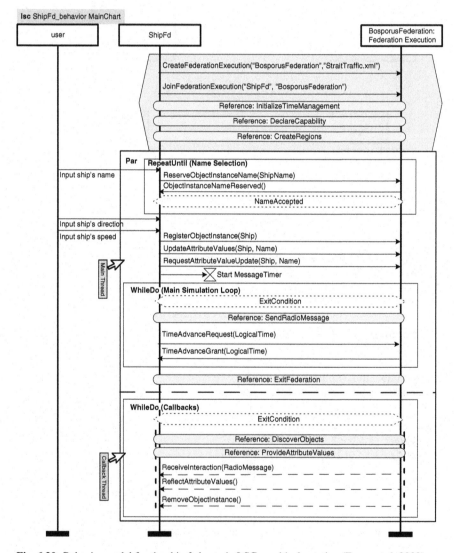

Fig. 6.20 Behavior model for the ship federate in LSC graphical notation (Topçu et al. 2008)

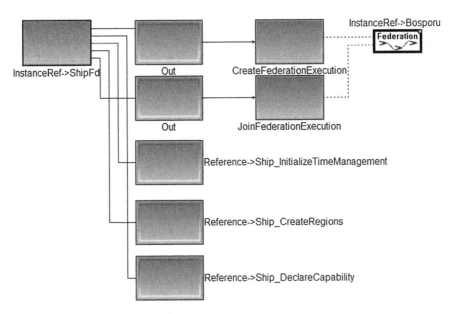

Fig. 6.21 Pre-chart part of ship federate's behavior model in abstract syntax (Topçu et al. 2008)

The behavior model for the Ship Federate (ShipFd), which is an instance of ship application, includes the federation execution and user interactions as well as the application logic. There are three instances (represented as rectangles): User, ShipFd, and Bosporus Federation (i.e., an instance of strait monitoring federation). The code generator only generates code for the federate instance (i.e., ShipFd). The vertical lines represent the lifelines for the instances. A typical LSC includes mainly two charts: a pre-chart (the diamond-shaped area on top) and a main chart (the rest of the chart). The pre-chart behaves like a conditional. If it is satisfied, the main chart is executed. In the pre-chart of the diagram, the ship federate first creates the Bosporus federation and then keeps interacting with it as it initializes its time management policy, declares its data interests, and creates data distribution regions. The behavior for these interactions is defined in separate LSC diagrams (not shown), namely, `InitializeTimeManagement`, `DeclareCapability`, and `CreateRegions`, and is referred to by references (the oval shapes) within the pre-chart. If the ship federate successfully completes the pre-chart, then the diagram proceeds with a parallel execution structure covering the rest of interactions with the user and the federation execution. This structure includes two operands that run in parallel: the main thread and the callbacks thread. A condition (`ExitCondition`) synchronizes the exit for these threads. In the callbacks part, the callbacks can occur in any order, and therefore they are connected to a coregion, designated by the vertical dotted line.

Figure 6.21 depicts the corresponding model of the pre-chart part of the diagram in the abstract syntax. The right pane shows the structure of the project while the left pane depicts the behavior model of the ShipFd corresponding to the pre-chart. The abstract syntax is in a one-to-one correspondence with the LSC. Therefore, the traceability is straightforward. As seen, the message-out events are connected to the HLA methods (specified in the methods library). The reference model elements are used to point to other LSCs.

The HLA methods can only be connected to the MSC message events (out and in) and method call events (call out, receive, reply in, and reply out).

6.7.3.1   Federates and Federation Executions

Federates and federation executions are the main instances that interacts in a behavioral model. Federate corresponds to the joined federates. It is created by instantiating the `FederateApplication` element. Federation execution corresponds to the federation executions created by RTI. A federation execution is the primary instance the federate interacts with (e.g., joining the federation, receiving an interaction, etc.). It is created by instantiating the `Federation` element. For example, Fig. 6.22 presents how to create federates and federation executions. ShipFd and StationFd, which represent two different types of joined federates, are instantiated from the federate applications: ship and station applications, respectively; while Bosporus Federation, a federation execution, is instantiated from the Traffic Monitoring Federation.

`FederateApplication` and `Federation` model elements in Federation Structure Model provide a template (type model) for the federate and federation execution, respectively. To create a federate and a federation execution;

• First, design the Federation Structure Model as described in the previous section,

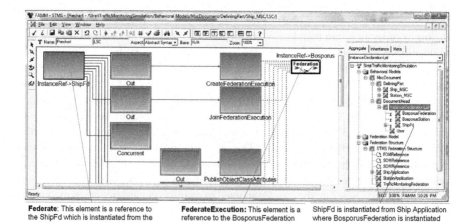

Federate: This element is a reference to the ShipFd which is instantiated from the Federate Application, ShipApplication.

FederateExecution: This element is a reference to the BosporusFederation which is instantiated from the Traffic Monitoring Federation.

ShipFd is instantiated from Ship Application where BosporusFederation is instantiated from TrafficMonitoringFederation

Fig. 6.22 Creating federates and federation executions (Topçu et al. 2008)

- Create an Instance Declaration List under the Document Head of the MSC Document,
- Instantiate the federate and federation execution elements by dragging the type models (i.e., FederateApplication and Federation) while pressing the [Alt] key, and dropping them into the Instance Declaration List.
- Rename their names as appropriate, for example, ShipFd.
- Now, they are ready to be used in the behavior charts. In the behavior charts (e.g., LSC), use only the instance reference elements that refer to the instantiated models. They are also used in HLA method calls such as JoinFederationExecution and CreateFederationExecution method calls.

6.7.3.2 Reserving Object Instance Names

After joining the federation, a federate may reserve object instance names with RTI. Although this step is not a compulsory step for a federate, sometimes, it is important to reserve unique names through federation executions. For example, in our case study, it is important to have unique ship names in the federation. Therefore, after joining the federation, first we seek a unique ship name and then try to reserve it (using a repeat-until block). This part of the federate's behavior also presents an example for how to connect a repeat-until block condition (i.e., until condition) with a Boolean indicator of an HLA method.

The LSC portion, extracted from Fig. 6.20, for reserving the object instance names is depicted in Fig. 6.23. If ObjectInstanceNameReserved callback returns a true indicator, then the repeat-until loop will be exited reserving the name successfully. Else, the loop will start over (i.e., the user will input a new name and the federate will try to reserve it again).

To preserve this semantic, the condition NameAccepted for the repeat-until loop must be connected to the indicator provided by the ObjectInstanceNameReserved callback. To do this, the modeler must define an indicator variable in the federate's variable list. For example, in Fig. 6.24, an indicator (Indicator_True) is defined to represent the true valued indicators. As seen in Fig. 6.24, both the callback method argument and the repeat-until construction condition refers to the same indicator. Thus, if callback returns true, then the loop is exited successfully.

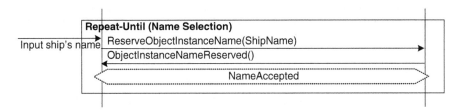

Fig. 6.23 LSC for reserving the object instance names

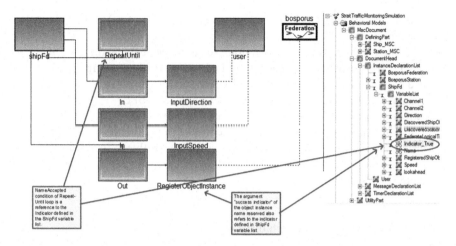

Fig. 6.24 Model for reserving the object instance names

6.7.3.3 Creating Elements for the Variable List

FAMM allows declaring the elements: message retraction designator, region, time-stamp, lookahead, and object instance in the variable list of the federate Instance. Message retraction designator and region are directly created inhere while others are instantiated from the templates (e.g., object instances are instantiated from the object classes).

Object instances are created by instantiating the ObjectClass elements declared in FOM. They are placed in the variable list of a federate application. The method calls that use or refer to the object instances have a reference to point to the instance declared in the variable list.

6.7.3.4 Creating Regions and Dimensions

As an example, a one-dimensional communication space for radios is created to illustrate a distribution region. In our example, radio communication is carried out using the radio channels: channel-1 for ship-to-ship communication and channel-2 for ship-to-shore communication. Channels are regions over the channel dimension (there are two channels from zero to 2). Channels are defined by the dimension numbers as shown in Fig. 6.25.

First, the dimensions, which constitute a region, must be defined in the federation object model. To do this, under the Federation Model Folder, create a Dimensions folder. Herein, we can create the dimensions. Each dimension has a type and a normalization function as described in (IEEE Std 1516.2-2010 2010). Type is a reference to a pre-defined type in Data Types folder. In the normalization function element, one can specify the upper limit. Second, in the `Variable List` of the federate under concern, the `Region` element can be created. Each region element has a reference to the dimension elements. Now, regions are ready to be used in the behavioral charts.

Regions are handled via the HLA DDM methods such as `CreateRegion` and `CommitRegionModifications` calls. All these methods have a reference to the regions defined in the variable lists. `CreateRegion` method call creates the regions while `SetRangeBounds` method call sets the boundaries for the regions. Figure 6.26 presents the corresponding model in FAM. Please note that the model is compliant with HLA 1.3 version.

Fig. 6.25 DDM example

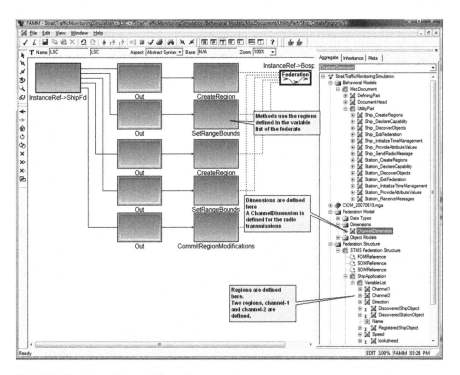

Fig. 6.26 Creating regions and dimensions

6.7.3.5   Modeling Callbacks

Discovering objects is done via the `DiscoverObjectInstance` method. A federate may discover many objects; it is the user responsibility to specify what the federate will do after object discovery. There are two modeling approaches for object discovery:

A loosely modeling approach is not to model the behavior after the federate discovers an object. If modeling each object discovery has no impact over the design, then it is sufficient to put only one `DiscoverObjectInstance` call to the model and to leave the arguments empty. After code generation, the modeler can weave the object discovery codes.

If the modeler wants to model each object-discovery and what-to-do-afterwards, then one way is to use PAR operator for each object discovery. In Fig. 6.27, object discovery for two different object classes: `Ship` and `Station` are modeled. After discovering the objects, the federate requests object updates for each of them. `DiscoverObjectInstance` calls are marked as cold messages as well as their locations in order to indicate that the call "may" be received.

6.7.4   Using the Model Libraries

GME supports model libraries, which are ordinary GME projects. Each GME project can be used as a library if both the library and the target project are based on the same version metamodel (i.e., FAMM). The primary ways of using libraries is to create sub-types and instances from the library objects. It is also possible to refer

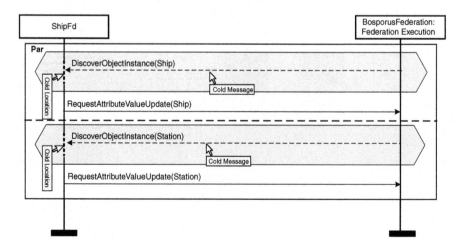

Fig. 6.27 Object discovery

library objects through references. Apart from being read-only, objects imported through the library are equivalent to objects created from scratch (ISIS 2015).

There are auxiliary libraries that can be readily attached to a project. Four libraries are currently provided: Methods Library for IEEE 1516.1 (IMLib) and HLA 1.3, IEEE 1516.1 Management Object Model Library (HMOMLib), and IEEE1516.2 HLA Defaults Library (HDefLib). All are available in (FAMM 2011).

Libraries are provided in ".mga" format. In order to attach a library into a project, right click to the root folder, and select Attach Library option. Choose the library file in the opened dialog box. Please, note that before attaching a library, first register the base paradigm of the library that will be attached to the project. The base paradigm is HLA Federation Metamodel (HFMM).

When a library version is changed, it is sufficient to refresh the library in the project, do not re-attach or delete the library. To do this, select the library in the project, right click, and select Refresh Library option.

6.7.4.1 IEEE 1516.1 Methods Library

An IEEE 1516.1 HLA Methods library serves the template methods (a type model) of the HLA services specified in (IEEE Std 1516.1-2000 2000) for the actual use (an instance model). This library is required to model the federate behavior. In order to use this library, we simply attach it to the model concerned.

Using Template Methods Defined in the Library

There are three ways to use the template methods found in the library. First and the common way to use the library is the Instantiation Approach. In this approach, whenever the modeler wants to use a template method in the library, he/she instantiates the template method (in other words, he/she creates an instance model from the type model). In GME, instance models can be created by dragging the type model and dropping it while pressing alt key. The modeler cannot change the number and type of the arguments, but only the argument values. This approach is the common way to use the HLA methods in the library and must be preferred to the other approaches in general. An example for the usage of this library is already presented in Fig. 6.21 for STMS federation. The method calls, such as CreateFederationExecution and JoinFederationExecution, are instantiated from the template models specified in the HLA Services Library attached to the project.

Another way is to use a *Method Reference* to refer to a template method in the library. This approach can be preferred only if the argument values are not specific for each method call and where the template method is appropriate for each call. The non-argument HLA methods are typical examples for such a use. For instance, QueryFederationRestoreStatus method has no supplied and returned arguments. So, when calling it, instead of instantiating it each time, the modeler may choose to use a reference pointed to it.

The last way to use a template method is to sub-type it first, and then instantiate it. As presented in the first approach, the instantiation of a template method does not allow changing the number of arguments in a call. But, some HLA methods use the sets, collections, and lists as supplied or returned arguments. These containers may include a number of elements. Since the template method provides only one element for these containers, the modeler may need to modify the number of the elements in the template method. Therefore, first a sub-type of the template method must be created in the declaration list of the MSC document head. Then, the modeler can modify the number and type of the arguments as needed. Lastly, the sub-type can be instantiated as described in instantiation approach. For example, `PublishObjectClassAttributes` method has a "set of attributes" supplied argument to specify the attributes to be published. The library provides a template method for it, but the set argument of the method has only one attribute reference. To add new attribute references, the modeler must sub-type it to add needed attribute references and then use (instantiate) it in the model.

Using Arguments of the Template Methods

The modeler must be familiar with the HLA methods and their arguments. Arguments are provided to the modeler inside the template methods. Most of the arguments are provided as null references for the object model such as federation reference, federate application reference, and object class reference. While modeling the federation architecture, the modeler must (re)direct the reference at any time by dropping a new target model element on top of them. For instance, `CreateFederationExecution` method has a federation reference, as a supplied argument. This argument is provided as a null reference in the template method. The modeler must manually direct which federation execution this null reference refers to.

Some arguments are provided in form of the Boolean and string type values. These are the indicator and string type arguments. When a method has this type of argument, the library provides both the element itself and its reference in the arguments of the template method. Only one must be utilized in modeling where the modeler may prefer to use the element itself in case specifying the value directly or its reference in case referring to other arguments defined in another method. A code interpreter must check the reference first, if it is null, then it must interpret the value assigned to the element itself.

The order type element provides an enumerated list for the representation of the order type arguments such as the sent message order type. Message retraction designator, object instance, and region are new model elements used to represent the counterpart arguments.

Exception Handling

Each exception of an HLA method found in the library is empty by default. The code generator only generates the skeleton for the exception (i.e., catch block), and the user introduces the advice code by hand.

If the modeler wants to specify a behavior for handling the exception instead of coding, then he can add an MSC reference to the exception in order to point a behavior chart.

6.7.4.2   IEEE 1516.1 Management Object Model Library

This library provides the required object models, specified in (IEEE Std 1516.1-2000 2000), to model HLA MOM. Whenever HMOMLib is attached to a FAM project, MOM automatically becomes a part of the FOM. There is no need an additional association among federation, MOM, and FOM. Which federates are using MOM is easily understood from the behavioral model.

After attaching this library, predefined object and interaction classes are loaded, and then they can be used just as the federation object models do. If there is no need for a FOM, for example, in case of modeling the architecture of a federation monitor, it is just sufficient to attach the MOM library as the object model. Federation element can be attached to the MOM instead of FOM.

6.7.4.3   IEEE1516.2 HLA Defaults Library

This library provides the predefined object model elements specified in (IEEE Std 1516.2-2000, September 2000).

6.8   Summary

This chapter presents what a federation architecture is and how to represent it. We introduce metamodeling, a powerful method, to represent federation architectures. In this regard, a metamodel, designated as FAMM, is presented to realize the concepts. FAMM is used to enable a broad range of tool support for the HLA federation development process. A significant part of this metamodel is adoption of Live Sequence Charts for the behavioral specification of federates.

There have been numerous calls to apply MDA to HLA-based distributed simulations (cf. for example, (Tolk 2002, 2004; Parr and Keith-Magee 2003; Kewley and Tolk 2009)). These papers provide an account of the tenets of MDE/MDA and the potential benefits of applying it to simulation development. Some go on discussing how these benefits can be achieved. In the scope of this book, we indeed do not argue for the desirability of applying MDE to HLA, instead, we rely on the cogent arguments made in the relevant literature. We adopt the view that model integrated computing is well suited for HLA development and we try to show that how to actually build a workable domain-specific metamodel to realize the vision, where the domain is HLA.

There are also some studies (Guiffard et al. 2006; Etienne et al. 2006), albeit limited in scope, represent attempts at building and utilizing metamodels to realize the potential of MDA/MDE. One is the Capsule study which aims to apply the MDE methodology to the simulation study. In this work, a metamodel for HLA related to the other simulation platforms (e.g., LIGASE and ESCADRE) is created, but the metamodel is not intended to be a universal metamodel of HLA, rather it is specific to its intended project (Guiffard et al. 2006). The (Etienne et al. 2006) discusses their "FRG (Federation Rapid Generation) metamodel", which is based on the HLA metamodel.

An earlier use of MSCs in the HLA realm has been reported by Loper (1998), where MSCs are used to specify the procedures to test individual federates for HLA Interface Specification compliance. Providing both static and dynamic views of a federation is a tenet of the Base Object Model (BOM) as well (SISO 2006). BOMs are reusable model components and "they provide a mechanism for defining a simulation conceptual model and optionally mapping to the interface elements of a simulation or federation using HLA OMT constructs" (SISO 2006). BOM effort aims to support component-based development of simulations, starting with the simulation conceptual model. BOM template specification extends the HLA OMT to cover the conceptual entities and events, and contains information on how such entities relate and interact with each other.

Some studies propose extending UML using its extension mechanisms (primarily, profiling). Such a study is UML Profile for HLA Federation Design, which can be seen as development of HLA-specific extensions to UML to support a more formalized and standardized description of the federation, federate design, and documentation issues (Topçu and Oğuztüzün 2000; Topçu et al. 2003). Another similar study (Dobbs 2000) presents an extension as stereotyped in Rational Rose for the HLA OMT. The model is simply a rendering of OMT, where stereotyping is a mechanism of UML profiling.

In this chapter, we also present the federation architecture verification methods. Verifying that all the preconditions of the RTI services used in a behavioral model are satisfiable allows the federation designer to have some confidence that the interface behavior (in terms of services in the behavioral model) is modeled according to the HLA Federate Interface Specification. Thus, as a result of the static verfication of a federation architecture, the well-behavedness of a FAM can be checked, facilitating to generate the federation code successfully for a prototype federation. The federation designer can detect the mistakenly modeled interface behavior of federates in the FAM by using the preconditions of the RTI services for verification.

The chapter concludes with a modeling case study implemented in GME. The reader may download all the required tools, metamodels, libraries, and the case study from FAMM (2011) in order to follow the practices presented in the case study section.

References

Adak, M., Topçu, O., & Oğuztüzün, H. (2009, February). Model-based code generation for HLA federates. *Software: Practice and Experience, 40*(2), pp. 149–175.

Bezivin, J. (2005). On the unification power of models. *Journal of Software and System Modeling, 4*(2), 171–188.

Brill, M., et al. (2004). Live sequence charts: An introduction to lines, arrows, and strange boxes in the context of formal verification. In *Integration of software specification techniques for applications in engineering* (Lecture notes in computer science, Vol. 3147, pp. 374–399). Berlin: Springer.

Çetinkaya, D. (2005). *A metamodel for the high level architecture object model*. Ankara: Middle East Technical University.

Dobbs, V. (2000). Managing a federation object model with rational rose: Bridging the gap between specification and implementation. In *Fall Simulation Interoperability Workshop*. Orlando: SISO.

Etienne, S., Xavier, L., & Olivier, V. (2006). Applying MDE for HLA federation rapid generation. In *European Simulation Interoperability Workshop (SIW)*. Stockholm: SISO.

FAMM. (2011). *FAMM web site*. [Online] Available at: https://sites.google.com/site/okantopcu/famm. Accessed 19 Dec 2015.

Gray, J., Bapty, T., Neema, S., & Tuck, J. (2001). Handling crosscutting constraints in domain-specific modeling. *Communications of the ACM, 44*(10), 87–93.

Guiffard, E., Kadi, D., & Mauget, R. (2006). CAPSULE: Application of the MDA methodology to the simulation domain. In *European Simulation Interoperability Workshop (SIW)*. Stockholm: SISO.

Holzmann, G. J. (2003). *The SPIN model checker, the primer and reference manual*. Addison-Wesley Professional.

IEEE Std 1516-2010. (2010). *IEEE standard for modeling and simulation (M&S) high level architecture (HLA) – Framework and rules*. New York: IEEE.

IEEE Std 1516.1-2000. (2000). *Standard for modeling and simulation (M&S) high level architecture (HLA) – Federate interface specification,* IEEE.

IEEE Std 1516.2-2000. (2000, September). *Standard for modeling and simulation (M&S) high level architecture (HLA) – Object model template specification*. IEEE.

IEEE Std 1516.3-2003. (2003). *Standard for IEEE recommended practice for high level architecture (HLA) federation development and execution process (FEDEP)*. IEEE.

IEEE Std 1516.1-2010. (2010). *Standard for modeling and simulation (M&S) high level architecture (HLA) – Federate interface specification*. IEEE.

IEEE Std 1516.2-2010. (2010). *Standard for modeling and simulation (M&S) high level architecture (HLA) – Object model template specification*. IEEE.

IEEE Std 1730-2010. (2011). *IEEE recommended practice for distributed simulation engineering and execution process (DSEEP)*. New York: IEEE.

ISIS. (2015). *GME manual and user guide* (GME 15 ed.). Institute for Software Integrated Systems Vanderbilt University.

ITU-T. (1998). *Formal semantics of message sequence charts*. s.l.: International Telecommunication Union (ITU-T).

ITU-T. (2004). *Formal description techniques (FDT) – Message sequence charts*. s.l.: International Telecommunication Union (ITU-T).

Kewley, R. H., & Tolk, A. (2009). A systems engineering process for development of federated simulations. In *SpringSim '09 Proceedings of the 2009 Spring Simulation Multiconference*. San Diego: ACM.

Kızılay, V. (2010). *Verifying the interface compliance of federates using pre- and postconditions of RTI services*. Istanbul: Institute of Informatics, Istanbul Technical University.

Kızılay, V., Topçu, O., Oğuztüzün, H., & Buzluca, F. (2009). RTI-related behavior verification of HLA federates using pre- and postconditions. In *Proceedings of 2009 Fall Simulation Interoperability Workshop (SIW)*. Orlando: SISO.

Kühne, T. (2006). Matters of (meta-) modeling. *Software & Systems Modeling, 5*(4), 369–385.

Ledezci, A., et al. (2001). Composing domain-specific design environments. *Computer, 34*(11), 44–51.

Lindland, O., Sindre, G., & Solvberg, A. (1994). Understanding quality in conceptual modeling. *IEEE Software, 11*(2), 42–49.

Loper, M. (1998). *Test procedures for high level architecture interface specification.* Georgia Tech Research Institute, Georgia Institute of Technology.

Molla, A., et al. (2007). Federation architecture modeling: A case study with NSTMSS. In *Fall Simulation Interoperability Workshop (SIW)*. Orlando: SISO.

OMG. (2014). *Object constraint language (OCL) v2.4.* Object Management Group (OMG).

OMG. (2015). *OMG unified modeling language (OMG UML) version 2.5.* s.l.: Object Management Group (OMG).

Özhan, G., & Oğuztüzün, H. (2006). Model-integrated development of HLA-based field artillery simulation. In *Proceedings of 2006 European Simulation Interoperability Workshop.* Stockholm: SISO.

Özhan, G., Oğuztüzün, H., & Evrensel, P. (2008). Modeling of field artillery tasks with live sequence charts. *The Journal of Defense Modeling and Simulation: Applications, Methodology, Technology, 5*, 219–252.

Pace, D. K. (2000). Ideas about simulation conceptual model development. *Johns Hopkins APL Technical Digest, 21*(3), 327–336.

Parr, S., & Keith-Magee, R. (2003). Making the case for MDA. In *Fall Simulation Interoperability Workshop (SIW)*. Orlando: SISO.

Schmidt, D. (2006). Model-driven engineering. *IEEE Computer, 39*(2), 25–32.

SimGe. (2015). *SimGe web site.* [Online] Available at: https://sites.google.com/site/okantopcu/simge. Accessed 19 Dec 2015.

SISO. (2006). *Base object model (BOM) template specification.* s.l.: Simulation Interoperability Standards Organization (SISO).

SPIN Web Site. (2015). *SPIN.* [Online] Available at: http://spinroot.com/spin/whatispin.html. Accessed 15 Aug 2015.

Stytz, M., & Banks, S. (2001). *Enhancing the design and documentation of high level architecture simulations using the unified modeling language.* Proceedings of 2001 Spring Simulation Interoperability Workshop (SIW). Orlando: SISO.

Tolk, A. (2002). Avoiding another green elephant – A proposal for the next generation HLA based on the model driven architecture. In *Fall Simulation Interoprability Workshop (SIW)*. Orlando: SISO.

Tolk, A. (2004). Metamodels and mappings – Ending the interoperability war. In *Fall Simulation Interoperability Workshop.* Orlando: SISO.

Topçu, O. (2007). *Metamodeling for the HLA federation architectures.* Ankara: Middle East Technical University (METU).

Topçu, O., & Oğuztüzün, H. (2000). Towards a UML extension for HLA federation design. In *Conference on simulation methods and applications* (pp. 204–213). Orlando

Topçu, O., & Oğuztüzün, H. (2005, Winter). Developing an HLA based naval maneuvering simulation. *Naval Engineers Journal, 117*(1), 23–40.

Topçu, O., Oğuztüzün, H., & Hazen, M. (2003). Towards a UML profile for HLA federation design, Part II. In *Proceedings of Summer computer and simulation conference* (pp. 874–879). Montreal: SCS.

Topçu, O., Adak, M., & Oğuztüzün, H. (2008, July). A metamodel for federation architectures. *Transactions on Modeling and Computer Simulation (TOMACS), 18*(3), 10:1–10:29.

Topçu, O., Adak, M., & Oğuztüzün, H. (2009). Metamodeling live sequence charts for code generation. *Software and Systems Modeling (SoSym), 8*(4), 567–583.

Chapter 7
Federate Architecture: Simulation Member Design

This chapter presents a practical approach to the design of federate architectures (i.e., simulation member design) for the simulation developers by applying a well-known architectural style, layered architecture. Adopting layered architecture for an HLA-based simulation provides a clear separation of the following concerns: the user interface, where the user can be a human or an external system such as a GIS server, the simulation logic, and the HLA-specific communication. Thus, the layered simulation architecture allows the simulation developers to focus on each concern separately and gives them the freedom to implement each layer in a different programming language and to encapsulate the tedious implementation details of the HLA federate interface specification. Moreover, this chapter introduces a wrapper for the current HLA run-time infrastructure and gives an account of the suggested implementation practices through a case study.

7.1 Introduction

Software engineering has a long history, advanced by academic and industrial efforts toward developing quality software at acceptable cost. While developing software, the engineers and programmers often confront similar kinds of design and implementation problems, which are affected not only by the user requirements but also by technological advances. By observing the problems and solutions, architectural styles and software design patterns emerged to provide useful abstract frameworks and templates (Buschmann et al. 1996). Additionally, the need to develop quality software prompted the use of architectural design patterns, and computer simulations are no exception.

Today, high-level architecture (HLA) (IEEE Std 1516-2010, 2010; IEEE Std 1516.1-2010, 2010; IEEE Std 1516.2-2010, 2010) is widely adopted framework and standard for distributed simulation applications, particularly in the military domain. This distributed simulation framework emphasizes the interoperability and reuse of

© Springer International Publishing Switzerland 2016
O. Topçu et al., *Distributed Simulation*, Simulation Foundations,
Methods and Applications, DOI 10.1007/978-3-319-03050-0_7

simulation components (i.e., federate applications in HLA terminology) in a distributed simulation (i.e., federation).

The architectural design of an HLA-based distributed simulation can be grouped into two broad categories:

- The architectural design of a federation (a federation architecture model)
- The architectural design of each federate (a federate architecture)

The federation architecture model deals with the structure and the observable interactions among federates (inter-federate behavior) and the environment. A formalization of a federation architecture model, called FAMM, which is introduced in Chap. 6, shows us how a formal federation architecture supports RTI-related code generation (Adak et al. 2009). The approach taken in Adak et al. (2009) for code generation is aspect oriented in that federate interactions within a federation execution are generated as the base code, and then the computation aspect of the simulation is expected to be woven by the developer on a per federate basis.

The federate architecture focuses on the internal structure of a federate (intra-federate behavior). Either generated or coded manually, the federate internal structure can be enhanced by the best practices in architecture and design patterns in order to develop quality simulation applications. For many large-scale simulation projects, new federate applications have to be built. Therefore, it is best to give attention to federate architectures using some good software practices. In this respect, some federation architectures have been reported in the literature such as Etienne et al. (2006) and Topçu and Oğuztüzün (2013). In this chapter, we will promote a layered architecture for federate application design (Topçu and Oğuztüzün 2013) to benefit from modern software architectures and patterns to facilitate code generation. A module perspective is adopted in the presentation of the architecture (Clements et al. 2011). This chapter aims to present good practice in the area of software design for distributed simulation members by:

- Elucidating a layered software architecture
- Introducing an abstraction (wrapper) for the current HLA RTI
- Exemplifying key implementation details of the architecture through a case study

The following sections present the layered architecture by giving the details of the inner structure of each layer using a case study Environment Federate. Before that, we present the requirements for the architecture with a related discussion of the relevant literature, and then the case study, used as a running example throughout the chapter, is introduced.

7.1.1 Requirements

The major requirements that affect the architecture of an HLA-compliant federate application are:

- The obligation to conform to the HLA rules (IEEE Std 1516-2010, 2010) and federate interface specification (IEEE Std 1516.1-2010, 2010).
- Loose coupling among federates due to the publish/subscribe interaction paradigm for object exchange. HLA uses RTI to exchange the simulation objects by employing the well-known publish-and-subscribe paradigm of interaction (Eugster et al. 2003).
- The nature of the HLA federates involves various areas of expertise and technical complexity such as RTI programming, graphics programming, and the simulation model programming. This dictates the involvement of individuals having a wide spectrum of expertise to implement each layer independently.

  - One of the HLA rules (IEEE Std 1516-2010, 2010) states that all inter-federate communication shall be through the RTI. However, RTI programming is an area requiring specific expertise. Moreover, RTI programming introduces an overhead. Gianni et al. report that the effort required for HLA-based version of a local simulation has been estimated to be up to 60 % and coding of extra 3500 lines of code per federate (Gianni et al. 2010).
  - Many distributed interactive simulations require elaborate user interfaces and make heavy use of three-dimensional graphics.
  - Simulation modeling (e.g., physical model, computational model, domain-specific algorithms, and preprocessing of model inputs and post-processing of model outputs) may require expertise in the problem domain.

- Furthermore, there is a need to encapsulate legacy simulations or non-HLA-compliant simulations as federates to allow those simulations to interoperate. An example study is presented in Sect. 7.6.

All concerns in those areas can be separated and the complexity can be mitigated by layering. Each layer groups common functionalities in a coherent way.

7.1.2 Introduction to the Case Study: The Environment Federate

A synthetic environment application is common in many distributed simulations; therefore, an Environment Controller Federate (EnviFd) is selected as a sample federate. EnviFd creates a common virtual environment for the participating entities such as ships (i.e., federate applications) in a distributed simulation for naval operations, called Naval Surface Tactical Maneuvering Simulation System (NSTMSS) (Topçu and Oğuztüzün 2005). EnviFd controls the environmental (i.e., sea) effects (e.g., sea state and waves) and the atmospheric (i.e., weather) effects (e.g., fog, wind, and time of day) in the virtual environment. EnviFd also periodically broadcasts weather reports to the NSTMSS federation at scheduled intervals specified in the scenario file. As seen in Fig. 7.1 the snapshot of the graphical user interface (GUI), EnviFd provides both federation and environment control. It is used

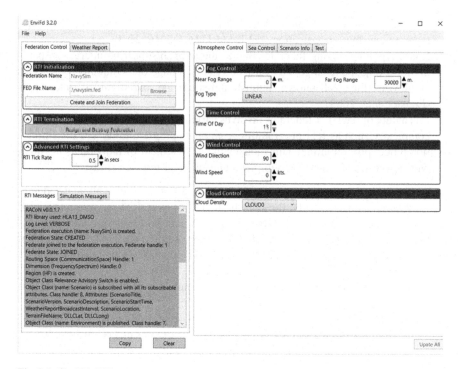

Fig. 7.1 EnviFd GUI

interactively during the federation execution, and at any time, it can be used to control the environmental parameters by a simulation trainer.

A simulation trainer can adjust the time of day for the virtual environment and
the cloud density and select four different types of waves at the same time; and can
change the behavior of waves by configuring direction, speed, length, amplitude,
and exponential properties of a wave; the fog type (e.g., linear and exponential fog);
minimum and maximum fog ranges; the wind direction and speed; the sea state,
where a sea state represents a predefined configuration for the wave, wind, and
cloud; and the sky, all of which varies according to the virtual environment weather
conditions (e.g., cloudy, clear sky).

The case study is used as a running example in particular to present the
application-specific concerns of the architecture. The HLA connection with the case
study is explained for each layer in Sects. 7.3 and 7.4 of this chapter.

7.2   Federate Application Design

Layered architectural style (Microsoft 2009) is a promising candidate choice for the
design of a federate. Layering is an encapsulation of the components by providing
separation of concerns of these three types of tasks: the user interaction (graphical

output, user input, and synchronization of data between view and simulation), the simulation logic and computation model (representation of the system of interest), and the communication which provides the federation-wide data (objects). The architecture mainly consists of a presentation layer, a simulation layer, and a communication layer (see Fig. 7.2). The crosscutting concerns between the simulation and the presentation layers are the federation-specific data structures in form of a shared federation foundation library (FFL) (Topçu and Oğuztüzün 2013).

The separation between the functionality of the layers is clear, and each layer is focused on its own responsibilities (tasks). This maximizes the cohesion within the layer as it diminishes the coupling between layers by clearly separating and defining the boundaries of layers. All the layers are loosely coupled to each other, and they are located on the same physical tier (computer) and operate within the same process. The interaction between layers is carried out only in one way by well-defined layer boundary interfaces that abstract many methods within the layer to encapsulate the inner details of the components. The communication technique between the layers is direct method calls, where the upper layers call the public methods of the lower layers and (may) react/handle the events in those layers. For instance, a class in the presentation layer can call the methods in the simulation layer. A non-strict layering approach can be adopted in the sense that the presentation layer can also use the public methods (in terms of object-oriented programming) of the communication layer. Event-based notification is used to inform the upper levels about the changes in lower layers, thus avoiding circular dependencies.

The developer can implement any appropriate architectural style within any layer. Here, we provide the overall architecture, but the sub-architectures are not restricted. The architecture is technology independent to the greatest extent possible, and it can be implemented with currently available technologies. The architec-

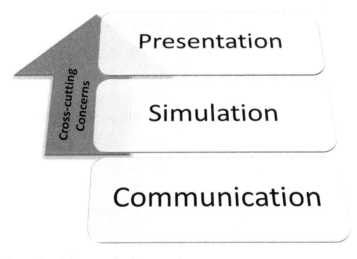

Fig. 7.2 Layers in a federate application

ture and the major components are shown in Fig. 7.3. Please note that the implementation described here is MS.NET based (Microsoft .NET 2014).

The presentation layer (also called the user interface layer) includes the pure presentation (view), input, and interaction with the user (if involved). The main components are the graphical user interface, which can be developed using a GUI library (e.g., Windows Presentation Foundation (Microsoft WPF 2015), Java Swing (Java 2015)) and a user interface controller. The UI controller binds the user interface widgets with simulation data, manages and handles the user events, and iterates the simulation flow (i.e., the main simulation loop). The presentation layer is separately developed for each federate.

The simulation layer (also called the processing layer) includes the computation (the simulation) and the local data (the federate-specific objects). Its purpose is to generate the federate behavior. The simulation layer is federate application specific.

The communication layer (also called the access layer) deals with the HLA-RTI-level communication in order to access the federation-wide data (viz., the objects and interactions exchanged in the federation execution). RTI is a middleware that manages the federation execution and object exchange through a federation execution.

Within the scope of an HLA federation, data are dispersed through federates and accessed through the RTI services (perhaps with the support of shared databases). In the next section, we show how this architecture overcomes the differences in HLA specifications by giving the details of the communication layer.

The federation foundation library (FFL) provides common data types, structures, and supporter classes for the federation object model (FOM)[1] to the federate applications. In addition, it provides crosscutting concerns for each layer. This library encapsulates the federation-specific data structures (i.e., classes and data types), and each federate application uses this library in order to construct its local data structures (i.e., simulation object model (SOM)). The FFL supports code reuse and facilitates code maintenance by keeping the common code in a central library.

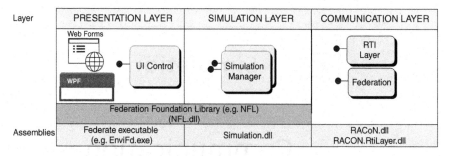

Fig. 7.3 An instantiation of the layered federate architecture (Topçu and Oğuztüzün 2013)

---

[1] See Chap. 3.

Consequently, a change in the FFL is reflected in all the federates using the FFL. One example is the NSTMSS foundation library (NFL) which is a specific library for NSTMSS federation. The details of the FFL and the discussion about its effect on the layered architecture are described in Sect. 7.5. It is useful to explain the details of the library as far as it presents a good practice in that it hides the complexity of many federation-wide data structures and FOM.

7.3 Communication Layer

The communication layer can be thought as a data access layer, but it also coordinates the use of all the functionality provided by management services such as federation management (e.g., creating a federation execution) and time management (e.g., coordinating time). Therefore, its functionality and its structure are deeply related to RTI. Many HLA simulations are developed on top of an abstraction layer over RTI as developing an abstraction layer (wrapper) over RTI is a popular approach in many HLA-based development projects (Savaşan 2008; PNP-Software 2007; Chen et al. 2008), since this approach offers more maintainable, robust, and portable methods. Thus, in order to explain the details of this layer, we will first present an RTI abstraction component, called RACoN, targeted for Microsoft .NET environments, which provides the .NET wrapper classes for the RTI and RTI-specific data structures. There are also available COTS tools that provide abstraction layers for HLA such as MAK VR-Link.[2] Although the layered architecture described here is independent of any specific RTI abstraction, it is useful to give the implementation and integration details of the layers. Therefore, RACoN is provided as an example library to demonstrate how the layered architecture can be realized. When other RTI abstractions are needed, then a specific implementation and integration solution must be developed, which is specific to that RTI abstraction.

RACoN encapsulates the entire RTI low-level class interface in order to simplify the repetitive, error-prone, and low-level implementation details of the HLA federate interface. For instance, data contracts are used in order to enforce the federate interface specification in service usage to diminish the run-time errors caused by the use of wrong RTI services. With the help of RACoN, any .NET language can be selected to implement an HLA federate. The major rationale for the development of RACoN is to prepare an HLA version-free platform with the aim of code generation. RACoN is a free distributed library (RACoN 2015).

Adopting the bridge (Gamma et al. 1994) and the wrapper façade (Schmidt 1999) design patterns, the RTI implementation and the abstraction of services are separated in order to handle multiple HLA specifications and vendor-specific RTI. The bridge design pattern is employed "to decouple an abstraction from the implementation so that the two can vary independently" (Data & Object Factory, LLC. 2015). The wrapper façade design pattern is mainly used to hide the complex,

---

[2] VT MAK, http://www.mak.com, last accessed August 30, 2015.

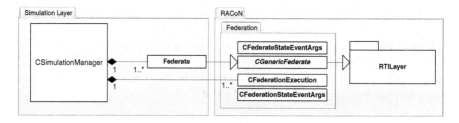

Fig. 7.4 The integration of the simulation layer and the RACoN (Reprinted from Topçu and Oğuztüzün (2013), Copyright (2015), with permission from Elsevier))

error-prone, and low-level functions behind a uniform class interface in order to simplify the application programming interface (API). Additionally, it is used to wrap the native C++ interface to obtain a .NET interface in order to provide language independency (only for .NET languages). RACoN is composed of two libraries: federation and RTI layer library.

7.3.1 Federation Library

The federation library (Federation) is the extension library for the simulations. The library implements a federation execution and a generic federate, which is an extension point inherited by each federate (i.e., the application-specific federate). The simulation layer classes directly include or extend the classes found in the federation library. The simulation layer is connected to the RACoN both by inheriting the generic federate (CGenericFederate) and by containing a reference to the federation execution (CFederationExecution) as presented in Fig. 7.4.

The generic federate is an abstract base class extended from the federate ambassador class found in the RTILayer. It includes a simulation object model (SOM) and the RTI ambassador (RTIAmb). See Fig. 7.5.

7.3.2 Generic RTI Library

The RTI library, called RTILayer, is the major portion of the .NET wrapper that abstracts the RTI services and makes transparent the use of both:

- The various HLA specifications (e.g., DoD HLA 1.3 specification (DMSO 2002), IEEE 1516-2000 Standard (IEEE Std 1516.1-2000, 2000), and HLA Evolved (IEEE Std 1516-2010, 2010).
- The various vendor-specific RTI implementation for the same specification (e.g., Portico (Portico 2013), DMSO 1.3 NG). Another approach to a generic RTI abstraction is to use the Dynamic Link Compatible HLA API Standard (SISO 2004).

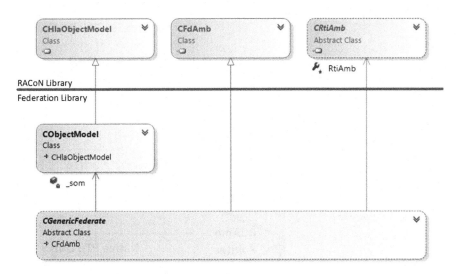

Fig. 7.5 The structure of the generic federate

The generic RTI library is implemented in .NET C++ (where it uses both managed (C++/CLI) and unmanaged (native C++) API). It encapsulates the RTI and federate ambassador classes as well as the common RTI-related data structures (CHlaObjectModel).

Figure 7.6 depicts how RTI library supports the vendor-specific native RTI implementations. The RTI ambassador (CRtiAmb) and federate ambassador (CFdAmb) are mainly wrapper classes that are responsible for communication with the RTI and for receiving callbacks. Both classes encapsulate the low-level native RTI method implementations and data structures found in the vendor-specific RTI to provide a uniform class interface. The support for two vendor-specific RTIs (Portico and DMSO 1.3) is depicted in Fig. 7.6. For instance, CRtiAmb_Portico is implemented to support the Portico RTI. The programmer specifies which native RTI he will use in the application-specific federate.

From the federate ambassador perspective, a native federate ambassador (e.g., CFdAmb_Dmso) must be inherited from the HLA version-specific null federate ambassador (e.g., NullFederateAmbassador). In order to add a new ambassador to support a new RTI specification, for example, HLA Evolved (IEEE Std 1516.1-2010, 2010), then (i) a native federate ambassador must be implemented overriding the abstract virtual functions found in the null ambassador provided by the HLA Evolved RTI implementation, and (ii) the actual pointer to the native ambassador (in the C++ sense) is to be supplied to the wrapper.

Every RTI call and callback is wrapped with try-catch blocks to manage native RTI exceptions. Furthermore, the events related to the RTI-initiated (RTI to federate) and federate-initiated (federate to RTI) methods are raised by the ambassadors in order to enable the event handling mechanism for the simulation layer. The object model and event management details are given in the following sections.

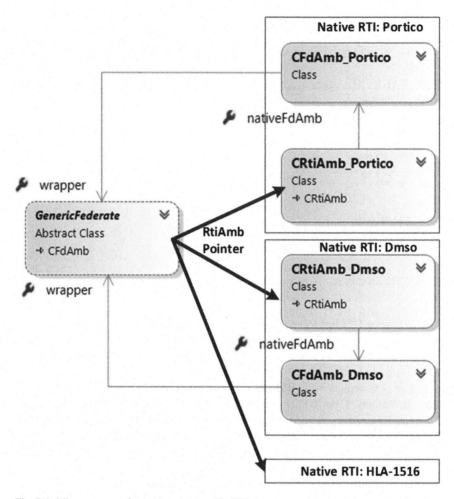

Fig. 7.6 Library support for two vendor-specific RTIs

7.3.3 Support for Multiple HLA Specifications

The approach for handling RTI-specific variation is to employ the bridge design pattern (Data & Object Factory, LLC. 2015) together with both the wrapper façade design pattern (Schmidt 1999). Figure 7.7 presents the applied pattern and shows how the wrapper classes refine and encapsulate the low-level RTI methods. The concrete implementation classes (e.g., CRtiAmb_HLA13 and CRtiAmb_1516_2000) implement the low-level functions and data structures of the related HLA specification. They can be seen as the plug-in modules. Whenever there is a requirement to support an HLA specification or implementation, then a concrete implementation must be created by implementing (overriding) all the virtual methods defined in the RTI ambassador class using inheritance.

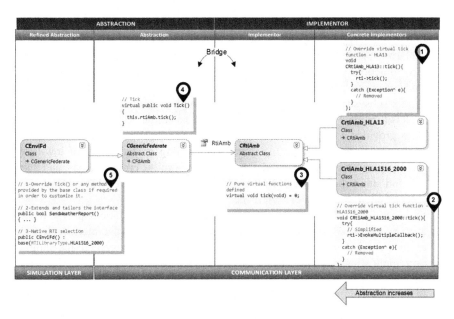

Fig. 7.7 Support for multiple HLA specifications

In order to illustrate how the wrapper classes encapsulate the low-level RTI methods and support the various HLA specifications, we provide a simple example. In our case, which is typical for federates, it is required for the application-specific federate to call the ticking service to allow the federate ambassador to receive the callback messages. Following the numbers in Fig. 7.7:

1. Two HLA specifications present two different services for ticking service. In the case of the HLA 1.3 specification, a `tick()` method is defined.
2. In HLA 1516-2000 federate interface specification, an `EvokeMultipleCallbacks()` service is defined for the EVOKED callback model (IEEE Std 1516.1-2010, 2010).
3. The RTI ambassador (`CRtiAmb`) is an abstract class and is implemented as a façade class. It provides a uniform interface for the concrete implementation classes by wrapping the low-level functions and data structures related to the various RTI implementations. For our example, `CRtiAmb` provides a virtual tick method prototype, where the concrete implementation classes must override and implement this method.
4. The generic federate (`CGenericFederate`) defines the abstraction and is implemented as a wrapper façade class. It also simplifies the interface by clustering the related functions and data structures to provide a higher-level abstraction and in order to ensure the appropriate order of the functions provided by the RTI ambassador. In the case of the ticking service, it just forwards the call to the implementer (see note 2 in Fig. 7.7); however, for other services the situation is different. For instance, a common action of each federate is the initiation and

initialization of a federation execution before interacting with other federates. Initialization typically involves the creation of a federation execution, joining it, declaring the federate interests, and creating the simulation objects. Each of those functions is related to the RTI subsystem. Most federate developers (mainly students or inexperienced simulation developers) are not interested in the details of this subsystem, which complicate their implementation; instead, their only need is to initiate and initialize the federation execution. Hence, the generic federate provides a higher-level interface. The developer calls only the method (InitializeFederation) rather than calling related series of low-level RTI methods (such as create federation, join federation, create regions, and publish and subscribe classes). On the other hand, the low-level RTI methods can still be called using the RTI reference.

5. In the simulation layer, the developer implements the application-specific federate (i.e., CEnviFd for our case study) that tailors (extends) the interface defined by the generic federate. Thus, the abstraction level is appropriate to the simulation application domain. The developer implements domain-specific methods such as SendWeatherReport(), as in our example federate. The selection of the concrete implementer for the RTI is specified as a constructor parameter.

When moving from one layer to the next higher level (right to left for Fig. 7.7), the level of abstraction in the methods' functionality increases as expected.

7.3.4   Code Contracts

Code contracts are employed to check the major pre- and postconditions of HLA federate interface services in order to ensure a well-behaved behavior in the sense that the preconditions of each invoked service are satisfiable when the federate runs. Let's explain how code contracts are used by giving an example. RTI register object instance service is wrapped as RegisterHlaObject() in RACoN. The code snippet for preconditions and postconditions is depicted in Fig. 7.8.

Whenever this method is called, the contracts check the preconditions are satisfied or not. For instance, it checks whether the federate is joined to a federation execution, and the object class is defined in FDD or not (see Contract. Requires calls in the code). When all conditions are satisfied (i.e., all are true), then native RTI method call is performed. If one of the conditions does not hold, then a contract failed exception is thrown reporting the precondition requirement to the programmer. At the end of method call, the postconditions are checked in the same manner (see Contract.Ensures calls in the code).

Beyond ensuring well-behaved RTI interface behavior, checking the pre- and postconditions in the library also provides fine-grained error messages to the programmer to ease the debugging the RTI.

```
virtual public bool RegisterHlaObject(RTILayer.CHlaObject theObject)
{
    #region Contracts
    // Preconditions
    //a) The federate is connected to the RTI.
    // This is ensured by the JOINED state
    //b) The federation execution exists.
    Contract.Requires(this.FederationExecutionState == FederationExecutionStates.CREATED, " at RegisterHlaObject().");
    //c) The federate is joined to that federation execution.
    Contract.Requires(FederateState == FederateStates.JOINED, " at RegisterHlaObject().");
    //d) The object class is defined in the FDD
    Contract.Requires(theObject.Type.ClassHandle != 0, " at RegisterHlaObject()."); // Class handle will be 0 if not P/S.
    //e) The joined federate is publishing the object class.
    Contract.Requires(theObject.Type.ClassPS == RTILayer.PSKind.PublishSubscribe || theObject.Type.ClassPS ==
RTILayer.PSKind.Publish, " at RegisterHlaObject().");
    // ... removed

    this._rtiAmb.registerObject(theObject, theObject.ObjectName);

    // Postconditions
    //a) The returned object instance handle is coadunated with the object instance.
    Contract.Ensures(theObject.ObjectHandle != 0, " at RegisterHlaObject().");
    // ... removed

    #endregion
```

Fig. 7.8 The code snippet for ensuring pre- and postconditions of an RTI interface service

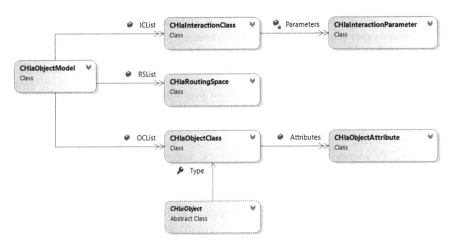

Fig. 7.9 Class diagram for object model class

7.3.5 The HLA Object Model

The HLA object model supports the construction of the simulation object model, which includes the HLA objects, interactions, and routing spaces. The class structure is shown in Fig. 7.9. The HLA object model includes three major lists: the interaction class (ICList), the object class (OCList), and the routing space (RSList). The routing space list is for backward compatibility and only used for HLA 1.3 federations.

One of the important aspects in the object model structure is the class for the HLA object (CHlaObject). This is a base class, from which the application-specific federate inherits its federation objects. Thus, the application-specific federate can encapsulate its objects to use them in RTI-specific interactions. Figure 7.12

presents an example usage of this class. The `CEnvironment` class, which represents a federation object, is inherited from the `CHlaObject`, so that it can be used in RTI object management services.

7.3.6 Events and Event Handling

RACoN provides notifications about HLA-related services to the application-specific federate by using events; this is known as event-based notification. Therefore, an application-specific federate can handle events triggered from the communication layer by overriding the event handlers that are registered by the base federate in order to customize their RTI-related behaviors (delegated event handling). For example, when the value of an attribute is updated through RTI, the RACoN assembly raises an object attribute reflected event. The application-specific federate that hooks the event is notified that the event has been triggered. Then, the application-specific federate can take action such as updating its local data or refreshing its user interface with the updated value.

The .NET event handling structures are used for implementing events and event handling mechanisms. Events are categorized according to their initiators, as follows:

(i) RTI-initiated events generated by federate ambassador callbacks such as an object discovered event

(ii) Federate-initiated events generated by the RTI ambassador such as a federate joined event

(iii) RACoN events generated by the generic federate such as a federate state-changed event (see Chap. 8 for the federate states)

The federate-initiated and RACoN event handlers are executed as soon as they are raised, but the RTI-initiated events (callbacks from the RTI to the federate ambassador) are queued as events for processing at the end of each simulation cycle. They are executed when the federate run method is called. The federate `Run()` method must be called in the main (simulation) loop of the application.

The native federate ambassadors add the related event instances (in fact, only the event arguments, not the event itself) to the event queue. A code snippet for reflecting an object attribute update implemented in EnviFd is given in Fig. 7.10, and it exemplifies the implementation of a callback.

```
// Reflect Object Attributes Callback - Override the one provided by RACoN
public override void FdAmb_ObjectAttributesReflectedHandler(object sender, RACoN.RTILayer.CHlaObjectManagementEventArgs data)
{
    // Call the base class handler
    base.FdAmb_ObjectAttributesReflectedHandler(sender, data);

    #region User Code
    // Find the updated object. Here, we look for the scenario object
    if (data.ObjectHandle == this.simManager.scenario.ObjectHandle)
    {
        // Update the value of the local data
    }
    #endregion
}
```

Fig. 7.10 Code snippet for reflecting an attribute update

7.4 Presentation and Simulation Layers

The presentation and the simulation layers are application-specific layers, and their structure is heavily dependent on the application requirements. Therefore, only the core parts of these layers and the integration with the communication layer are described here.

The separation of algorithms and the visual presentation of their results are points worthy of discussion. Consider, for example, a weather condition, such as fog. The algorithm that models the dynamics of fog dispersion will be implemented in the simulation layer, while the visualization of the fog dispersion will be handled in the presentation layer. The algorithm obtains the model inputs from the communication layer.

7.4.1 Presentation Layer

The presentation layer depends on its deployment platform. For instance, it can be implemented as a web client or a stand-alone desktop application. From the design point of view, it can take the advantage of the use of *separated presentation* patterns (Microsoft 2009) such as model-view-presenter (MVP) (Potel 1996) or Model-View-ViewModel (MVVM) (Smith 2009) in order to separate the user interface design and the code that drives it. Here, the controller corresponds to the presenter, which handles all requests from the UI controls. However, for small-scale applications, where either a simple user interface or simple simulation logic is required, the presentation and the simulation layers can be implemented in a single assembly.

MVP is a variant of the well-known model-view-controller (MVC) pattern (Burbeck 1992) to cope with modern UI libraries. In the presentation layer of the EnviFd application, a form of MVP, called the Passive View (Fowler 2006) presentation pattern, is employed. In the Passive View pattern, the view is only updated through the controller (called the presenter). Figure 7.11 shows the presentation layer of the class diagram for the case study. For the EnviFd, an interface class (IEnviFd_MainWindow) is implemented in order to provide both a standard interface to the presenter class (CUIControl) and a base for a GUI class. The MainWindow is the main GUI class implemented using the Microsoft Windows Presentation Foundation (WPF) library (Microsoft .NET 2014). A federate can have more than one GUI based on different architectures (e.g., web-based vs. windows-based) and/or libraries in order to support various working environments. As the entire burden is on the controller, it is easy to design and apply a different GUI by implementing the EnviFd presentation interface. The CUIControl is the controller/presenter for the view part. It processes the user input and accordingly updates the view and the simulation model deciding how to respond to external events. The other part of the controller is the simulation manager, which focuses on updating and managing the simulation model (see next section). The CEnviFdApp is the main entry point for the EnviFd application.

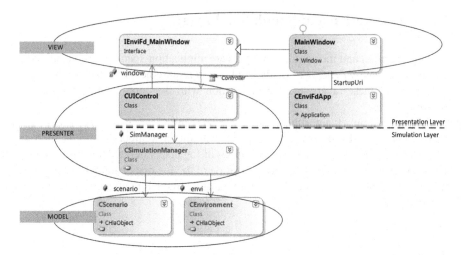

Fig. 7.11 The class diagram of EnviFd application for the presentation layer (Topçu and Oğuztüzün 2013)

7.4.2 Simulation Layer

Simulation layer is the layer where the local simulation is performed. For instance, for a ship simulation, it is the core, where all the hydrodynamic calculations (e.g., the forces affecting the ship hull) are performed. Therefore, it contains all the model-related data (e.g., inputs and parameters). We call these data structures *local data structures* as they are all related to the local simulation application.

In order to integrate the local simulation with the communication layer and the underlying RTI, one may use a manager class (i.e., CSimulationManager) to manage the (multiple) federation execution(s) and the (multiple instances of) federate(s). The application-specific federate, CEnviFd, is the representation of a joined federate. It is responsible for all the application-specific RTI behaviors (the observable behavior of a federate). For example, when a new object is discovered, CEnviFd implements the appropriate action for that object. It is derived from the abstract class CGenericFederate, which is the main extension point for application-specific federates (see Area-1 in Fig. 7.12) as described in the previous section. Therefore, for implementing the simulation layer, the federate application programmers must.

- Extend the abstract federate class by inheriting it
- Override the abstract methods found in the abstract federate class in order to implement application-specific behavior
- Encapsulate the simulation local data structures of the simulation and/or the data structures found in the FFL with the provided HLA object class (i.e., CHlaObject) (see Area-2 in Fig. 7.12)

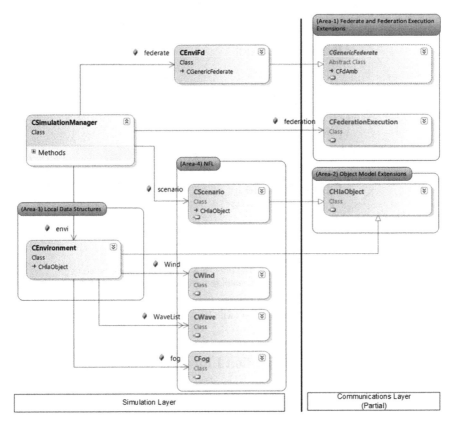

Fig. 7.12 The class diagram of EnviFd application for the simulation layer (Topçu and Oğuztüzün 2013)

7.4.3 Encapsulating the Simulation Local Data

A local data is encapsulated when it is needed to be exchanged in the federation execution. Encapsulation is not needed for all the local data structures. Only the relevant part of the data that will be shared in the federation by other federates must be considered. See Fig. 7.13 for an example. Here, the User class is the local data structure that represents a user with two data members – name and id. You encapsulate it (or a part of it) with HLA object, so it can be processed by RTI.

In the case study, the CEnvironment class (see Area-3 in Fig. 7.12) represents the simulation local data structures (e.g., wind, fog, and waves), and it is also needed as an HLA object in the federation, so that it is inherited from the abstract HLA object class. Another example is the scenario class, which is a federation-wide data structure provided by the NSTMSS foundation library (NFL) (see Area-4 in Fig. 7.12). It is also implemented as an HLA object.

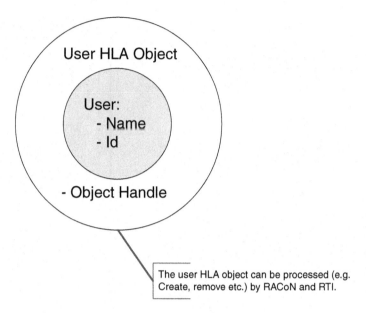

The user HLA object can be processed (e.g. Create, remove etc.) by RACoN and RTI.

Fig. 7.13 Encapsulation of local object (User) with HLA object

7.5   The Federation Foundation Library

The federation foundation library is a collection of classes and data structures that are commonly used in the implementation of federates in a specific federation. Its main goal is to handle the crosscutting concerns (e.g., the standardization of exception handling throughout the federation) implied by the federation architecture in a uniform way to each federate architecture. They are the shared components that address the crosscutting concerns of the federation both in functionality and structure. The major crosscutting concerns for many federations are the federation-wide data structures (object and interaction classes), support classes for FOM, exception management, logging, internationalization, standard look-and-feel GUI components (e.g., a federation clock for each federate), and security.

The use of an FLL is not mandatory from the architectural point of view, but when it is not used, each federate must implement the components (the functionality thereof) found in the FFL. For example, the NSTMSS FFL (NFL)[3] provides the scenario class, which is common for all NSTMSS federate applications. Another example is that the EnviFd informs each federate of the NSTMSS federation what the fog type (a part of FOM) is in an area of the virtual environment using an enumeration data structure (FogTypes). This data structure is currently implemented in the NFL and is shared by each federate.

---

[3] A particular in-house implementation of the FFL is the NSTMSS foundation library.

Whenever a change is required in the code (e.g., when a new fog type is added to the enumeration), it is sufficient to change the FFL code so that a single point of code maintenance exists, thus improving the maintainability. Consequently, a change in the FFL is reflected in all the federates that are using it.

The FFL is designed with the aim to support for code reuse. Thus, using the FFL classes reduces the effort involved in federate development, while providing a better encapsulation and standardization in the common interest of the federates.

The FFL is a heavily application-dependent auxiliary library accessed by presentation and simulation layers. The architecture presented here is not layered in the pure sense of the term due to the existence of the FFL. Clements et al. (Clements et al. 2011) remark that in practice many architectures presented as being layered are not strictly layered. It should explicitly be clarified how an FFL component in a layer interacts with the other FFL components in the other layers. We note that there can be different implementation strategies for an FFL ranging from using an existing common enterprise library (e.g., Microsoft Enterprise Library) or weaving advices (which address crosscutting concerns) by aspect-oriented programming methods to developing from scratch. Therefore, the federate developer should be able to use FFL without having the knowledge of how it was implemented.

7.6 Non-HLA-Compliant Simulations

The layered architecture can also be employed in the design of non-HLA-compliant simulations to obtain HLA-compliant federates. Here, we provide an example architecture for simulations based on Functional Mock-up Interface (FMI). The FMI is a tool-independent model interface standard targeting model reuse and exchange and co-simulation (MODELISAR Consortium 2010a, b). A simulation component conforming to FMI is called a Functional Mock-up Unit (FMU), whose contents include a model description file, user-defined libraries, source codes, model icons, and documentation (Yılmaz et al. 2014).

In order to connect FMUs to HLA federation, a wrapper is needed. In this respect, a Functional Mock-up Unit Federate (FMUFd) is proposed in (Yılmaz et al. 2014).

The architecture of FMUFd fully suits to the layered architecture presented in this chapter. In the presentation layer, a user interacts with the FMUFd application to load the configuration files and to observe the value changes of variables in real time. The communication layer is responsible to deal with the RTI service interaction to access the HLA objects and interactions exchanged in the federation execution. FMUFd also handles the HLA time management services in this layer. The simulation layer is the core of where the FMI-HLA mapping is performed. This layer is also responsible to run the FMU and generate the federate behavior. In general sense, the wrapping of a non-HLA-compliant simulation of a legacy simulation is generally carried out in the simulation layer. Some other layering proposals for legacy simulations are presented in the following section.

7.7 Related Work

This chapter focuses on the distributed simulation development, specifically on that of the HLA federates. There are studies (Sarjoughian et al. 2001; Gianni et al. 2011; Chen et al. 2008) that show how to design and architect the federates in a better way. Sarjoughian et al. (Sarjoughian et al. 2001) propose a layered architectural framework to support agent-based system development, which is particularly intended for both simulated agents and real-world agents.

Gianni et al. (2011) propose a layered architecture to facilitate the development of distributed simulations. Two prominent features are the support for the development of a distributed simulation derived from an existing local simulation (e.g., this can be a discrete event simulation) and the introduction of a domain-specific language for model specification. Support for the development of a distributed simulation from a local simulation brings two additional layers to the architecture in order to support discrete event simulations. In Gianni et al. (2011), simulation models must be specified in a domain-specific language. For the given architecture implementation (`SimArch`), this language is called jEQN.

Chen et al. (Chen et al. 2008) presents a decoupled federate architecture by decoupling the communication from the local simulation for the HLA-based distributed simulation. The aim of the architecture is to provide a solution, especially for distributed simulation cloning, fault tolerance, and web-/grid-enabled simulations. The decoupled federate architecture introduces a federate where it is separated into a virtual federate and a physical federate that are interlinked in order to achieve those aims. Although this brings an extra overhead, the benchmark experiments presented in Chen et al. (2008) show that a well-designed federate architecture performs as well as a normal federate.

7.8 Summary

This chapter has presented a non-strict layered simulation architecture adopting the layered architectural style for HLA federates. The architecture and its supporting framework support code generation and facilitate the development of HLA-compliant distributed simulations by separating the concerns of the system of interest. The architecture has been employed in a variety of small-scale projects (NSTMSS 2015; Yılmaz et al. 2014; Rabelo et al. 2013). It has been observed that the layered architectural style provides a good logical separation of the concerns of interface, simulation computation, and the HLA-specific communication, both at the conceptual and implementation levels. Layered architecture allows the separation of the layers so that each can be implemented and maintained individually. Moreover, layers become suitable for reuse in other applications, especially the lower levels, which are independent of the layers above. For example, RACoN is an application-independent component and can be reused in any HLA federation. On the downside, note that the federate architecture presented here does not aim to address specific nonfunctional requirements, such as fault tolerance (Li et al. 2010; Chen et al. 2008).

One of the layers of the architecture is the communication layer, where the entire RTI low-level class interface is encapsulated in order to simplify the repetitive, error-prone, and low-level implementation details of the HLA federate interface. This layer introduces RACoN component, which is a wrapper for some known RTI implementations (e.g., Portico). With the help of RACoN, any .NET language can be selected to implement an HLA federate. The approach has been demonstrated on the environment federate, a member of the NSTMSS federation (Topçu and Oğuztüzün 2005). In the design of the communication layer, the employment of the bridge design pattern assisted us in separating the abstraction and the implementation, whereas the wrapper façade design patterns helped to cope with the RTI-specific variation due to the various HLA specifications. The RACoN component also serves as a target platform for enforcing the architecture by (automated) code generation. The proposed architecture can guide code generation for realistic HLA federates. For instance, a code generator tool, SimGe, targets the RACoN component. It is a layer-aware tool that enforces the layered federate architecture.

Federation and federate architecture designs need to take advantage of the state-of-the-art not only software architectures but also hardware architectures. Many distributed simulations require powerful hardware to support real-time and complex computations such as trajectory simulations. This requirement strongly dictates a better design, architecture, and coding of simulation software. The layered simulation architecture could be tailored to take advantage of the recent advances such as multi-core processors and graphical processing units. The effect of the computer hardware architecture (e.g., multi-core or multithreaded) (Sodan et al. 2010) on the software architecture is an interesting topic to research.

Moreover, the base object model (BOM) components (Chen 2010) could be integrated into the architecture. Security in distributed simulations is gaining importance; therefore, "secure federates" can be developed by implementing a security-related sub-layer within the communication layer or by introducing a new security layer.

References

Adak, M., Topçu, O., & Oğuztüzün, H. (2009, February). Model-based code generation for HLA federates. *Software: Practice and Experience, 40*(2), 149–175.

Burbeck, S. (1992). *Applications programming in Smalltalk-80(TM): How to use Model-View-Controller (MVC)*. [Online] Available at: http://www.dgp.toronto.edu/~dwigdor/teaching/csc2524/2012_F/papers/mvc.pdf. Accessed 19 Dec 2015.

Buschmann, F., et al. (1996). *Pattern-oriented software architecture. Volume 1: A system of patterns*. West Sussex: Wiley.

Chen, B. (2010). Integrating base object model components into DEVS-based simulation. *The Journal of Defense Modeling and Simulation: Applications, Methodology, Technology, 7*(4), 241–246.

Chen, D., Turner, S., Cai, W., & Xiong, M. (2008). Decoupled federate architecture for high level architecture-based distributed simulation. *Journal of Parallel and Distributed Computing, 68*(11), 1487–1503.

Clements, P., et al. (2011). *Documenting software architectures: Views and beyond* (2nd edn). Addison-Wesley Professional.

Data & Object Factory, LLC. (2015). *Bridge.* [Online] Available at: http://www.dofactory.com/net/ bridge-design-pattern. Accessed 30 Aug 2015.

DMSO. (2002). *High level architecture run-time infrastructure RTI 1.3-next generation programmer's guide Version 6.* Department of Defense Modeling and Simulation Office.

Etienne, S., Xavier, L., & Olivier, V. (2006). Applying MDE for HLA federation rapid generation. In *European Simulation Interoperability Workshop (SIW)*. Stockholm: SISO.

Eugster, P., Felber, P., Guerraoui, R., & Kermarrec, A. (2003). The many faces of publish/subscribe. *ACM Computing Surveys, 35*(2), 114–131.

Fowler, M. (2006). *Passive view.* [Online] Available at: http://martinfowler.com/eaaDev/ PassiveScreen.html. Accessed 19 Dec 2015.

Gamma, E., Helm, R., Johnson, R., & Vlissides, J. (1994). *Design patterns: Elements of reusable object-oriented software* (1st edn). Addison-Wesley.

Gianni, D., D'Ambrogio, A., & Iazeolla, G. (2010). SimArch: A layered architectural approach to reduce the development effort of distributed simulation systems. In *The Workshop on Simulation for European Space Programmes (SESP)*. Noordwijk: ESA.

Gianni, D., D'Ambrogio, A., & Izazeolla, G. (2011, September). A software architecture to ease the development of distributed simulation systems. *Simulation Transactions of The Society for Modeling and Simulation International, 87*(9), 819–836.

IEEE Std 1516.1-2000. (2000). *Standard for Modeling and Simulation (M&S) High Level Architecture (HLA) – Federate interface specification.* New York: IEEE.

IEEE Std 1516-2010. (2010). *Standard for Modeling and Simulation (M&S) High Level Architecture (HLA) – Framework and rules.* New York: IEEE.

IEEE Std 1516.1-2010. (2010). *Standard for Modeling and Simulation (M&S) High Level Architecture (HLA) – Federate interface specification.* New York: IEEE.

IEEE Std 1516.2-2010. (2010). *Standard for Modeling and Simulation (M&S) High Level Architecture (HLA) – Object model template specification.* New York: IEEE.

Java. (2015). *Java.* [Online] Available at: www.java.com. Accessed 19 Dec 2015.

Li, Z., Cai, W., Turner, J., & Pan, K. (2010). A replication structure for efficient and fault-tolerant parallel and distributed simulations. In *Spring simulation multiconference*. Ottawa: SISO.

Microsoft. (2009). *Microsoft application architecture guide: Patterns & practices* (2nd edn). Microsoft Press.

Microsoft .NET. (2014). *MS.NET.* [Online] Available at: http://www.microsoft.com/net. Accessed 19 Aug 2015.

Microsoft WPF. (2015). *Windows Presentation Foundation (WPF).* [Online] Available at: blogs. msdn.com/wpf. Accessed 30 Aug 2015.

MODELISAR Consortium. (2010a, January). *Functional mock-up interface for model exchange version 1.0.*

MODELISAR Consortium. (2010b, October). *Functional mock-up interface for co-simulation version 1.0.*

NSTMSS. (2015). *Naval Surface Tactical Maneuvering Simulation System (NSTMSS) web site.* [Online] Available at: http://www.ceng.metu.edu.tr/~otopcu/nstmss/. Accessed 30 Aug 2015.

PNP-Software. (2007). *EODiSP.* [Online] Available at: http://www.pnp-software.com/eodisp/ index.html. Accessed 29 Oct 2014.

Portico. (2013). *The portico project.* [Online] Available at: http://www.porticoproject.org/. Accessed 30 Aug 2015.

Potel, M. (1996). *MVP: Model-view-presenter the Taligent programming model for C++ and Java.* [Online] Available at: http://www.wildcrest.com/Potel/Portfolio/mvp.pdf. Accessed 19 Dec 2015.

Rabelo, L., et al. (2013). Simulation modeling of space missions using the high level architecture. *Journal Modelling and Simulation in Engineering, 2013*, 12.

RACoN. (2015). *RACoN web site.* [Online] Available at: https://sites.google.com/site/okantopcu/simge. Accessed 19 Dec 2015.

Sarjoughian, H., Zeigler, B., & Hall, S. (2001). A layered modeling and simulation architecture for agent-based system development. *Proceedings of the IEEE, 89*(2), 201–213.

Savaşan, H. (2008). The RToolkit: An open source object oriented distributed simulation framework. In *Fall Simulation Interoperability Workshop*. Orlando: SISO.

Schmidt, D. (1999) Wrapper façade – A structural pattern for encapsulating functions within classes. *C++ Report Magazine, 11*, 1–10.

SISO. (2004). *Dynamic link compatible HLA API standard for the HLA interface specification.* SISO.

Smith, J. (2009). *WPF apps with the model-view-viewModel design pattern.* [Online] Available at: https://msdn.microsoft.com/en-us/magazine/dd419663.aspx. Accessed 08 Aug 2015.

Sodan, A., et al. (2010). Parallelism via multithreaded and multicore CPUs. *IEEE Computer, 43*(3), 24–32.

Topçu and Oğuztüzün, H. (2005, January). Developing an HLA based naval maneuvering simulation. *Naval Engineers Journal, 117*(1), 23–40.

Topçu, O., & Oğuztüzün, H. (2013, March). Layered simulation architecture: A practical approach. *Simulation Modelling Practice and Theory, 32*, 1–14.

Yılmaz, F., Durak, U., Taylan, K., & O   uztüzün, H. (2014). *Adapting functional mockup units for HLA-compliant distributed simulation.* Proceedings of the 10th international Modelica conference, Lund, Sweden, pp. 247–257.

Chapter 8
Scenario Management

Training in a distributed simulation involves carefully designed and constructed simulation scenarios to fulfill the training requirements. Simulation analysis, on the other hand, asks for engineered scenarios to investigate required aspects and behaviors of the system. Moreover, simulation scenarios (federation scenario) play an important role in the federation design and development as suggested in IEEE Recommended Practice for Distributed Simulation Engineering and Execution Process (DSEEP). The simulation scenarios are used in every step in distributed simulation life span from the beginning (analysis and design) of a distributed simulation development to the analysis of results. Such an extensive use of scenarios in a distributed simulation dictates a judicious management of scenarios. In a distributed simulation, scenario management includes the activities of scenario development, scenario loading and parsing, scenario distribution and event injection, and scenario-related data collection and logging. This chapter explains the major concepts of simulation scenarios, introduces a model-driven scenario development process, and discusses the main activities in scenario management in a distributed simulation with a practical slant. It also presents examples to illustrate the scenario management activities.

8.1 Introduction

A distributed simulation generally involves carefully designed and constructed simulation scenarios to fulfill the training or analysis aims. IEEE 1278 (IEEE 1993), the standard for distributed interactive simulation, defines scenario as the description of the initial conditions and timeline of significant events. Further, the high-level architecture glossary (US Department of Defense 1996) expresses that a scenario shall identify the major entities with their capabilities, behavior, and interactions over time with all related environmental condition specifications. In NATO Science and

© Springer International Publishing Switzerland 2016
O. Topçu et al., *Distributed Simulation*, Simulation Foundations,
Methods and Applications, DOI 10.1007/978-3-319-03050-0_8

Technology Organization Modeling and Simulation Group 053 (MSG-053 2010), scenario is defined as the description of the hypothetical or real area, environment, means, objectives, and events during a specified time frame related to events of interest.

In a distributed simulation, a common scenario is needed to be synchronized through all the simulation components. In a typical case, a scenario manager selects a simulation scenario and distributes it to the participants. Moreover, scenarios are part of testing and validation activities. For example, see Topçu (2004) for the ideas about how scenarios can be used in conceptual model validation.

Using scenarios (in noninteractive federations) will help:

• Increase the repeatability of a federation runs
• Decrease the non-determinism of the event flow

The simulation scenarios are used in every step in distributed simulation arena from the beginning (analysis and design) of a distributed simulation development to the analysis of results. Moreover, scenarios are used not only in distribution simulation but also in networked or stand-alone games (Ullner et al. 2008). Such an extensive use of scenarios in a distributed simulation dictates scenario management. As stated in Lofstrand et al. (2004), scenario management includes all activities involved with the development and execution of a scenario. In a distributed training simulation, major scenario management activities can be classified according to the time of the activity: (a) the activities in design and development time and (b) the activities at run time. There is one major activity in design and development phase of a distributed simulation: scenario development. In execution of a distributed simulation, scenario management activities include (i) scenario loading and parsing, (ii) scenario distribution and role casting, (iii) event injection, and (iv) scenario-related data collection and logging (see Fig. 8.1).

From the operator, sponsor, or user statement of scenario to the executable specifications for machine processing, the scenario development is a continuous process in which scenarios are also developed along with the simulations. Siegfried and colleagues identify three types of scenarios: operational scenario, conceptual scenario, and executable scenario, which are produced in successive stages of scenario development process (Siegfried et al. 2012, 2013). Following paragraphs summarize these scenario types. Readers are referred to Siegfried et al. (2012) for further details.

Operational scenarios are described in early stages by the user or the sponsor. The language of an operational scenario consists of terms that the users or the sponsors are familiar with. They can be documented in any textual or graphical format. The key elements are initial state, desired end state, and course of actions to reach the prescribed end state and entities with their capabilities and relations. Below is an example operational scenario introduced in Durak et al. (2014).

> The Airbus A320 Advanced Technologies Research Aircraft (D-ATRA) which is located at German Aerospace Center (DLR) in Braunschweig, gets ready for a test flight. Pilots ask the tower for taxi clearance. The tower provides taxi instructions towards RWY 08. Pilots then start taxiing according to the instructions. Then the tower provides information about

Fig. 8.1 Scenario
management activities

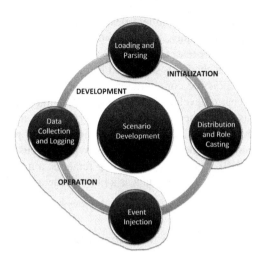

the departure like the weather, VRB05KT, R08/2800FT, overcast sky. Then the pilots ask
for a departure clearance and the tower grants the departure. (DFS Deutsche Flugsicherung
GmbH 2013; Ahmad and Sexana 2008)

Conceptual scenario can be understood as an M&S experts' specification of
operational scenario. It is a structured scenario specification that identifies and clari-
fies all points required for consistency and completeness.

An operational scenario belongs to the domain of application (problem area or
the mission space). It is stated in terms that are familiar with domain experts and
practitioners, who are not necessarily interested in simulation. Conceptual scenario,
however, is closely related with conceptual model and can be specified using the
terms and concepts from conceptual model. In other words, the conceptual scenario
and conceptual model should be at the same level of abstraction. More on conceptual models appears in Chap. 5.

The executable scenario, on the other hand, is defined as the specification of the
conceptual scenario to be processed by the simulation applications for preparation,
initialization, and execution. They are also employed for supporting scenario management activities like scenario distribution and role casting (Topçu and Oğuztüzün
2010). There is a need for a transformation from conceptual scenarios to executable
scenarios. Hereby, these assets can be processed by the member applications (federates). The conceptual scenario can be viewed as a specification for an executable
scenario. To put differently, an executable scenario is a refinement of the conceptual
scenario, enriched with platform-level details.

In IEEE Recommended Practice for Distributed Simulation Engineering and
Execution Process (DSEEP), which describes a process framework for development
and execution of distributed simulation environments (IEEE 2010a), introduces scenario development activity as a part of problem conceptual analysis. Scenario development activity is supposed to identify major entities that must be represented in the

simulation environment, description of their capabilities, behaviors and relationships, event time lines, the environment, initial conditions, and termination conditions. Design process, then, utilizes the outcomes of the scenario development activities.

This chapter is structured in a way that, first, scenario development will be introduced as the core activity of the scenario management activities. A model-based scenario development practice will be introduced based on the work of Durak and his colleagues (Durak et al. 2014). Then the surrounding activities of scenario development, namely, scenario loading and parsing, role casting, event injection, and data collection and logging, will be discussed referring to Topçu and Oğuztüzün (2010). Before the concluding remarks, a methodology is proposed to handle scenario management data as a part of federation agreements.

8.2 Scenario Management Activities

8.2.1 Scenario Development

Scenario development is the core activity of scenario management. This chapter introduces a model-driven approach to scenario development. Model-driven engineering (MDE) has been employed in simulation domain to generate elements of a simulation system or simulation environment from models via model transformations (Topçu et al. 2008; Adak et al. 2009; Gaševic et al. 2009; Durak et al. 2009; Durak et al. 2008; Cetinkaya et al. 2011). In various attempts, models are refined and transformed during the development process for obtaining an executable simulation. In this chapter, model-driven scenario development (MDScD) from Durak and his colleagues (Durak et al. 2014), which adopt these MDE practices to define a scenario development process, will be presented.

This MDScD process conforms to the process model recommended by the DSEEP (Fig. 8.2). In this process, we promote the construction of the conceptual scenarios as models and the utilization of model transformations for designing member applications, environment agreements, and executable scenarios.

8.2.1.1 MDScD

The worldview of MDE has two pillars: models and transformations. Model can only be described using a modeling language which possesses the constructs of models. A modeling language is usually specified by metamodeling. The Meta Object Facility (MOF) of the Object Management Group (OMG) introduces a metamodeling architecture. MOF specifies four levels for metamodeling: information (M0), model (M1), metamodel (M2), meta-metamodel (M3), and their relations (OMG 2011b). The top level structure and the semantics of the meta-metadata are specified in M3. In M2, the structure and the semantics of the metadata are described.

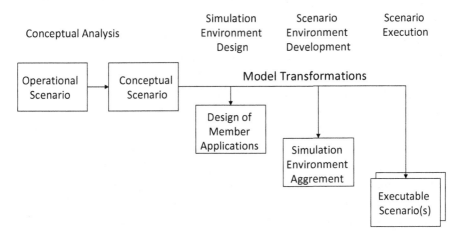

Fig. 8.2 Model-based scenario development process

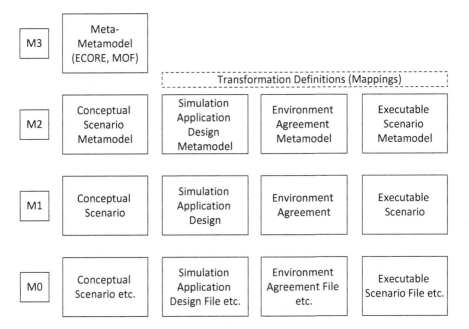

Fig. 8.3 Metamodeling for scenario development

M1 is the model; it describes the data. Lastly, the data to be accessed and manipulated resides in M0 (Arboleda and Royer 2012) (Fig. 8.3).

MDScD process is framed according to this four-layer metamodeling architecture of MOF. At the top level, practitioner shall choose a meta-metamodel. ECORE of Eclipse Modeling Framework can be regarded as an option (Steinberg et al. 2008). First a conceptual scenario metamodel shall be developed for conceptual

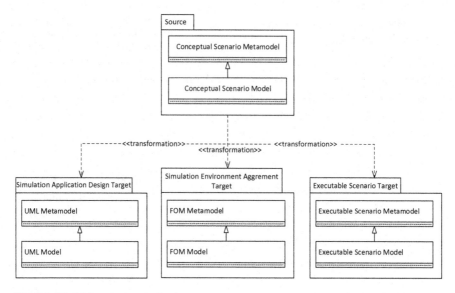

Fig. 8.4 Model-based scenario development

scenarios. The aim is to start with a metamodel to support model transformations from the source, i.e., the conceptual scenario, to the target, comprising simulation application design, simulation environment agreement, and executable scenario. But for sure, targets need to possess a metamodel as well as the source. So the introduced approach requires either to select or to develop a metamodel for simulation application design, simulation environment agreements, and executable scenarios.

Then both model-to-model and model-to-text transformations can be employed on the conceptual scenario model. To accomplish those transformations, one needs to specify the mappings between the constructs of the source metamodel and the target metamodel. Then the model conforming to the source metamodel is transformed into the model conforming to the target metamodel (Gronback 2009).

The process is depicted in Fig. 8.4. As mentioned in the previous paragraph, depending on the simulation environment development process, either a completely new metamodel can be developed or an existing one can be used for these targets. If component diagrams are used to specify the simulation application design, the UML metamodel can be pronounced as the target. If HLA object models are employed to specify an environment agreement, then FOM metamodel is the target (Topçu et al. 2008). The executable scenarios can be defined by a domain-specific language, mostly referred as scenario definition language. For instance, the Military Scenario Definition Language (MSDL) (SISO 2008) is an emerging standard from Simulation Standards Organization (SISO) for defining military scenarios. For a simulation environment that uses MSDL, it can be used as a target metamodel for the executable scenario.

Further, it should be noted that a single scenario can only give a partial view of the system requirements. For design and simulation environment agreements, a

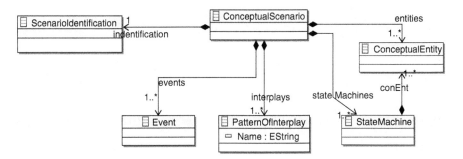

Fig. 8.5 Conceptual scenario metamodel top level diagram

complete view, which implies many (ideally, all interesting) scenarios, is required. Thus, it is more realistic to check designs and agreements against available scenarios.

8.2.1.2 BOM-Based Metamodeling

In this section, the metamodeling will be further explained over a sample conceptual scenario metamodel from Durak et al. (2014) that has been developed adopting base object model (BOM) metamodel.

BOM is also a SISO standard for fostering reuse in HLA-based distributed simulation environments. It introduces the reusable patterns, the interplay, and the sequence of events between simulation elements and provides a standard to capture the interactions (SISO 2006). It has been exercised as a method for capturing the conceptual scenarios by Siegfried and colleagues (Siegfried et al., 2013). Based on this work, BOM metamodel specified in the standard is adopted to construct a conceptual scenario metamodel.

Eclipse Modeling Framework (EMF) is a framework for describing models and then generating other constructs, like other models, code, or text from them. It allows its users to implement the four-level metamodeling architecture. ECORE is the model used to describe models in EMF (Steinberg et al. 2008). It is the meta-metamodel of the EMF. In the following paragraphs, how the conceptual scenario metamodel is build using EMF will be introduced.

There are four ECORE classes, namely, `EClass`, `EAttribute`, `EReference`, and `EDataType`. They are the building blocks of a metamodel. `EClass` is defined as the modeled class with attributes and references. `EAttribute` is the modeled attribute with a name and a type. `EReference` is specified as an association between classes. `EDataType` is the type of an attribute.

At the top level (Fig. 8.5), there are six `EClass`: `ConceptualScenario`, conceptual entity, `StateMachine`, `PatternOfInterplay`, event, and `ScenarioIdentification`. Their associations are defined by `EReference` constructs: entities, `stateMachines`, interplays, events, and identification. These relate `ConceptualScenario` to others.

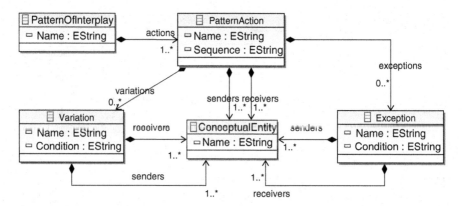

Fig. 8.6 Pattern of interplay in conceptual scenarios

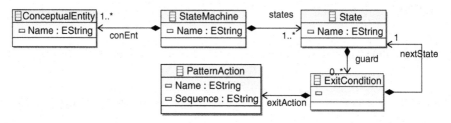

Fig. 8.7 State machines in conceptual scenarios

All classes have attributes that are defined by `EAttributes`. As an example, each `PatternOfInterplay` has a `Name` attribute. `Name` attribute is defined as string (`EString`) data type (`EDataType`).

Patterns of interplay are used to capture the pattern actions as well as their exceptions and variations. The classes and their association within the scope of pattern of interplays are depicted in Fig. 8.6. Actions are initiated by the sender conceptual entities, and the receivers are the intended recipients. Exceptions are defined as the actions that cause a remaining sequence to fail. Variations are however defined as alternative ways of an action that does not affect the completion or success.

As shown in Fig. 8.7, the state machines are used to capture states and their transitions in a conceptual scenario. A state machine possesses a number of states, each of which has an exit condition and a next state. Exit actions, which are pattern actions, depend on exit conditions. When the exit condition is satisfied, the corresponding exit action takes place, and a state transition occurs.

The conceptual entities appear in patterns of interplay as senders and receivers, and they are associated with a state machine. Entities possess characteristics, such as their position and mass. The BOM metamodel is enhanced by adding values to these characteristics to define scenario parameters (Fig. 8.8).

Events are used to capture the messages and triggers. Triggers represent undirected events when a change in the characteristic of an entity creates a response

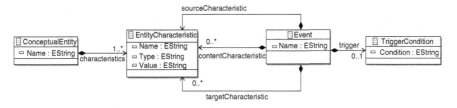

Fig. 8.8 Conceptual entities and events in conceptual scenarios

from other entities. The condition of change is captured in a trigger condition. Messages are directed events from one entity to another one that are uniquely identified by source and target characteristic. The content of a message is given in content characteristics.

In the next section, we introduce a sample excerpt from a conceptual scenario to illustrate the concepts introduced in this section.

8.2.1.3 Sample Scenario

This section is based on an operational scenario that was introduced previously for the departure activity of the D-ATRA aircraft. This is a typical example operational scenario from the users or sponsors of a flight simulator. As discussed earlier in this chapter, it is defined in natural language. It is neither complete nor entirely accurate. Data that is required to run this scenario is not completely available. An M&S expert needs to augment the missing information and develop a conceptual scenario.

EMF.Edit is a facility to build functional viewers and editors to display and edit the instances of the developed metamodels via automatic code generation. It is employed to generate the conceptual scenario editor that is used to develop a sample conceptual scenario based upon the operational scenario above.

The basic presentation capabilities of the conceptual scenario editor are presented using a tree viewer and a properties sheet for each conceptual scenario element. The hierarchical structure of the sample conceptual scenario is given in Fig. 8.9 as depicted by conceptual scenario editor. The tree organizes the conceptual entities from the operational scenario like aircraft, pilot, and weather. The main pattern of interplay is defined as take-off procedure. Flight status is captured as a state chart.

Various characteristics are specified for the aircraft entity. Initial location, fuel weight, and gross weight are some of them. The value of these characteristics then determines the scenario parameters.

The properties viewer is used to specify the attributes of the model elements. As an example, the attributes of initial location entity characteristics are its name (*initial location*), type (*string*), and value (*52°18′57″N 010°33′58″E*) (Fig. 8.10). M&S expert here specifies the implicit reference to the initial location of the aircraft in the operational scenario explicitly.

Fig. 8.9 Conceptual
scenario editor tree viewer

▲ ◆ **Conceptual Scenario**
   ▲ ◆ **Conceptual Entity Aircraft**
      ◆ **Entity Characteristic Call Sign**
      ◆ **Entity Characteristic Initial Location**
      ◆ **Entity Characteristic Fuel Weight**
      ◆ **Entity Characteristic Gross Weight**
    ◆ **Conceptual Entity Pilot**
    ◆ **Conceptual Entity Air Traffic Control**
   ▲ ◆ **Conceptual Entity Weather**
      ◆ **Entity Characteristic Temperature**
      ◆ **Entity Characteristic Visibility**
      ◆ **Entity Characteristic Sky Condition**
      ◆ **Entity Characteristic Wind Direction**
      ◆ **Entity Characteristic Wind Velocity**
    ◆ **Pattern Of Interplay Take-off Procedure**
    ◆ **State Machine Flight Status**

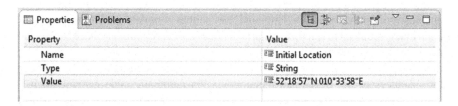

Properties Problems	
Property	Value
Name	Initial Location
Type	String
Value	52°18′57″N 010°33′58″E

Fig. 8.10 Conceptual scenario editor properties

The take-off procedure is presented in Fig. 8.11 as a sample pattern of interplay. There are six consecutive actions, starting from aircraft requests to taxi from air traffic control till its takeoff. The sender and receiver entities are all captured. While one can specify exceptions and variations, this sample does not possess them. As an example, the first pattern of action is request for taxiing. The sender entity is the aircraft, and the receiver entity is the air traffic control.

Flight status is presented in Fig. 8.12 as a sample state machine. Taxiing, takeoff, climbing, cruise, and landing are identified as the aircraft states. Taxiing state is followed by the takeoff, and the exit action of the taxiing state is issue of takeoff clearance. The consecutive state after takeoff is climbing.

The next section demonstrates how to transform a conceptual model to a simulation environment design, a simulation environment agreement, and an executable scenario over some sample model transformations.

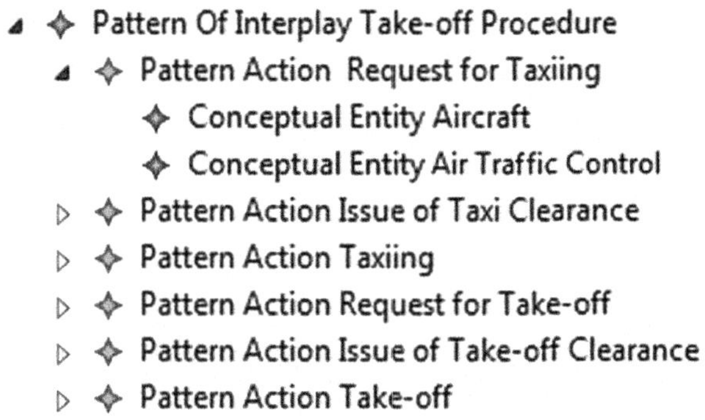

⊿ ✦ Pattern Of Interplay Take-off Procedure
  ⊿ ✦ Pattern Action Request for Taxiing
      ✦ Conceptual Entity Aircraft
      ✦ Conceptual Entity Air Traffic Control
  ▷ ✦ Pattern Action Issue of Taxi Clearance
  ▷ ✦ Pattern Action Taxiing
  ▷ ✦ Pattern Action Request for Take-off
  ▷ ✦ Pattern Action Issue of Take-off Clearance
  ▷ ✦ Pattern Action Take-off

Fig. 8.11 A sample pattern of interplay

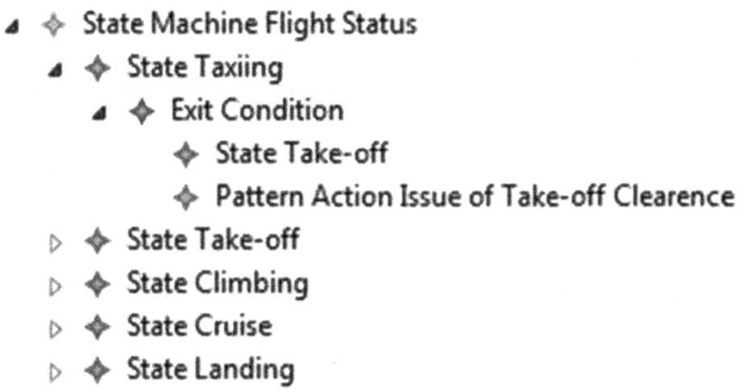

⊿ ✦ State Machine Flight Status
  ⊿ ✦ State Taxiing
    ⊿ ✦ Exit Condition
        ✦ State Take-off
        ✦ Pattern Action Issue of Take-off Clearence
  ▷ ✦ State Take-off
  ▷ ✦ State Climbing
  ▷ ✦ State Cruise
  ▷ ✦ State Landing

Fig. 8.12 A sample state machine

8.2.1.4 Sample Transformations

MDE promotes the use of model transformations throughout the engineering process. Models are proposed as the main artifacts and transformations that enable to carry over the information captured in one model to another one. Model transformations are the enabling mechanisms of MDE. In the model-based scenario development process, model transformations are proposed for transforming the information that is captured in a conceptual model to simulation environment design, simulation environment agreement, and executable scenarios. A model transformation language is required to define transformations from a source to a target. ATLAS Transformation Language (ATL) (Jouault et al. 2006), Graph Rewriting and Transformation (GReAT) (Agrawal 2003), and Query/View/Transformation (QVT) (OMG 2011a) are some of these languages. Rather than addressing a specific model transformation language, it is recommended to evaluate model transformation languages according to the project requirements such as development environments or target models and pick the right one.

In this section, sample transformation specifications, or mappings, are developed using QVT utilizing Eclipse Model-to-Model Transformation (MMT) project (The

Eclipse Foundation 2014). MMT supports QVT operational, which is a partial implementation of defined in QVT specification (Barendrecht 2010).

```
-- model type declaration to conceptual scenario metamodel
modeltype CS uses 'ConScen.ecore';
-- model type decleration to UML
modeltype UML uses 'UML.ecore';
-- transformation definition from Conceptual Scenario to UML
transformation scenario2UML(in CS :ConSce, out UML);
-- main is the trigger for the transformation
main (in scenario: CS ::ConSce, out umlModel: UML ::Model)
{
    umlModel := scenario. map scenario2UML ();
}
```

Above is an example of transformation defined using QVT. It presents a certain structure, which consists of model type definitions, transformation declarations, and a main function. Model type definitions declare the metamodels. Input and output metamodels are specified in transformation declarations. The main function finally starts the transformation process by calling the first transformation.

Mappings specify which object from an instance of a source metamodel will be transformed to a specific object in the instance of the target metamodel. The source class name and the target class name are specified by the declarations. Variables and parameters are initialized in the init section, mappings are specified in the population section, and post processing can be done in the end section of mapping body.

```
mapping CS::CS:: scen2UML() : UML::Model
{
    states     := self.states2staClasses();
    packages   := self.entities2packages();
    interfaces := self.entChar2intClasses();
}
```

Above is an excerpt from the top level mapping that is called in the main function. Mapping function *self.entites2packages()* map conceptual entities in the conceptual scenario metamodel to packages in the UML model. Similarly, entity characteristics in the conceptual scenario metamodel are mapped to the interface classes and states to state classes in the UML model.

```
mapping CS::CS:: scen2FOM() : FOM::Model
{
    interactions := self.events2intact();
    intParam     := self.contChar2intParam();
    objects      := self.entities2objects();
    objectAttr   := self.entChar2objAttr();
}
```

In the above excerpt, sample portion is provided for the conceptual scenario to FOM transformation. Excerpt shows how entities are mapped to HLA objects and entity characteristics to object attributes. Events in the conceptual scenario metamodel can be mapped to HLA interactions in a FOM and content characteristics to interaction parameters.

```
mapping CS::CS:: scen2Exec() : Exec:File
{
   logData       :=self.states2logging();
   entitites      := self.entities2entities();
   initialCond   := self.entChar2iniCond();
}
```

For creating an executable scenario from a conceptual scenario, the entities in the conceptual scenario need to be mapped to entities of the executable scenario as above. For example, initial conditions are collected from entity characteristic values. Conditional clauses can be used to filter event instances, as an example, whose name starts with "log" can be transformed to log data.

8.2.2   Scenario Loading and Parsing

In a distributed simulation, it is not necessary for every federate to load the entire scenario. Because (i) the federate does not necessarily need to know the entire scenario and (ii) simulation scenarios can be dynamic. Dynamic means that the flow or an element of the scenario can be changed by the user at run time. For example, a trainer can inject events (e.g., emergency events). This enforces to distribute the dynamic elements of the scenario as simulation objects or interactions. Therefore, it is reasonable to develop a scenario manager federate specifically to manage the dynamic aspects of scenarios in the federation.

Naval Surface Tactical Maneuvering Simulation System (NSTMSS) (Topçu and Oğuztüzün 2005) will be used to exemplify the concepts. Conceptually, NSTMSS is a distributed virtual environment, where some of players interactively control the virtual frigates in real time and some players behave as tactical players that command the groups of the frigates. All share a common virtual environment, with its environment characteristics (e.g., time of day) and parameters (e.g., the wind direction). The environment is managed by an environment application, obeying a common scenario that is distributed (e.g., role casting), controlled (e.g., injection messages), and monitored by an exercise planner. Technically, NSTMSS is an HLA-based distributed simulation system that is composed of 3D ship-handling simulators such as a frigate, a tactical level simulation of operational area, a virtual environment manager, and simulation management processes.

In NSTMSS, the exercise manager federate (ExMFd), also called scenario manager, selects the training scenario and distributes it to the participants (i.e., the ship federates), injects events defined in the scenario into the federation execution, collects data, and generates a report about the federation execution. The ExMFd operates as the orchestra conductor (Fig. 8.13). One possible sub-module of a scenario manager is the scenario parser, which selects and loads a (part of) scenario from the scenario data store. The implementation of a scenario parser can be simplified when

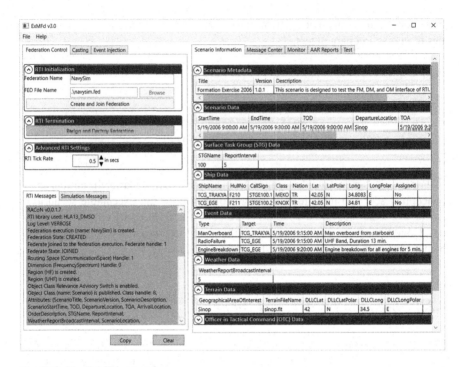

Fig. 8.13 The ExMFd screenshot

the scenario definition language (SDL) is based on the XML. A generic XML parser can be used (or customized) as a scenario parser.

8.2.3   Scenario Distribution and Role Casting

Initially, prior to a scenario run (execution), scenario distribution and role casting are used to initialize federation according to the scenario. During the scenario run, distribution mechanism is used to update the scenario status. In this respect, scenario distribution activity is the distribution of the scenario (initialization) data to the relevant simulation entities in the distributed environment. Role casting is distributing the roles of the scenario entities specified in the scenario to the actual federates in the federation.

8.2.3.1   Scenario Distribution

Scenario can be distributed using some distribution patterns specified in Lofstrand et al. (2004). Using a centralized pattern, a scenario is distributed and projected onto the federation execution via a specific-purpose federate and scenario manager (federate) using the federation object model (FOM) (IEEE 2010c). A FOM is required

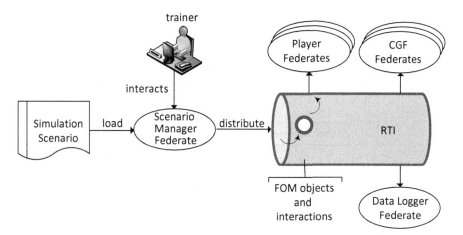

Fig. 8.14 Scenario distribution using RTI (Topçu and Oğuztüzün 2010)

for each federation execution. It defines the shared objects and interactions of a federation. A typical scenario distribution environment is seen in Fig. 8.14. A player federate is a federate that uses and needs the scenario during the federation execution. A computer-generated force (CGF) federate is an implementation of a software agent such as an agent ship.

For distributing the scenario via FOM classes, the types of the scenario entities must be mapped to the FOM classes. Thus, the FOM will contain the classes of the scenario domain entities and the scenario management-specific elements.

Another approach, instead of distributing of a (part of) scenario at run time, is to choose an offline approach, where participating federates load and parse the entire scenario at start-up. Other ways of distributing a scenario such that referencing and hard coding can be found in Lofstrand et al. (2004).

In NSTMSS, the scenario distribution is done via the scenario object class (in the form of the HLA object class (IEEE 2010c)) over the HLA RTI (IEEE 2010b) after the scenario file is selected in the scenario manager (i.e., the ExMFd). Whenever a new federate is discovered, the scenario object class is updated by the scenario manager through the federation so that the newly joined federate can set the initialization data.

8.2.3.2   Role Casting (Tasking)

Role casting is to decide which roles in the scenario will be played by which federate and to cast the role to the appropriate federate. For example, in the scenario, there can be two Meko class frigates, with their class, name, call sign, location, and nationality (e.g., blue vs. red or neutral) that are defined. When one frigate federate joins the federation, if its frigate class is Meko, then it must be cast to its role in the specific federation execution.

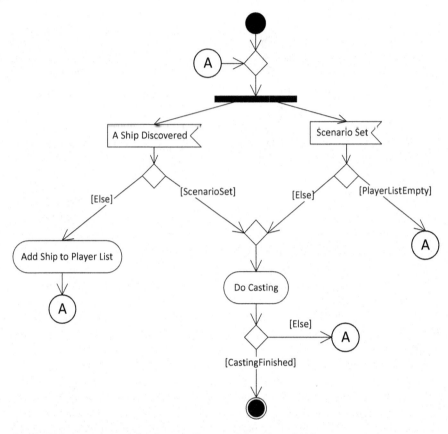

Fig. 8.15 Role casting activity diagram (Topçu and Oğuztüzün 2010)

Role casting can be done automatically or manually (by the simulation manager or trainer, respectively). In automatic role casting, whenever a federate is discovered, if it is suitable for the scenario, then role casting is done automatically by the scenario manager tool. In manual role casting, the trainer determines which federate will play which role. After a new simulation entity is discovered, the ExMFd checks that there is an unassigned scenario element in the scenario or not, and then if there is and the new entity is eligible for the scenario, it does casting. In more specific terms, it checks whether the scenario element class and the ship class are the same or not based on the enumerated class types. Casting rules are as follows:

- Casting begins after the scenario file is selected.
- Casting is done immediately (if the ship is eligible), when a new ship is discovered.
- Roles are encapsulated in the task order message for each ship.
- Task order messages are sent via data distribution management interface of RTI (IEEE 2010b).

Casting flowchart is presented in Fig. 8.15. The casting activity is triggered by two parallel signals (i.e., received events from an outside process). When a ship federate joins to the federation, then a-ship-discovered event is generated. If the scenario is not set (not selected) yet, the information of the ship is saved in a player list for a future cast till the scenario is set. Otherwise, casting is done immediately if the discovered ship meets its role specifications. When the scenario is selected, the first thing checked is the player list. If there are saved ships, then casting is done for each until the list gets empty. The whole activity repeats until all elements in the scenario are cast (i.e., casting is finished).

On the other hand, role casting is done via sending a message to the federation members in the form of the HLA interaction classes (IEEE 2010c). For instance, in our case study, this is done by sending a task order message over the Tactical Messaging System (Topçu and Oğuztüzün 2005). A task order message contains the object id's of the ships. So, a unique task order is sent for each ship object. In military applications, role casting, known as tasking, can be done using Coalition Battle Management Language (C-BML) orders (SISO 2010).

8.2.4 Event Injection

Event injection is essential for augmenting the training value of an exercise. The events, generated during the federation execution, change the course of events in the exercise. Events can be scheduled (defined in scenario) or unscheduled (activated by the trainer at run time). Therefore, events are seen as part of the scenario. It is possible to schedule events at scenario composition time (scheduled event injection) or to inject them at run time (unscheduled event injection). The timeline for events in the scenario can be specified using a sequence chart such as UML sequence diagrams (Fowler 2003) or live sequence charts (Brill et al. 2004). The scenario manager federate injects the events defined in the scenario file at their target time of occurrence to the target federate(s). Event injection is done using the event injection interactions defined in the scenario management classes (see Sect. 8.2.6) as part of the scenario object model in FOM. To separate the communication channel of the event injection interactions for an easier data logging, a special data distribution region can be created specific to the scenario management.

In NSTMSS, the injected events (e.g., man overboard, engine failure) are delivered to human player. When an event injection message is received by a ship, the ship loses of her steering capability and the functionality of the ship is automatically reduced according to the type of the event. For example, as far as a rudder malfunction emergency event is received, the helm of the ship becomes unusable.

8.2.5   Data Collection and Logging

Data collection is performed by listening to the activities occurring during the exercise (i.e., messaging activities). Logging can be implemented in two abstraction levels. Implementation of a data logger can be either federation (application)-specific level or federation nonspecific level. The federation-specific data loggers can be used for after-action review, replay, and results (output) validation for credibility. For instance, in our case study, for replaying ship movements in real time or in faster/slower time pace, the data logger must log the ship's posture (the three-dimensional position and angular velocities) in sampling time. The federation nonspecific data loggers are also known as federation execution/RTI monitoring tools. They are generally intended for collecting RTI-related data for the purposes for RTI parameter and network infrastructure optimization and enhancement and RTI debugging.

In NSTMSS, the ExMFd collects simple data about messaging activities, such as counting the formation messages using the federation-specific implementation approach. Moreover, the ExMFd provides the interface to monitor the simulation run. The monitor tab displays the ship status reports that indicate the location of the ships in the scenario. The simulation clock displays the simulation time and the time spanned till scenario began (i.e., physical (exercise) time). The real-time clock displays the current system time. Data logging capability is needed for an after-action review. In the ExMFd, the user can save the log file in text format for further logging and investigations on simulation status data. The ExMFd provides the means to generate various kinds of reports in order to review the scenario run (after-action review). A typical federation execution report that gives an account of the simulation scenario events is seen in Fig. 8.16.

There are commercial data loggers independent of any specific federation. They collect generic data related to the usage of the RTI services, not to a specific scenario.

In NSTMSS, the federation monitor federate (FedMonFd) enables generic data collection and reporting of the HLA federates about their usage of underlying RTI services by using the HLA Management Object Model interface (IEEE 2010c). The FedMonFd is a stealth federate that also controls the federation reporting behaviors. The FedMonFd provides a basis for implementation of an observer federate and provides user interfaces to monitor the status of the federation and the federates. The FedMonFd monitors and logs the RTI data (e.g., interactions and objects published and subscribed, interactions sent and received, objects updated and reflected, etc.). The FedMonFd also provides detailed reports for review of the monitoring activity. The FedMonFd is not specific to NSTMSS federation. It can be run in any federation. It has a reporting module that generates two kinds of reports: one is a federate-based report that shows all the RTI service usage per federate and second is the RTI service-based usage report that shows all the RTI services used by the federates grouped by the service name (e.g., report for object published service). A sample RTI-based usage report is presented in Fig. 8.17.

Federation Execution (Events) Report

3/5/2006 2:54:32 PM

All Federation Events

Simulation Time	Real Time	Event Type	Event
5/19/2006 9:00:00 AM	3/5/2006 2:40:38 PM	06	Task Order. To:MekoFd
5/19/2006 9:00:00 AM	3/5/2006 2:40:59 PM	06	Task Order. To:MekoFd
5/19/2006 9:00:00 AM	3/5/2006 2:41:02 PM	01	Scenario is being started.
5/19/2006 9:04:48 AM	3/5/2006 2:45:51 PM	03	Formation Message. From:TCG_TRAKYA
5/19/2006 9:04:59 AM	3/5/2006 2:46:02 PM	04	Ship Status Report. From:TCG_TRAKYA
5/19/2006 9:05:01 AM	3/5/2006 2:46:04 PM	04	Ship Status Report. From:TCG_EGE
5/19/2006 9:05:43 AM	3/5/2006 2:46:59 PM	02	Injection Event. Event Type: EngineBreakdown Description: Parameter 1: Both Parameter 2: 1
5/19/2006 9:07:18 AM	3/5/2006 2:48:22 PM	05	Weather Report. Sea State: SS0 Fog Type: FOG OFF Wind Direction: 90 Wind Speed: 2 Explanation: -

Total Number of Events	8
Total Duration (in minutes)	7

Legend:	Event Type Code	Event Type Explanation
	01	Scenario Management Event
	02	Event Injection Message
	03	Formation Message
	04	Ship Status Message
	05	Weather Report
	06	Task Order

1 of 1

Fig. 8.16 Federation-specific data logging – execution report sample (the report data is related to a fictitious scenario)

Service-based RTI Usage Report

2/19/2006 8:23:54 PM

Federation Information

Federation Name	NSTMSS
FED File Name	nstmss.fed
RTI Version	RTI-1.3NGv6
Last Save Name	
Last Save Time	0.0000000000
Next Save Name	
Next Save Time	0.0000000000

Federates in Federation

Federate Id	Federate Name	Hosted By
1	FedMonFd	iy0434231

Objects Published

Object No	Object Name	Attribute No	Attribute Name

Objects Subscribed

Object No	Object Name	Attribute No	Attribute Name	Active
Federate: 1		Number of Classes: 2		
4	objectRoot.Manager.Federate	2	FederateHandle	
4	objectRoot.Manager.Federate	3	FederateType	
4	objectRoot.Manager.Federate	4	FederateHost	
4	objectRoot.Manager.Federate	10	FederateState	
5	objectRoot.Manager.Federation	25	FederationName	
5	objectRoot.Manager.Federation	26	FederatesInFederation	
5	objectRoot.Manager.Federation	27	RTIversion	
5	objectRoot.Manager.Federation	28	FEDid	
5	objectRoot.Manager.Federation	29	LastSaveName	
5	objectRoot.Manager.Federation	30	LastSaveTime	
5	objectRoot.Manager.Federation	31	NextSaveName	
5	objectRoot.Manager.Federation	32	NextSaveTime	

Objects Updated

1 of 3

Fig. 8.17 RTI-based RTI usage report sample

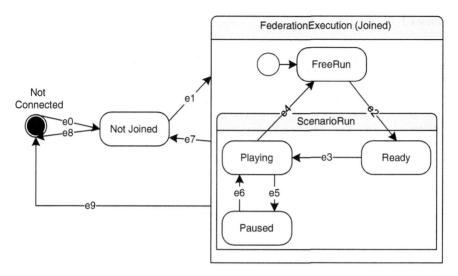

Fig. 8.18 Federate state diagram regarding to scenario management

The generic data loggers are very useful for troubleshooting the federation execution at the RTI level and for troubleshooting the scenario distribution and event injection problems as well.

8.2.6   Federate States

In Chap. 4, we presented the lifetime of a federate. When scenario is involved in the federation execution, then some new federate states are introduced. Scenario management, specifically distribution and role casting activities, must account for the states of the federates in the federation. When a scenario is involved, the states of a federate regarding to the scenario management and pause/resume support are depicted in Fig. 8.18. Here, we assume that the federate is initially in not connected state, and we depict only the scenario involved states. All states are sub-states of the Connected state.

The explanation of each state and the transitions are presented in Table 8.1 and in Table 8.2, respectively.

As an example, Fig. 8.19 presents an activity diagram that depicts the preparation activity of the ship federate in transition (e2) from the FreeRun state to the scenario run (Ready) state. When the ship federate receives the scenario data (e.g., scenario object class) and/or the role casting message (e.g., task order interaction class), the federate prepares itself (e.g., a ship (tele)transports to its scenario

Table 8.1 Federate states

States	Description			
Not joined	Federate is connected to RTI. Federate is ready for joining a federation execution. Federate also enters to this state after federate resigns from the federation execution			
Federation execution (joined)	This state is a compound state formed by `FreeRun` and `ScenarioRun` states. Federation execution is begun. This state also indicates an Active State			
	FreeRun	Federate is joined to a federation execution. Federate is an active federate and can freely run in the federation execution without adhering to a specific scenario		
	Scenario run	This state is a compound state formed by `Ready,` `Paused,` and `Playing` states. Scenario is in execution		
		Ready	Federate received the scenario updates and its role and completed its initialization according to the scenario and its role. Federate is ready to play	
		Playing	The scenario has begun and the federate is running the scenario	
		Paused	The scenario and the federate execution are paused	

Table 8.2 Transitions for federate states

Transitions	Description
e0	Trigger event: Federate application connects to RTI
e1	Trigger event: Federate joins a federation execution. Federate joined event is raised
	Guard: Federation execution exists
e2	Trigger event: Role casting interaction is received
	Guard: Scenario update is received
	Activity during transition: Prepare by doing federate-specific initialization (e.g., set terrain file and load the terrain data for rendering) related to the scenario received and report the readiness
e3	Trigger event: `BeginToPlay` interaction is received. Scenario run is begun
	Activity during transition: Begin the scenario play. Start the federate clock
e4	Trigger event: `EndToPlay` interaction is received. Scenario run is ended
	Activity during transition: Stop federate clock. End scenario play
e5	Trigger event: Pause the scenario run. This state is specific to scenario run, not related to federation save and restore
	Activity during transition: The federate will suspend the scenario and its execution
e6	Trigger event: Resume the scenario run. This state is specific to scenario run, not related to federation save and restore
	Activity during transition: The federate will resume its execution and the scenario play
e7	Trigger event: Federate resigns from a federation execution. Federate resigned event is raised
	Activity during transition: Delete RTI-specific objects. A typical federate will also try to destroy the federation execution
e8	Trigger event: Federate disconnects from RTI
e9	Trigger event: The connection is lost between federate and RTI

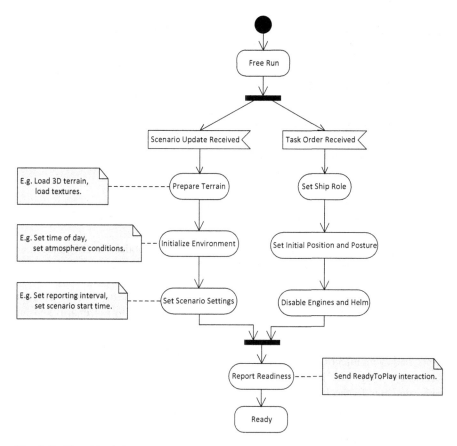

Fig. 8.19 The ship federate activity diagram for preparing for the scenario run (Topçu and Oğuztüzün 2010)

location) according to the scenario and sends a `ReadyToPlay` (i.e., I am ready) message in transition to the ready state. In ready state, the federate waits for the scenario to begin. For example, it waits on a synchronization point and freezes its federate clock. After the scenario begins (e3 transition), the federate moves to the playing state.

8.3   Scenarios and FOM

As already pointed out in the scenario distribution, the scenario or a part of it is required to be distributed using the HLA classes specified in FOM. Thus, we hold that a FOM must involve an object model related to the scenario and its

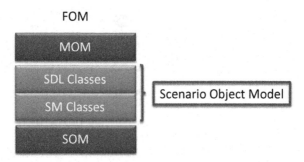

Fig. 8.20 Scenario object model (Topçu and Oğuztüzün 2010)

management. We name this model as the scenario object model (ScOM) as seen in Fig. 8.20. The ScOM includes two parts: the SDL classes and the scenario management (SM) classes.

The SM classes include the scenario management-specific classes defined beforehand for all kind of scenarios. They are not specific to a scenario and an SDL. The SM classes are generally in form of the HLA interaction classes. These include `BeginToPlay`, `ReadyToPlay`, `EndToPlay`, pause, resume interactions, and event injection interactions such as `InjectEmergencyEvent`. When necessary, they can be extended according to the simulation object model requirements. To the best of our knowledge, there is no standardized set of scenario management classes. Some proposed sets can be found in Lofstrand et al. (2004).

Scenarios and their specifications (i.e., the SDL) can be used to generate the requirements for the object model. And, then an FOM can be synthesized to satisfy these requirements. In a broader sense, the main idea is to use the scenarios in the scope of requirement analysis of FOMs. The SDL classes can be partially obtained from the scenario and its specification (i.e., SDL). The SDL provides us the necessary classes, attributes, and relations among the classes, while the scenario helps to determine the application-specific properties such as the resolution of an object class attribute. The SDL entities and events can be mapped to the HLA object classes and interaction classes, respectively. When the SDL (schema) changes, then the SDL classes in the ScOM must reflect the change.

The FOM requirement generation using scenarios can be noted as a future work where many research questions arise such as what forms an object model requirement can take or what elements it can involve.

8.4   Summary

Scenario management in a distributed simulation involves many activities. Scenario development is regarded as the design and development activity. Scenario loading and parsing, scenario distribution, role casting, event injection, and data collection are presented as run-time activities. The scenario development involves all effort starting from operational scenario to executable scenario and utilization of scenario simulation environment design. The scenario loading is not necessary for all simulation entities in a distributed simulation, but this creates a need for a distribution mechanism of the scenario elements using the distributed simulation communication infrastructure (RTI in HLA). In HLA, the scenario elements can be distributed using object exchange mechanisms (in terms of object and interaction classes). This dictates to define the appropriate scenario objects and interactions in the FOM. Role casting can be done manually or automatically. Event injection increases the effectiveness of training, and data collection allows a complete after-action review.

In this chapter, we first introduced a model-based approach for scenario development with an example from flight simulation domain, and then we explained all run-time activities using a real-life distributed simulation system, namely, NSTMSS. Finally, this chapter introduces a scenario object model as a part of a FOM.

References

Adak, M., Topçu, O., & Oğuztüzün, H. (2009, February). Model-based code generation for HLA federates. *Software: Practice and Experience, 40*(2), 149–175.

Agrawal, A. (2003). *GReAT: A metamodel based model transformation language.* Nashville: Institute for Software Integrated Systems (ISIS), Vanderbilt University.

Ahmad, S., & Sexana, V. (2008). Design of formal Air traffic control system through UML. *Ubiquitous Computing and Communication Journal, 3*(6), 11–20.

Arboleda, H., & Royer, J. C. (2012). *Model-driven and software product line engineering.* Hoboken: John Wiley & Sons, Inc..

Barendrecht, P. (2010). *Modeling transformations using QVT operational mappings.* Eindhoven: Eindhoven University of Technology Department of Mechanical Engineering Systems Engineering Group.

Brill, M., et al. (2004). Live sequence charts: An introduction to lines, arrows, and strange boxes in the context of formal verification. *Lecture Notes in Computer Science, 3147*, 374–399.

Cetinkaya, D., Verbraeck, A., & Seck, M. (2011). MDD4MS: A model driven development framework for modeling and simulation. In *Proceedings of the 2011 summer computer simulation conference* (pp. 113–121). The Hague: SCS.

DFS Deutsche Flugsicherung GmbH. (2013). *Aerodome chart -ICAO Braunschweig-Wolfsbug.* Langen: DFS Deutsche Flugsicherung GmbH.

Durak, U., Oguztuzun, H., & Ider, K. (2008, March). Ontology based trajectory simulation framework. *Journal of Computing and Information Science in Engineering, 8(1),* 014503.
DOI:10.1115/1.2830845

Durak, U., Oguztuzun, H., & Ider, K. (2009). Ontology based domain engineering for trajectory
simulation reuse. *International Journal of Software Engineering and Knowledge Engineering,*
9(8), 1109–1129.

Durak, U., Topcu, O., Siegfried, R., & Oguztuzun, H. (2014). Scenario development: A model-
driven engineering perspective. In *Proceedings of the 4th international conference on simulation and modeling methodologies, technologies and applications*. Vienna: SCITEPRESS.

Fowler, M. (2003). *UML distilled a brief guide to the standard object modeling language*. Boston:
Addison-Wesley.

Gašević, D., Djuric, D., & Devedžic, V. (2009). *Model driven engineering and ontology development*. Berlin: Springer.

Gronback, R. C. (2009). *Eclipse modeling project: A domain-specific language*. Upper Saddle
River: Addison-Wesley.

IEEE. (1993). *Protocols for distributed interactive simulation applications-entity information and
interaction*. IEEE Std 1278-1993. New York: IEEE.

IEEE. (2010a). *IEEE recommended practice for Distributed Simulation Engineering and Execution
Process (DSEEP)*. IEEE Std 1730-2010. New York: IEEE.

IEEE. (2010b). *Standard for Modeling and Simulation (M&S) High Level Architecture (HLA) –
Federate interface specification*. IEEE Std 1516.1-2010. New York: IEEE.

IEEE. (2010c). *Standard for Modeling and Simulation (M&S) High Level Architecture (HLA)
-object model template*. IEEE Std 1516.2-2010. New York: IEEE.

Jouault, F., et al. (2006). ATL: A QVT-like transformation language. In *Proceedings of the 21st
ACM SIGPLAN Symposium on Object-Printed Programming Systems, Languages, and
Applications (OOPSLA '06)* (pp. 719–720). New York: ACM.

Lofstrand, B., et al. (2004). Scenario management – Common design principles and data interchange formats. In *Proceedings of European Simulation Interoperability Workshop (SIW)*.
Edinburgh: SISO.

MSG-053. (2010). *Rapid scenario generation for simulation applications*. RTO-TR-
MSG-053. Neuilly sur Seine: NATO RTO.

OMG. (2011a). *Meta Object Facility (MOF) 2.0 query/view/transformation specification*.
Needham: OMG.

OMG. (2011b). *Object Management Group, meta object facility, MOF specification version 2.4.1*.
Needham: OMG.

Siegfried, R., et al. (2012). Scenarios in military (distributed) simulation environments. In
Proceedings of the Spring Simulation Interoperability Workshop (SSIW). Orlando: SISO.

Siegfried, R., et al. (2013). Specification and documentation of conceptual scenarios using Base
Object Models (BOMs). In *Proceedings of the 2913 Spring Simulation Conference*. San Diego:
SISO.

SISO. (2006). *Base Object Model (BOM) template specification*. Orlando: Simulation
Interoperability Standards Organization (SISO).

SISO. (2008). *Standard for Military Scenario Definition Language (MSDL)*. Orlando: SISO.

SISO. (2010). *Coalition Battle Management Language (C-BML)*. Orlando: Simulation
Interoperability Standards Organization (SISO).

Steinberg, D., Budinsky, F., Merks, E., & Paternostro, M. (2008). *EMF: Eclipse modeling framework*. Upper Saddle River: Pearson Education.

The Eclipse Foundation. (2014). *Model-to-Model Transformation (MMT)*. [Online] Available at:
https://projects.eclipse.org/projects/modeling.mmt. Accessed 10 Feb 2014.

Topçu, O. (2004). *Development, representation, and validation of conceptual models in distributed
simulation*. Halifax: Defence R&D Canada – Atlantic (DRDC Atlantic).

Topçu, O., & Oğuztüzün, H. (2005, Winter). Developing an HLA based naval maneuvering simulation. *Naval Engineers Journal, 117*(1), 23–40.

Topçu, O., & Oğuztüzün, H. (2010). Scenario management practices in HLA-based distributed simulation. *Journal of Naval Science and Engineering, 6*(2), 1–33.

Topçu, O., Adak, M., & Oğuztüzün, H. (2008, July). A metamodel for federation architectures. *Transactions on Modeling and Computer Simulation (TOMACS), 18*(3), 10:1–10:29.

Ullner, F., Blomberg, J., & Andersson, N. (2008). The lessons learned from implementing a MSDL scenario editor. In *Proceedings of the 2008 Fall Simulation Interoperability Workshop*. Orlando: SISO.

US Department of Defense. (1996). *High level architecture glossary*. Washington, DC: US DoD.

Part IV
Implementation and Execution

Chapter 9
Implementation, Integration, and Testing

Implementation can be regarded as one of the important steps of simulation engineering in which all the concepts and ideas, abstracted as models, are transformed to an executable form. MDE had a major effect on the practices of this step. Models became the major artifacts for implementation. MDE proposed that model development and code generation replace the traditional coding practices. This also disrupted and changed the other major implementation practices like static code analysis, integration, and testing. As models are regarded as the major artifacts, the model development is pronounced as the major activity. Guidelines have been developed for increasing the readability and maintainability of the simulation models and the efficiency and performance of the generated code. Along with them, methods and techniques have been developed for model checking and repair. Advancements in model-to-text transformation enabled effective and flexible code generation. Integration requirements could then be attacked by retargeting the code generator for particular platforms. In the same vein, model-based testing (MBT) introduced generation of executable test cases from a model. This chapter explains the activities of implementation that have been changing with introduction of MDE. These activities include model development, model checking, code generation and integration, and testing. These activities are first explained and introduced with examples from an off-the-shelf modeling and simulation environment, and then a recent methodology research on that particular activity is presented.

9.1 Introduction

Implementation is introduced in DSEEP as an activity that targets member applications for the distributed simulation that can represent corresponding objects and associated behavior as described in the conceptual model (IEEE 2010). IEEE Standard 12207–2008 for Systems and Software Engineering – Software Life Cycle

© Springer International Publishing Switzerland 2016
O. Topçu et al., *Distributed Simulation*, Simulation Foundations,
Methods and Applications, DOI 10.1007/978-3-319-03050-0_9

Processes (IEEE 2008) defines implementation as the realization of the specified system elements. Implementation transforms the specified behavior, interfaces, and implementation constraints to a software product. It may consist of architecture design, detailed design, construction, and integration and testing steps. The architecture defines the top-level structure and identifies the components and their interaction scheme. The detailed design, on the other hand, provides sufficient information that will permit coding in a programming language or a simulation language. While the construction step produces the executable units (simulation components), in the integration step, these units are combined into integrated units (subsystems, and eventually, the system). Lastly, system testing targets at confirming that the integrated product conforms to its requirements. Construction should yield individual simulation components (federates), tested and documented properly. Then, integration will yield a integrated simulation system (federation).

The implementation in MDE relies on transforming models to other models and eventually to code. Implementation will lead to the realization and test of the executable units which are called components. While model-to-model (M2M) translations are used to move from one technical or conceptual space to another, basically for specification, model-to-text (M2T) transformations are mainly used for code generation. While M2M transformations are usually applied for design and testing, M2T transformations are applied for construction and integration.

Architecture and detailed design steps following the MDE approach turns out to be model development. Here modeling languages are employed. The abstract syntax of the models expressed in these languages is defined in their metamodels. The mappings among the abstract syntax and simulation models that preserve the semantic and behavior while introducing new information, enable transformations to generate executable simulation code.

In this chapter, the simulation modeling practices for MDE will be explained rather than software system modeling for MDE, which is well introduced in various books (Kleppe et al. 2003; Mellor and Balcer 2002; Pastor and Molina 2007; Frankel 2003). The causal block diagrams (CBD) can be introduced as one of the formalisms that is widely utilized in modeling and simulation of technical systems. They have their roots in design of control systems (Astrom and Wittenmark 1984). Well-known implementations are MATLAB/Simulink (The MathWorks Inc. 2015d, e, f) and Scilab/Xcos (Scilab Enterprises 2015). The concrete syntax may display tool-specific variations, but when we investigate the abstract syntax, a block diagram is composed of number of entities and their directed relationships (Denckla and Mosterman 2005). Blocks, input ports, and output ports are the types of entities. The connections between the output ports and input ports specify a directed relationship. Blocks and ports are the basic elements. Input and output ports may be bound to blocks or they may stay free. Ports are bound with a variable, either used as an input or calculated as an output. And the behavior of a block is defined by a function that maps the explicit inputs on the input ports and implicit inputs to explicit outputs on the output ports and implicit outputs. An execution manager executes the block diagram, usually repeatedly. It is responsible to assign the external and implicit inputs to the block diagram and collect external and implicit outputs.

While temporal interpolation can be enabled by incrementing the time between repeated evaluations, using special blocks like integrator, the continuous state of the system can be represented and further evaluated using time integration operation that employs a numerical solver. A hybrid dynamic system can be modeled using explicit rate transition blocks between the discrete and continuous parts of the models.

While other modeling formalisms like UML are more popular for MDE in software engineering and SysML in systems engineering, this chapter will introduce the implementation process over the CBDs, which are particularly popular in modeling and simulation community. The examples and particulars of the practice will be introduced over MATLAB/Simulink and Scilab/Xcos.

Model Development section introduces the basics of model building using CBDs in MATLAB/Simulink and Scilab/Xcos. In Model Checking and Refactoring section, modeling guidelines and static model checking approaches will be explained. Model refactoring will be discussed as the methodology for model enhancement and evolution. Besides the available tool sets that are currently provided by modeling environments, the implementation of model-based approaches to refactoring will be presented using a sample implementation in Scilab/Xcos.

In the Code Generation and Integration section, as an example, the code generation mechanism of MATLAB/Simulink will be summarized. Then a sample case study will be acquainted to exemplify how available code generation tool sets of the modeling environments can be extended to support model integration. Later, Testing section will provide reader with an overview of testing approaches proposed for MDE of simulation using CBDs. Further, a particular model-based approach will be revealed for MATLAB/Simulink models.

9.2 Model Development

Simulink provides its users a library that is composed of various predefined source, sink, linear, and nonlinear blocks that represent the mathematical models of commonly occurring components in dynamic systems (Klee and Allen 2011). The full list of available predefined blocks and their details can be found in Simulink® Reference (The MathWorks Inc. 2015e). Building a Simulink model can be described as selecting the appropriate blocks and connecting them to represent the mathematical model. As an example, to generate inputs, blocks from the *sources* sub-library are employed (Fig. 9.1). And the outputs are displayed or saved using blocks from *Sinks* sub-library.

The Simulink Library Browser, which is presented in Fig. 9.1, is the source of blocks. The selected blocks are copied to the Simulink Editor, and the links, which establish the mathematical relations between the blocks, are created in this editor environment. Models can be hierarchical and can encapsulate groups of blocks in subsystems.

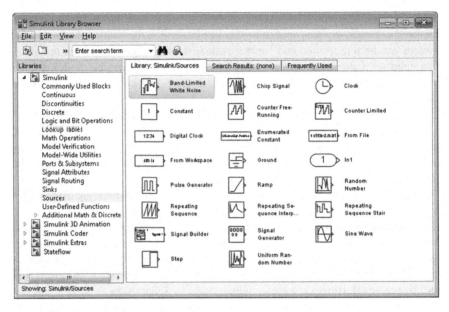

Fig. 9.1 Simulink library browser

To model a differential equation $x' = 3x(t) + u(t)$, we can use a sine wave generator for the $u(t)$, an integrator to integrate x' and compute x, a gain block, and a sum block. After locating the blocks, the links are created, and the resulting model is presented in Fig. 9.2. Simulink® User's Guide (The MathWorks Inc. 2015f) presents an extensive guide on how to use Simulink.

Very much like MATLAB/Simulink, Scilab/Xcos provides a modular approach to construct complex dynamical system models using a CBD editor, which has been presented in Fig. 9.3 (Campbell et al. 2006). Besides utilizing the available set of block libraries that are provided in palettes, using Xcos, the user can develop libraries of reusable blocks.

The graphical editor is employed to construct CBDs of dynamic systems. The main source of building blocks is palettes. Figure 9.4 depicts the Scilab/Xcos palette browser. The blocks are copied from the palette to the editor. Figure 9.3 depicts an example model for which three blocks are copied from *sources* and *sinks* palettes, namely, a sine wave generator, a scope, and a clock event generator. *Sources* palette contains blocks that generate signals without any input where the *sinks* palette contains blocks without output like data display or logging blocks. The sine wave generator generates an output signal with the value of the *sin(t)* function at every time step of the simulation. The clock activates the scope block in a desired frequency to read the input signal and construct the curve to be displayed. There are basically two types of links in Xcos: regular links, which are black, carry signals, whereas activation links, which are red, carry activation timing information. Scilab Online Help (Scilab Enterprises 2015) provides detailed information on how to use Scilab/Xcos and the blocks provided in palettes.

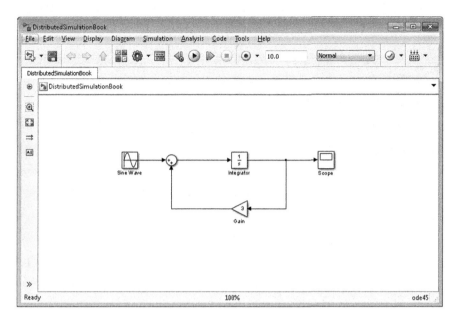

Fig. 9.2 Simulink editor

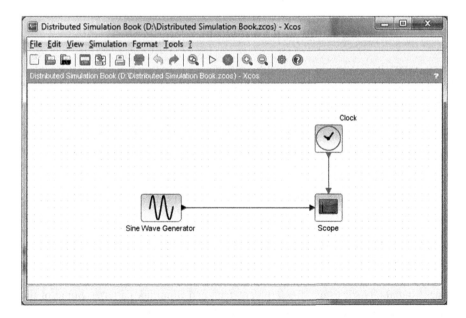

Fig. 9.3 Scilab/Xcos editor

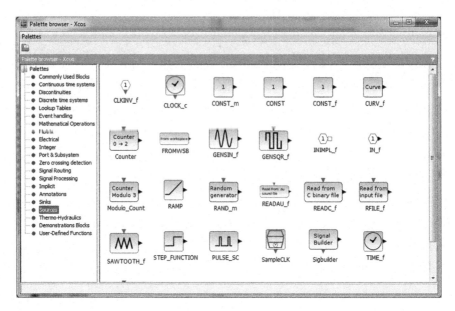

Fig. 9.4   Scilab/Xcos palette browser

9.3   Model Checking and Refactoring

9.3.1   Modeling Rules and Guidelines

With MDE, the quality of the resulting simulation software depends on the quality of the models; therefore, all possible effort is spent to ensure the highest quality of the model (Farkas et al. 2006). Coding rules and style guides are long been applied in traditional software development process. These rules and style guides try to ensure the quality of the code by fostering clearness and readability. Further, there are also guidelines for increasing the run-time performance as well as safety. Now rules and style guides are being developed and applied on models for MDE to achieve higher quality in modeling.

In 2009, MathWorks Automotive Advisory Board (MAAB) proposed modeling guidelines using MATLAB, Simulink, and Stateflow, and since then they have been maintaining these guidelines (MathWorks Automotive Advisory Board 2015). The motivations of these guidelines are achieving reusable and readable models, well-defined interfaces, understandable presentation, and uniform appearance of models, code, and documentation. Simulink guidelines are grouped under diagram appearance, signals, block usage, block parameters, and Simulink patterns. Some of the guidelines from diagram appearance group can be exemplified as Simulink model appearance, Simulink font and font sizes, or Simulink signal appearance.

The guidelines are defined with identification, title, priority, scope, applicable MATLAB versions, prerequisites, description, rationale, change history, and the related Model Advisor check. As an example guideline from MAAB, *db_0032: Simulink signal appearance* is given in Table 9.1.

Later in aerospace domain, the Orion Crew Exploration Vehicle Flight Dynamics Team from NASA enhanced MAAB rules and guidelines set to support guidance and navigation and control model development in Orion program (Henry 2011).

Both rules and guidelines from MAAB and NASA are commonly applied by the modeling and simulation community. Further, MathWorks provided a tool within MATLAB, namely, Model Advisor that enables the automatic model checking against these guidelines.

9.3.2 Model Checking and Repair

Considering that the modeling guidelines are usually large in size, checking huge models against this large number of guidelines and fixing all the identified violations are almost impossible and require automation (Legros et al. 2009). For Simulink, MathWorks provides Model Advisor to check a model for adherence to modeling guidelines and rules (The MathWorks Inc. 2015g). From its GUI, depicted in Fig. 9.5, its users can select and run the selected model checks, review the results,

Table 9.1 Simulink signal appearance guideline

ID: title	db_0032: Simulink signal appearance	
Priority	Strongly recommended	
Scope	MAAB	
MATLAB version	All	
Prerequisites		
Description	Signal lines	
	Should not cross each other, if possible	
	Are drawn with right angles	
	Are not drawn one upon the other	
	Do not cross any blocks	
	Should not split into more than two sublines at a single branching point	
	Correct	Incorrect
Rationale	Readability	
Last change	V2.00	

MathWorks Automotive Advisory Board (2015)

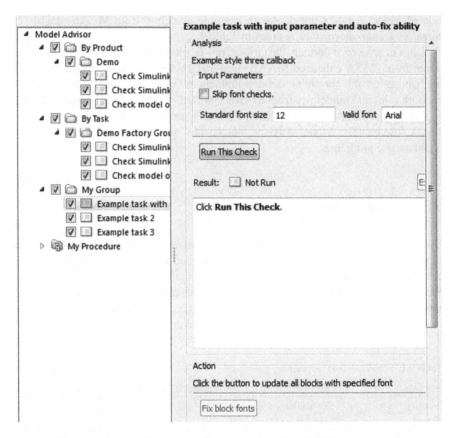

Fig. 9.5 Model Advisor GUI (Reprinted with permission of The MathWorks, Inc)

fix warnings and failures, and view and save the Model Advisor reports. Further, Model Advisor provides a programming interface to create custom checks and fix operations using MATLAB scripting.

There are also active academic research groups on model checking and repair. In 2006, Giese and coworkers proposed to utilize the model transformation capabilities of Fujaba for Simulink model checking and repair. They aimed at repairing the model for complying with generally accepted MATLAB/Simulink modeling guidelines (Giese et al. 2006). They claim that rule-based model checking and repairing methodologies, like the Simulink Model Advisor, are disadvantageous, because they require extensive programming and maintenance effort. Hence, they claim that a more abstract description of guidelines is a better approach. Fujaba is an opensource model-based software engineering tool (Nickel et al. 2000). The graph transformation capabilities of Fujaba are employed for formally specifying graphical rules, the so-called pattern rules for guideline violations, which refer to the MATLAB/Simulink metamodel. On the other hand, the complex and large pattern rules developed using Fujaba turned out to be not readable and maintainable.

Therefore, Giese and coworkers attempted to develop an approach to model guideline violations using concrete MATLAB/Simulink syntax.

Stürmer and his colleagues (Amelunxen et al. 2008; Stürmer et al. 2007; Stürmer and Travkin 2007) proposed a graph-based description of guideline violations in the model and introduced the transformations to repair them in their Model Advisor Transformation Extension (MATE) approach. MATE targets MathWorks Automotive Advisory Board's Control Algorithm Modeling Guidelines using MATLAB, Simulink, and Stateflow (MathWorks Automotive Advisory Board 2015). It provides automatic repair functions, interactive repair functions, design pattern instantiations, and model beautifying operations for conforming modeling guidelines. MATE follows the approach from Giese et al. (2006). The guideline violations are described as graph patterns. Graph transformations are then employed as repair mechanisms. Since these transformations exceed the boundaries of MATLAB during execution (other model transformation tools), the accessibility of the methodology and its adaptability and maintainability by the typical MATLAB user are regarded as challenging.

The following two studies were implicitly targeted at MATLAB users' capability set. In 2013, Tran and coworkers (Tran et al. 2013) proposed a scripting level application programming interface (API) for the basic guideline checking and repairing steps as the building blocks of complex refactoring operations. In 2014, Denil et al. (2014) introduced rule-based model transformations for MATLAB/Simulink models that are specified and executed in Simulink in order to employ model checking and repair.

9.3.3   A Model-Based Approach to Model Checking and Repair in Scilab/Xcos

While there are various approaches to model checking and repair in MATLAB/Simulink, Scilab/Xcos is currently lacking readily available capability. Here in this section, a model-based approach to model checking and repair in Scilab/Xcos will be presented (Durak 2015).

Like the other graphical modeling tools, Scilab/Xcos also possesses a formalized model specification conforming to its implicit metamodel. This Scilab/Xcos metamodel is utilized to conduct in-place M2M transformations for model checking and repair. The Scilab/Xcos metamodel is explicitly presented using its physical representation as the Scilab model structure *scs_m* (Scilab Enterprises 2015). Based on this metamodel, the modelers are provided with Scilab script level API to execute overall model transformation, as well as the atomic model transformation functions for find-, add-, delete-, and replace-type basic operations on the blocks and the links. Thus, while the modelers are equipped with ready-to-use refactoring functions, they are also provided with building blocks for developing their tailored applications. All functions basically manipulate the Scilab model structure *scs_m*, thus enabling a native and seamless model checking and repair.

Model transformations are defined by a precondition pattern, which can be described as the left-hand side (LHS), and the outcome pattern, which can be introduced as the right-hand side (RHS). In-place transformation approach comprises matching the LHS pattern in the model being transformed (model checking) and replacing it with the RHS pattern (repair) in place (Czarnecki and Helsen 2006). Patterns are the definition of guidelines and can be very similar to the model itself. A relaxation is usually applied to the modeling language to define the LHS pattern (Denil et al. 2014). So the search patterns are proposed to be developed using the scs_m structure. As the relaxation, in order to define the constraints, regular expressions are proposed as the values of attributes in LHS pattern structure. Since not all the fields of Xcos metamodel is suitable for constraint definition, Xcos metamodel is simplified for refactoring purposes. Further, in the simplification, all the data types of the parameter values are specified as strings in order to enable the application of regular expressions. The RHS pattern, which is the replace pattern, is to be specified using the same structure with the model. It is regarded as an incomplete model specification that represents a model segment, namely, sub-diagram.

Using Eclipse Modeling Framework (EMF) (Steinberg et al. 2009), the metamodeling hierarchy has been constructed as presented in Fig. 9.6. ECORE is at the meta-metamodeling (M3) level of the metamodeling hierarchy. Two

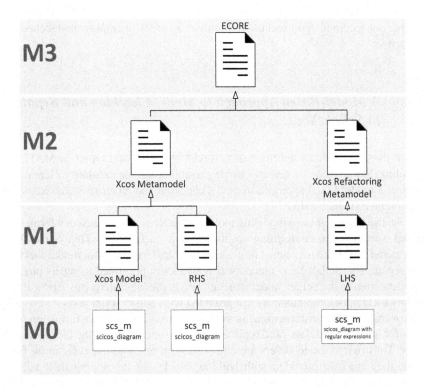

Fig. 9.6 Metamodeling hierarchy

metamodels, Xcos metamodel and Xcos refactoring metamodel, are described using ECORE in metamodel (M2) level. The reader will find the Xcos models and RHS patterns that are specified using Xcos metamodel and the LHS pattern that is defined using Xcos refactoring metamodel in model (M1) level. In the physical level (M0), scs_m data structure that represents scicos_diagram will be used for all Xcos and RHS pattern and relaxed scs_m with regular expressions as attribute values for LHS patterns.

The variables, patterns, and logic are used to specify LHS and RHS (Czarnecki and Helsen 2003). Variables are defined as the elements from the source and target. Patterns are defined as model fragments with zero or more variables. An abstract or a concrete syntax of the source or target modeling language can be employed to define the patterns. Both textual and graphical syntax can be utilized. Logic, on the other hand, holds the constraints on the model elements. It may be either executable or non-executable, and executable ones can be either declarative or imperative.

The variables of the transformation are proposed as the objects of the Xcos diagram with their attributes. Patterns are then introduced as the composition of these elements. The graphical concrete syntax of Xcos is employed to define the patterns as depicted in Fig. 9.7. Any executable logic specification is recommended that employs regular expressions (Watt 2005) as the declarative constraints to retrieve elements from the source model. Then, the LSH scs_m structure can be altered with scripting to assign a constraint on any variable.

Atomic functions of the proposed API include finding, adding, deleting, and replacing a block and, likewise, finding, adding, deleting, and replacing a link. Further, getting the list of connected blocks and the list of connecting links between the blocks are also an atomic function. While these atomic model transformation functions will provide the modeler with the building blocks for developing their own algorithms to manipulate or transform their models, they are also used to construct, basically, the composite model transformation functions `find_subdiagram`, `add_subdiagram`, `delete_subdiagram`, `replace_subdiagram`, and an overall `find_and_replace`. An excerpt from the definition of the API is provided in Table 9.2.

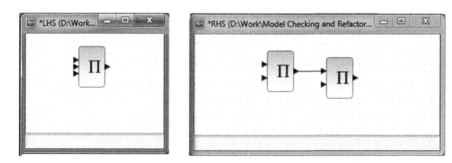

Fig. 9.7 Sample LHS and RHS specifications using Xcos concrete syntax

Table 9.2 An excerpt from the API definition

Function name	Input arguments	Output arguments
find_block	scs_m structure for the diagram	List of indexes for matching blocks
	Block structure to be searched	
	List of constraining attributes	
	List of constraints	
add_block	scs_m structure for the diagram	scs_m structure for the updated diagram
	Block structure to be added	
find_subdiagram	scs_m structure for the diagram	List of indexes for matching blocks
	scs_m structure to be searched	List of indexes for matching links
	List of indexes for the constraining objects	
	List of constraining attributes	
	List of constraints	
find_and_replace	scs_m structure for the diagram	scs_m structure for the updated diagram
	scs_m structure to be searched (LHS)	
	List of indexes for the constraining objects (logic)	
	List of constraining attributes (logic)	
	List of constraints (logic)	
	New scs_m structure (RHS)	

Durak (2015)

A simple example of guideline checking and repair task includes identifying all the Scope blocks and replacing them with To Workspace blocks (Fig. 9.8). The proposed set of functions enables the user to conduct this refactoring task in more than one way. While it can be conducted only just using the find_and_replace composite model transformation function, it is also possible for the modeler to write a script using the atomic model transformation function. A sample implementation is presented in the below listing.

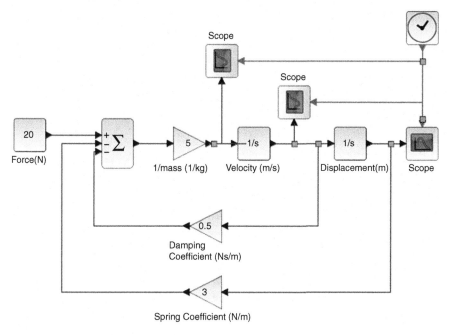

Fig. 9.8 Sample model with scopes

```
//import the diagram to be refactored
importXcosDiagram('springmassdamper.xcos')
//no particular selection constraints
attribute_list=[]
constraint_list=[]
//get a scope block
scope_block=CSCOPE("define")
//get the list of scope blocks
scope_list=find_block(scs_m,scope_block,attribute_list,constraint_
list)
//get a to workspace block
tows_block = TOWS_c("define")
//replace the scopeblocks with
for i = 1: size ("scope_list")
  replace_block(scs_m,scope_list(i),tows_block)
end
```

Here find_block is used to check the model against having a scope block,
then replace_block is used to repair the model by replacing the scope blocks
with To Workspace blocks. In this example, the repaired model is represented in
Fig. 9.9.

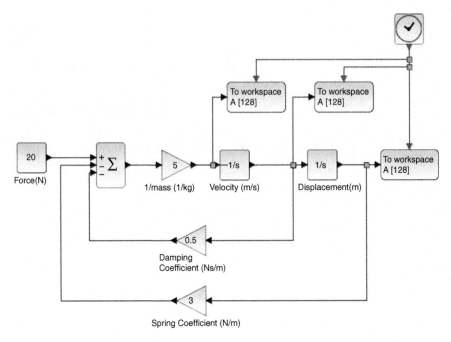

Fig. 9.9 Repaired sample model

9.4   Code Generation and Integration

The main aim of MDE is to get a running system out of the model at the end of the day (Brambilla et al. 2012). So code generation is the most important application of M2T transformations. While code generator can be implemented as a program in a general-purpose programming language that parses the model using its metamodel and prints out the corresponding code statements to a file, a more effective approach of MDE is using M2T transformation languages.

Static and dynamic code is separated in M2T approach. Static text elements are stored in templates, whereas the dynamic content is located in the text as meta-markers which are then interpreted during the code generation as the data queries from the model. To discuss how M2T is employed for MDE of simulation, Simulink Coder and SimGe code generator will be introduced in the next sections as sample generators.

9.4.1   Code Generation in MATLAB/Simulink

MathWorks provides Simulink Coder (previously Real-Time Workshop) product to generate C and C++ code from the Simulink diagrams (The MathWorks Inc. 2015a). Then the generated source code can be employed in both real-time and non-real-time applications. It supports single-rate, multi-rate, and asynchronous models with single task and multitask execution.

As introduced in the Simulink Coder User's Manual (The MathWorks Inc. 2015c), the code generation starts with a compilation process which ends up with an intermediate representation of the model that is stored in an ASCII file *model.rtw*. Then the code generator uses the Target Language Compiler (TLC) and the supporting TLC function library to transform the intermediate model in *model.rtw* into code.

TLC script can be viewed as an interpreted programming language that converts a model description into code (The MathWorks Inc. 2015b). The TLC scripts that specify how to generate code from the model are executed by the TLC. This can be categorized as a template-based M2T approach. The scripting is used for meta-markers and it works as M2T transformation language, and TLC as the code generator, interprets the script to query the dynamic content from *model.rtw*.

The top-level record of a *model.rtw* is *CompiledModel*. It constitutes various subdata elements for the properties and the content of a model. Consider the following sample *model.rtw* extract:

```
CompiledModel {
  Name "SampleModel"
  ...
  GeneratedOn "Sun Jul 05 16:42:05 2015"
  ...
  Solver FixedStepDiscrete
  SolverType FixedStep
  ...
}
```

The TLC script consists of a series of statements of either in the form `text` or `%<expression>`. While the statements of the first type cause the text to be passed to the output stream unmodified, the expressions enclosed in %< > are evaluated before being written to output. There are various directives to be interpreted. Some of the examples would be `%assign`, `%copyrecord`, or `%include`. For the extensive list of directives and details of TLC, the reader may refer to Simulink® Coder™ Target Language Compiler document (The MathWorks Inc. 2015b). Below is a sample TCL script that will be applied on the above *model.rtw* excerpt.

```
%with CompiledModel
  My model is called %<Name>.
  It was generated on %<GeneratedOn>.
  It has %<SolverType> type solver %<Solver>.
%endwith
```

The output of sample TLC script will be as follows:

```
My model is called SampleModel.
It was generated on Sun Jul 05 16:42:05 2015".
It has FixedStep type solver FixedStepDiscrete.
```

9.4.2 Code Generation in SimGe

Another template-based code generation approach is to use Microsoft T4 text templates. T4 text template "is a mixture of text blocks and control logic that can generate a text file" (Microsoft 2015). The control logic is written in C#, and the text generated can be a C# source code file (.cs).

SimGe (SimGe 2015) uses this approach for a fast federation prototyping. The target platform of SimGe code generation is the layered federation architectures that use the RACoN as the communication layer. The generated code files are intended for a fast start-up to the layered federate development. In order to employ the generated code files, a RACoN project must be created, and the generated code files must be added to the project in Visual Studio Integrated Development Environment (IDE). SimGe code generator uses the federation architecture model (FAM) and simulation object models as source. Before generating code, the user must construct an object model and a FAM that includes the federate applications. Code is generated for each federate application separately. So, it is important to specify the simulation object models for each federate.

SimGe code viewer showing sample generated code and the code explorer is depicted in Fig. 9.10a, b, respectively.

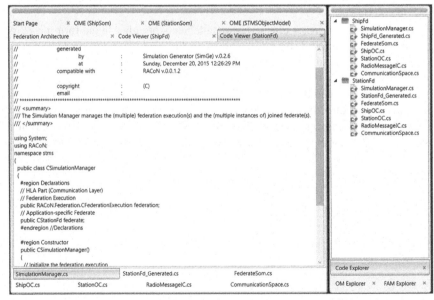

(a) SimGe code viewer – a generated C# code is depicted.   (b) The code explorer

Fig. 9.10 SimGe code viewer, generated code sample, and the code explorer

The modeler can change the code generator behavior such as code indenting size using the setting parameters provided.

The structure of the generated code conforms to the layered architecture introduced in Chap. 7. Referring to that chapter, we may recap the layers as the communication, simulation, and presentation layer. As the presentation layer heavily depends on the project, the SimGe code generator only generates code partially for the simulation layer and the communication layer. The class structure of the generated code for a simple chat federation (ChatFd) is presented in Fig. 9.11.

Each generated class is placed in a separate C# file. The generated classes are grouped as follows:

- Simulation Layer

  - Simulation manager class (i.e., CSimulationManager)
  - Application-specific federate class (e.g., CChatFd)
  - Federation execution class (i.e., CFederationExecution)

- Federate Object Model

  - Federate SOM class (i.e., FederateSOM)
  - Interaction classes for each interaction defined in FOM. For instance, CChatIC class
  - Object classes for each object defined in FOM. For instance, CUserOC class

The application-specific federate class includes the skeleton code for federate ambassador callback event handlers. Typically, the user will manually edit this class. Therefore, in order not to lose the changes when it is generated again, it is in form of a partial class, an approach provided in MS.NET languages, where it can be dispersed to multiple files. Here, two files are generated for the application-specific federate class. The first one contains the automatically generated code, and the other one is used by the user for manual coding.

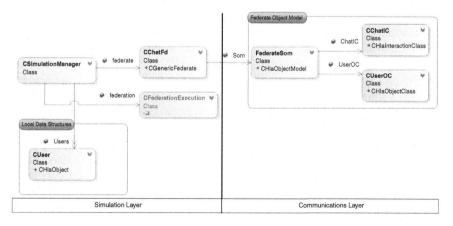

Fig. 9.11 Class diagram for sample chat federation

9.4.3 Model Integration

The code generation facility provided by the modeling environments usually gener-ates code for a predefined set of target platforms. These targets can be specific operating systems, compilers, hardware components like I/O devices, and their driv-ers. Simulink Coder product is also bundled with various targets that are suitable for many different applications and development environments. But in many occasions, the particular target that is required is not supported. Either the target can be so special for the domain, like there is no predefined HLA target, which is particularly applied in distributed simulation, specifically in military simulation domain, or it can be application specific, like an in-house developed real-time simulation framework.

There are some efforts for the standardization of model interfaces in order to enable easy model exchange and integration. Functional Mock-up Interface (FMI) and Simulation Model Portability 2 (SMP2) are two recent efforts that deserve a short introduction.

FMI is an interface to be implemented by an executable called Functional Mock-up Unit (FMU) in order to support both model exchange and co-simulation of dynamic models using a combination of xml-files and compiled C-code (Modelica Association 2014). Co-simulation can be effective when FMUs have their own solv-ers, and model exchange is applicable when FMU requires the simulation environ-ment to perform numerical integration. FMU is composed of FMU description file, C sources including required libraries, and additional FMU data. FMU description file captures the FMU variables and their attributes such as name or unit.

A large set of modeling and simulation tools and environments are supporting FMI either natively or by a third party. FMI Toolbox can be introduced as an exam-ple of third-party product that enables export and import of FMUs from and to MATLAB/Simulink (Modelon AB 2015). There are further efforts for using FMI for integrating HLA federates (Yilmaz et al. 2014).

SMP2 is developed by European Space Agency (ESA) as an open standard for enabling portability and reuse of simulation models (ESA 2005c). SMP2.0 metamodel (ESA 2005d) introduces the Simulation Model Definition Language (SMDL), which describes platform-independent mechanisms to design models, integrate model instances, and schedule them. SMP 2.0 Component Model (ESA 2005b) presents a platform-independent definition of the components employed for an SMP2 simulation. These components include models, services, and the simula-tor. And lastly SMP 2.0 C++ Mapping (ESA 2005a) expresses a mapping of the platform-independent models to the ANSI/ISO C++ target platform.

Besides the readily available target platforms in the M&S tools and environ-ments and standardization of model interfaces, it is also possible to extend M&S tools and environments by defining new target platforms. As an example, DLR Institute of Flight Systems extended generic real-time target (GRT) from Simulink Coder to generate code for their in-house real-time distributed simulation frame-work, 2Simulate (Gerlach et al. 2014).

2Simulate is a C++ real-time distributed simulation framework that facilitates integrating a wide range of models and simulation components like external devices, data recorders, or image generators for particularly developing flight simulators (Gotschlich et al. 2014). It is composed of three components, namely, 2Simulate Real-Time Framework (2SimRT), 2Simulate Model Control (2SimMC), and 2Simulate Control Center (2SimCC).

2SimCC is the graphical user interface that can run, pause, and stop 2SimRT applications and manage their data. 2SimRT is the core simulation framework of 2Simulate that provides deterministic scheduling and controlling of real-time tasks. TSimModel is one of these real-time tasks used for integrating Simulink models. 2SimMC is the enabler of model integration. It is composed of 2Simulate Model Control Source (2SimMC-Source) that abstracts model interfaces for 2SimRT and 2Simulate Model Control Scripts (2SimMC-Scripts) that include Simulink Coder Target Language Compiler files (TLC files) to specify the 2Simulate target and m-files to conduct the code generation and build process.

A target specification called *grt_2Simulate* is implemented by 2SimMC-Scripts TLC files. These files extend GRT provided by Simulink Coder. The top-level entry point is *grt_2Simulate.grt*. It first calls *codegenentry.tlc* to generate model code and then calls all eight 2Simulate TLC files to generate 2SimMC-Component code (Fig. 9.12).

Figure 9.13 shows 2SimMC-Component classes. 2SimMC-Component code includes sources for a 2SimRT task, model, data dictionary, and model definitions and specifications for input and output signals. Task and model TLC files extend the 2SimRT API and glue it with generated model code. The <Name>TSimSimulinkModel class inherits from TSimMcModelCtrl from

Fig. 9.12 2Simulate TLC Scripts

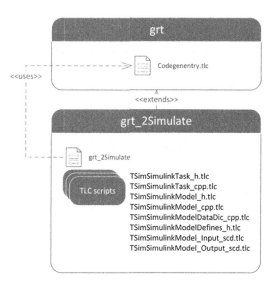

Fig. 9.13 2SimMC-
Component classes

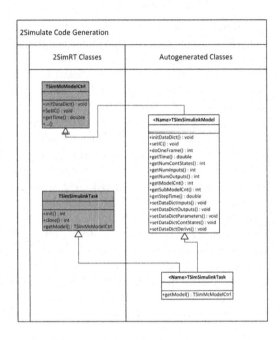

2SimRT API and includes <name>.h which enables it to access Simulink model
code. Finally, <Name>TSimSimulinkTask class inherits from both model
classes and TSimSimulinkTask from 2SimRT API, so that one can use this
class to create a schedulable 2SimRT task for the Simulink model.

9.5   Testing

After introducing modeling, code generation, and integration approaches of MDE-
based simulation implementation practices, as the last step, model-based testing
will be presented with a particular adaptation for MATLAB/Simulink.

Testing a model has been defined as simulating it under various conditions and
comparing it with the system it represents (Hollmann, et al. 2012). Considering the
infinite number of scenarios that can be simulated to test a model against the system
it represents, testing in modeling and simulation is traditionally a tedious and labor-
intensive task. Thus, automation can be introduced as the key practice for the success of testing in modeling and simulation.

While automating test case execution can be regarded as the one step, the application of model-based practices in testing enabled the automation of test case generation as well (Utting and Legeard 2007). MBT was introduced as a methodology
for automating test case generation from a test model that specifies the test cases,
instead of implementing test cases manually (Zander et al. 2012). It is widely used
in the software testing community, and there are some recent efforts on its applica-

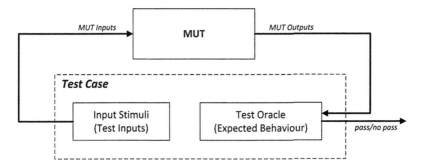

Fig. 9.14 Test case with model under test

tion in modeling and simulation (Hollmann et al. 2012; Schmidt et al. 2015; Durak et al. 2015).

A test case is composed of a system under test or model under test (MUT) for modeling and simulation, an input stimuli, and a test oracle (Fig. 9.14). Input stimuli generates test inputs to be fed to the model, and the test oracle compares model outputs against the expected behavior and makes a pass or no pass decision.

Aligned with the rest of the chapter, MATLAB/Simulink will be picked as the example environment to present MBT approaches in modeling and simulation. It was 2004, when MathWorks released the first version of Simulink of Verification and Validation (The MathWorks Inc. 2006). Starting from the very first versions, the model verification blocks were introduced. They were providing the user to monitor model signals and define assertions against leaving a specified limit or range. Recent versions of the tool further provide an integrated workflow for open- and closed-loop testing from model to generated code and deployed system via Model-in-the-Loop (MIL), Software-in-the-Loop (SIL), and Hardware-in-the-Loop (HIL) approaches (Fig. 9.15) (The MathWorks Inc. 2015a, b, c, d, e, f, g). Further, MathWorks supports automated test case generation to some extent using heuristic and formal methods with the capabilities distributed in a handful of products and conducts active research on it (Lee and Friedman 2013).

On the other hand, in 2006, Zander et al. proposed model-driven architecture-based MBT approach for MATLAB/Simulink (Zander-Nowicka et al. 2006) in which they specify two metamodels: Simulink metamodel for system modeling and Simulink test metamodel for test modeling. Then they propose model transformations for automated test model generation. Zander later presented Model-in-the-Loop for Embedded System Test (MiLEST) infrastructure that provides structured tools and mechanisms for test data generation, test control, and test validation employing model-based principles (Zander-Nowicka 2008).

Both tools and techniques offered by MATLAB and MiLEST can be used for testing simulation models, but their basic motivation is to provide a methodology to test the controller models that are basically employed to generate code to be deployed in an embedded system. Recently Schmidt, Durak, and Pawletta proposed an MBT infrastructure for Simulink that is based on the system theoretical

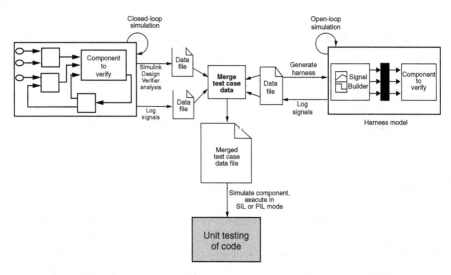

Fig. 9.15 Simulink model testing workflow (The MathWorks Inc. 2015a, b, c, d, e, f, g) (Reprinted with permission of The MathWorks, Inc.)

approaches adopted in the simulation theory (Schmidt et al. 2015; Durak et al. 2015; Durak et al. 2014). They proposed using the experimental frame as the basic formalism to specify and run tests for simulation models. The concept of experimental frame (EF) was introduced by Zeigler (Zeigler 1984). It specifies a limited set of circumstances under which a model has to be observed. The formal specification of EF is given by the 7-tuple:

$$EF = \langle T, I, O, C, \Omega i, \Omega c, SU \rangle$$

where:

T is the time base.
I is the set of input variables.
O is the set of output variables.
C is the set of control variables.
Ωi is the set of admissible input segments
Ωc is the set of admissible control segments.
SU is a set of summary mappings.

EF has been recommended as a coupled model, consisting of a generator, an acceptor, and a transducer, which are connected to the model. In our context, the model is the model under test (MUT).

As a test case is formalized by an EF, the structure is proposed as in Fig. 9.16. Test inputs are produced by the generator. They have to be admissible input segments of MUT and influence its behavior. The acceptor and the transducer form a test oracle. Based on the output variables, the transducer calculates outcome measures in the form of performance indices, comparative values, statistics, etc. The

Fig. 9.16 Experimental
frame as a test case

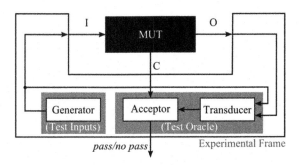

acceptor corresponds to a decision unit that decides if an experiment is valid or not. The acceptor monitors its inputs and maps them to a specified admissible control segment. If the admissible control segment is violated, the experiment is not accepted.

The system entity structure and model base (SES/MB) framework (Zeigler et al. 2000) is proposed for test modeling and automatic generation of executable test cases. The SES is a high-level ontology, which was introduced for the specification of a set of system structures and parameter settings for modeling and simulation. It is composed of four node types: (1) entity, (2) aspect, (3) specialization, and (4) multiple aspect (Zeigler and Hammonds 2007). Entity represents real or artificial system components. The other node types describe the relationships between their parent and child entities. Aspect nodes denote the decomposition relationship of an entity, and specialization nodes represent the taxonomy of an entity. The multiple aspect nodes, finally, represent a multiplicity relationship which specifies that the parent entity is a composition of multiple entities of the same type. Specific suffixes are employed for a clear separation of the node types.

The SES is a directed and labeled tree with links to base models (BMs) in the model base (MB). A distinct system structure can be derived from an SES using a *pruning* operation. The result is called pruned entity structure (PES). Then, a *translation* operation is employed to generate an executable simulation model (ESM) based on the information of the PES and BMs from the MB.

The testing infrastructure is built upon the SES Toolbox for MATLAB/Simulink which has been developed by the Computational Engineering and Automation research group of the Wismar University of Applied Sciences (Pawletta et al. 2014). It comprises a graphical editor for designing system entity structures and pruning and translation methods. The pruning method is based on a modified depth-first search algorithm for directed graphs. The translation method is implemented using the Simulink API.

A sample SES that specifies eight different test scenarios is given in Fig. 9.17. All aspect nodes have the suffix *Dec*, specialization nodes have the suffix *Spec*, and the multiple aspect nodes have the suffix *MAsp*. Nodes without the pre-defined suffixes correspond to entity nodes. The test scenario is described as a coupled system containing an MUT and an EF using the node `TestScenarioDec`. An EF is decomposed into a generator (*G*), an acceptor (*A*), and a transducer (*T*) using the

Fig. 9.17 SES specifying
various test cases (Schmidt
et al. 2015)

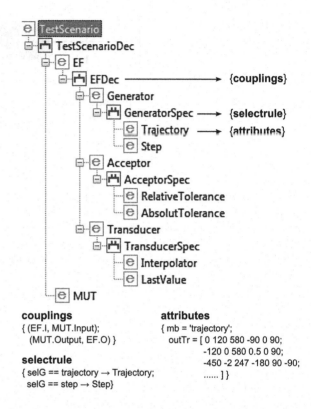

node EFDec. The nodes GSpec, ASpec, and TSpec are used to specialize entity nodes *G*, *A*, and *T* to their successor nodes. *G* is specialized in an entity Step or a RandomNumber (RN), *A* in InRelativeTolerance (IRT) or LessThenThreshold (LTT), and *T* in MeanComputing (MC) or LastValue (LV).

Attributes attached to aspect nodes, such as TestScenarioDec and EFDec, define the coupling relationship between their direct predecessors and successors as attributes. For example, the tuple *(MUT.out, EF.in)* specifies that the output of the MUT is connected with the input of the EF. In specialization nodes, a set of selection rules, labeled with *{selectrule}* and hinted with *{...}*, are described as attributes which are then used for the pruning operation. The attributes that reference to BMs in the MB and the parameter setting of BMs are described in leaf nodes. For example, the leaf node *Step* has three attributes, *mb*, *step value* (*sv*), and *step time* (*st*). The attribute *mb* indicates a link to a BM, a Simulink block in a corresponding MB, and a Simulink library.

As the user defines a specific test case with specifying a set of selection variables, using the selection rules, a pruning operation can be carried out. The result is then a tree, namely, PES, which specifies a single test case with the links to the Simulink

Fig. 9.18 Automatically
generated MATLAB/
Simulink model (Schmidt
et al. 2015)

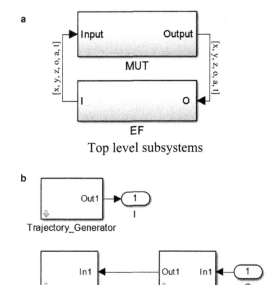

Top level subsystems

Components of subsystem EF

blocks in the Simulink library that contains all the leaf blocks in SES. A translation script is then employed to automatically construct a new executable test model in Simulink (Fig. 9.18) using the blocks (BMs) from the library (MB) following the description in tree (PES).

9.6 Summary

The activities of implementation in MDE of distributed simulation systems are introduced in this chapter. The current practices of model development, model checking, code generation and integration, and testing are presented by providing examples from off-the-shelf modeling and simulation environments such as MATLAB/Simulink or Scilab/Xcos. While the activities presented are being practiced by the industry, it is hard to contend that the methodologies and techniques employed in these activities are mature enough. There is a vast amount of active research about MDE. Following software intensive systems, the modeling and simulation community is actively developing new MDE methodologies and techniques for various simulation engineering activities including implementation. Recent research has been presented for each activity in this chapter in order to provide the reader with an insight about the research directions as well as the industrial applications.

References

Amelunxen, C., Legros, E., Schürr, A., & Stürmer, I. (2008). Checking and enforcement of modeling guidelines with graph transformations. In *Applications of graph transformations with industrial relevance* (pp. 313–328). Berlin: Springer.

Astrom, K., & Wittenmark, B. (1984). *Computer controlled systems: Theory and design.* Englewood Cliffs: Prentice Hall.

Brambilla, M., Cabot, J., & Wimmer, M. (2012). *Model-driven software engineering in practice.* San Rafael: Morgan & Claypool Publishers.

Campbell, S., Chancelier, J., & Nikaukhah, R. (2006). *Modeling and simulation in scilab/scicos.* New York: Springer.

Czarnecki, K., & Helsen, S. (2003). Classification of model transformation approaches. In *Proceedings of OOPSLA'03 workshop on generative techniques in context of model driven architecture.* Anaheim: ACM.

Czarnecki, K., & Helsen, S. (2006). Feature-based survey of model transformation approaches. *IBM Systems Journal, 45*(3), 621–645.

Denckla, B., & Mosterman, P. (2005). Formalizing causal block diagrams for modeling a class of hybrid dynamic systems. In *Proceedings of 44th IEEE conference on decision and control and the European control conference.* Seville: IEEE.

Denil, J., Mosterman, P., & Vangheluwe, H. (2014). *Rule-based model transformations for and in Simulink.* Proceedings of the Symposium on Theory of Modeling and Simulation-DEVS Integrative (pp. 314–421). San Diago: SCS.

Durak, U. (2015). Pragmatic model transformations for refactoring in Scilab/Xcos. *International Journal of Modeling, Simulation, and Scientific Computing.* doi:10.1142/S1793962315410044

Durak, U., Schmidt, A., & Pawletta, T. (2014). Ontology for objective flight simulator fidelity evaluation. *Simulation Notes Europe, 24*(2), 69–78.

Durak, U., Schmidt, A., & Pawletta, T. (2015). Model-based testing for objective fidelity evaluation of engineering and research flight simulators. In *AIAA modeling and simulation technologies conference.* Dallas: AIAA.

ESA. (2005a). *SMP 2.0 C++ mapping.* Paris: European Space Agency.

ESA. (2005b). *SMP 2.0 component model.* Paris: European Space Agency.

ESA. (2005c). *SMP 2.0 handbook.* Paris: European Space Agency.

ESA. (2005d). *SMP 2.0 metamodel.* Paris: European Space Agency.

Farkas, T., Hein, C., & Ritter, T. (2006). Automatic evaluation of modelling rules and design guidelines. In *Proceedings of the 2. workshop "From code centric to model centric software engineering: practices, implications and ROI".* Bilboa: ESI.

Frankel, D. (2003). *Model driven architecture: Applying MDA to enterprise computing.* New York: Wiley.

Gerlach, T., Durak, U., & Gotschlich, J. (2014). Model integration workflow for keeping models up to date in a research simulator. In *Proceedings of 2014 International Conference on Simulation and Modeling Methodologies, Technologies and Applications (SIMULTECH)* (pp. 125–132). Vienna: SCITEPRESS.

Giese, H., Meyer, M., & Wagner, R. (2006). A prototype guideline checking and model transformations in MATLAB/Simulink. In *Proceedings of the 4th international Fujaba Days* (pp. 56–60). Bayreuth: University of Bayreuth.

Gotschlich, J., Gerlach, T., & Durak, U. (2014). *2Simulate: A distributed real-time simulation framework.* Workshop der ASIM/GI-Fachgruppen STS und GMMS. Reutlingen: ARGESIM.

Henry, J. (2011). *Orion GN&C MATLAB/Simulink standards.* Houston: NASA.

Hollmann, D., Cristia, M., & Frydman, C. (2012). Adapting model-based testing techniques to DEVS models validation. In *Proceedings of the 2012 symposium of theory of modeling and simulation – DEVS integrative.* San Diego: SCS.

IEEE. (2008). *Systems and software engineering – Software life cycle processes.* IEEE SA - 12207-2008. New York: IEEE.

IEEE. (2010). *IEEE recommended practice for Distributed Simulation Engineering and Execution Process (DSEEP)*. IEEE Std 1730-2010. New York: IEEE.

Klee, H., & Allen, R. (2011). *Simulation of dynamic systems with MATLAB and Simulink*. Boca Raton: CRC Press.

Kleppe, A., Warmer, J., & Bast, W. (2003). *MDA explained: The model driven architecture: Practice and promise* (1st ed.). Boston: Addison-Wesley Professional.

Lee, C., & Friedman, J. (2013). Requirements modeling and automated requirements-based test generation. *SAE International Journal of Aerospace, 6*(2), 607–615.

Legros, E., Amelunxen, C., Klar, F., & Schürr, A. (2009). Generic and reflective graph transformations for checking and enforcement of modeling guidelines. *Journal of Visual Languages & Computing, 20*(4), 252–268.

MathWorks Automotive Advisory Board. (2015). *MathWorks® automotive advisory board control algorithm modeling guidelines using MATLAB®, Simulink®, and Stateflow®*. Natick: The MathWorks, Inc.

Mellor, S., & Balcer, M. (2002). *Executable UML: A foundation for model-driven architecture* (1st edn.). Boston: Addison-Wesley Professional.

Microsoft. (2015). *Code generation and T4 text templates* [Online]. Available at: https://msdn.microsoft.com/en-us/library/bb126445.aspx. Accessed 9 July 2015.

Modelica Association. (2014). *Functional mock-up interface for model exchange and co-simulation*. Linköping: Modelica Association.

Modelon, A. B. (2015). *FMI toolbox user's guide*. Lund: Modelon AB.

Nickel, U., Niere, J., & Zündorf, A. (2000). Tool demonstration: The Fujaba environment. In *Proceedings of the 22nd International Conference on Software Engineering (ICSE)* (pp. 742–745). Limerick: ACM Press.

Pastor, O., & Molina, J. (2007). *Model-driven architecture in practice: A software production environment based on conceptual modeling*. Secaucus: Springer.

Pawletta, T., Pascheka, D., Schmidt, A., & Pawletta, S. (2014). Ontology-assisted system modeling and simulation within MATLAB/Simulink. *Simulation Notes Europe, 24*(2), 59–68.

Schmidt, A., Durak, U., Rasch, C., & Pawletta, T. (2015). Model-based testing approach for MATLAB/Simulink using system entity structure and experimental frames. In *Proceedings of symposium on theory of modeling and simulation '15*. Alexandria: SCS.

Scilab Enterprises. (2015). *Scilab online help* [Online]. Available at: https://help.scilab.org/. Accessed 1 July 2015.

SimGe. (2015). *SimGe web site* [Online]. Available at: https://sites.google.com/site/okantopcu/simge. Accessed 15 Aug 2015.

Steinberg, D., Budinsky, F., Paternostro, M., & Merks, E. (2009). *EMF: Eclipse modeling framework* (2nd ed.). Boston: Pearson Education, Inc.

Stürmer, I., & Travkin, D. (2007). Automated transformation of MATLAB Simulink and Stateflow Models. In *Proceedings of 4th workshop on object-oriented modeling of real-time embedded systems* (pp. 57–62). Padeborn: University of Paderborn.

Stürmer, I., Kreuz, I., Schäfer, W., & Schürr, A. (2007). The MATE approach: Enhanced Simulink and stateflow model transformations. In *Proceedings of mathworks automative conference*. Dearborn: Mathworks, Inc.

The MathWorks, Inc. (2006). *Simulink® verification and validation release notes, V1.1.2 (R2006a)*. Natick: The MathWorks, Inc.

The MathWorks, Inc. (2015a). *Simulink® Coder™ getting started guide*. Natick: The MathWorks, Inc.

The MathWorks, Inc. (2015b). *Simulink® Coder™ target language compiler*. Natick: The MathWorks, Inc.

The MathWorks, Inc. (2015c). *Simulink® Coder™ user's guide*. Natick: The MathWorks, Inc.

The MathWorks, Inc. (2015d). *Simulink® getting started guide*. Natick: The MathWorks, Inc.

The MathWorks, Inc. (2015e). *Simulink® reference*. Natick: The MathWorks, Inc.

The MathWorks, Inc. (2015f). *Simulink® user guide*. Natick: The MathWorks, Inc.

The MathWorks, Inc. (2015g). *Simulink® Verification and Validation™ user's guide*. Natick: The MathWorks, Inc.

Tran, Q., Wilmes, B., & Dziobek, C. (2013). Refactoring of Simulink diagrams via composition of transformation steps. In *Proceedings of 8th international conference on software engineering advances* (pp. 140–145). Venice: IARIA XPS Press.

Utting, M., & Legeard, M. (2007). *Practical model-based testing* (1st ed.). San Francisco: Morgen Kaufmann Publishers, Inc.

Watt, A. (2005). *Beginning regular expressions*. Indianapolis: Wiley.

Yilmaz, F., Durak, U., Taylan, K., & Oguztuzun, H. (2014). Adapting functional mockup units for HLA-compliant distributed simulation. In *Proceedings of the 10th International Modelica Conference*. Lund: Linköping University Press.

Zander, J., Schieferdecker, I., & Mostermann, P. (2012). *Model-based testing for embedded systems*. Boca Raton: CRC Press Taylor & Francis Group.

Zander-Nowicka, J. (2008). *Model-based testing of real-time embedded systems in the automotive domain*. Berlin: Technical University Berlin.

Zander-Nowicka, J., Schieferdecker, I., & Farkas, T. (2006). Derivation of executable test models from embedded system models using model driven architecture artefacts – automotive domain. In *Tagungsband Dagstuhl-Workshop MBEES:Modellbasierte Entwicklung eingebetteter Systeme II* (pp. 131–140). Braunschweig: Technische Universität Braunschweig.

Zeigler, B. (1984). *Multifaceted modelling and discrete event simulation*. San Diego: Academic Press Professional, Inc.

Zeigler, B., & Hammonds, P. (2007). *Modeling and simulation-based data engineering: introducing pragmatics in ontologies for net-centric information exchange*. Amsterdam: Academic Press.

Zeigler, B., Praehofer, H., & Kim, T. (2000). *Theory of modeling and simulation: Integrating discrete event and continuous complex systems*. Orlando: Academic.

Chapter 10
Simulation Evolution and Modernization

The evolution of simulations and models during their operational use is inevitable. Constant change in technology and user requirements is the core reason. It comes up with aging and erosion of the software systems. Thus, in time, assets are started to be categorized as legacy. Software modernization has been introduced as the methodology for comprehending and transforming legacy software systems. Basically inspired by MDE, model-driven reverse engineering (MDRE) is proposed as the major approach to tackle knowledge extraction from available assets. Then canonical model transformations and forward engineering MDE practices are promoted for transforming legacy software. The Object Management Group (OMG) promoted architecture-driven modernization (ADM) as the process of understanding and transformation of existing software assets with model-driven principles that have been supported by various metamodels, tools, and languages. This chapter introduces simulation evolution and modernization. It presents and adopts the software modernization approaches, particularly ADM, for simulation modernization. After providing a background on tools, methods, and approaches that have been proposed for software modernization, a recent research effort is revealed that adopts and extends ADM, particularly the knowledge discovery metamodel (KDM), for simulation modernization.

10.1 Introduction

Simulations, as all other software-intensive systems, are subject to evolution. Remembering the early work of Lehman from the 1980s, software systems which are actively used and embedded in a real-world domain are subject to an inevitable change and evolution (Lehman 1980a, b).

Evolution comes with constant maintenance. IEEE Std. 14764-2006 (Software Engineering-Software Life Cycle Process-Maintenance) defines maintenance as an

© Springer International Publishing Switzerland 2016
O. Topçu et al., *Distributed Simulation*, Simulation Foundations,
Methods and Applications, DOI 10.1007/978-3-319-03050-0_10

effort to ensure that the software product continues to satisfy its end users' requirements (IEEE 2006). Various types of maintenance including preventive, adaptive, and perfective maintenance have been introduced by the standard. Preventive maintenance is introduced as modifications to prevent potential errors. Adaptive maintenance is modifying the software to accommodate the changing environment. And finally perfective maintenance targets at increasing performance and maintainability.

Software systems encounter software aging and erosion. The measures of aging and erosion have been claimed as sourceless executables, dead data, dead code, inconsistencies, and missing capacities (Visaggio 2001). Parnas argues that there are two basic causes for aging and erosion: the first one is *lack of movement* which is explained as not making the required changes, and the second one is *ignorant surgery* which is to make changes haphazardly (Parnas 1994).

Due to inevitable changes in technology, user expectations, environments in which they execute, and systems they simulate, simulations also age. Additionally, they age due to successive changes with limited understanding of original or previous design concepts and decisions. Both result in simulations becoming less maintainable (Lehman et al. 1998).

Paradauskas et al. describe legacy systems with the following characteristics: (i) they are mostly deployed on obsolete hardware that are slow and hard to maintain, (ii) they are difficult and expensive to maintain since there is a lack of comprehensive understanding of these systems, (iii) they require an extensive effort to be integrated to other systems since the interfaces and borders are not clearly defined or maintained, and (iv) they are almost impossible to expand (Paradauskas and Laurikaitis 2006).

Legacy simulation is characterized with the words "often originating from the seventies" and "domain-specific, not reusable, complex monoliths" by Trcka Radosevic et al. in 2006 (Trcka Radosevic et al. 2006). In 2011, Sonntag and colleagues described legacy simulations as "developed without adhering to known software engineering guidelines, lack of acceptable software ergonomics, run sequentially on single workstation and require tremendous manual task" (Sonntag et al. 2011).

The tendency of the modeling and simulation community for legacy simulations has been reusing them by developing a wrapper that provides interfaces to modern systems. Trcka Radosevic et al. propose a methodology for run-time information exchange between legacy simulations (Trcka Radosevic et al. 2006). Likewise, White and Pullen recommend wrapping legacy simulations using the Java Native Interface and making them available over Web services (Pullen and White 2003). Perry et al. proposed DIS/HLA gateways for legacy training simulators (Perry et al. 1998).

Meanwhile, the software engineering community introduced reengineering for software systems to tackle aging and erosion. Chikofsky and Cross defined reengineering as the examination and alteration of the existing system with respect to new requirements that could not be met (Chikofsky and Cross 1990). The reengineering of software systems was promoted as a methodology that does not discard the system as whole but preserves the embedded knowledge embedded in the legacy system by proposing an evolutionary maintenance of the legacy systems for reducing the risk and the cost (Sneed 2005).

The efforts to define a standard reengineering process for software systems have led to architecture-driven modernization (ADM), which was introduced by the Object Management Group (OMG) as a standard approach for the modernization of existing systems (OMG 2003a). ADM has a broad focus on all aspects of the current system and a promise of transformation to target architectures. It advocates a model-based approach to software modernization.

This chapter will present a simulation modernization perspective adapting the practices and standards from software modernization. The next section will provide a gentle introduction to ADM. A section will then present tools and languages that support ADM. Finally a particular enhancement to ADM will be presented that targets simulation modernization.

10.2 Architecture-Driven Modernization

10.2.1 Overview

ADM was offered as "the process of understanding and evolving existing software assets" by the OMG ADM Task Force. They set the most important point of the ADM as a standard metamodel that will be used to represent existing software assets (OMG 2003b).

In the late 1990s, the Software Engineering Institute introduced the horseshoe model. Software reengineering is defined in this model by three processes: reverse engineering, restructuring, and forward engineering. Reverse engineering is the analysis of an existing system and it is conceptualized as the left leg of the horseshoe that goes up. Restructuring is the transformation that goes across the top of the horseshoe, and forward engineering is the development of the new asset. It goes down the right leg of the horseshoe (Bergey et al. 1999). The OMG ADM Task Force adapted the horseshoe metaphor by introducing level of abstraction that is reached during modernization. They defined three levels of modernization which are, namely, technical modernization, application/data modernization, and business modernization (Khusidman 2008). Technical modernization is introduced as the most common modernization effort that targets mostly language or platform change. Application/data modernization is described as the one that targets a change in systems design. And lastly business modernization is expressed as an effort that addresses the business rules and processes that are governed by the software. The OMG ADM Task Force claimed that any software modernization effort, no matter in which abstraction level it is, will follow the horseshoe model but will require different tool sets (Fig. 10.1).

ADM asserted that the well-known model-driven development principles that have been well employed for forward engineering, like generative techniques to obtain source code from UML, can be applied to reverse engineering and restructuring in an effective manner (Perez-Castillo et al. 2011). In reverse engineering, the

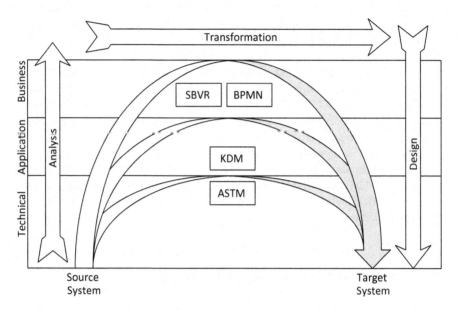

Fig. 10.1 ADM horseshoe

implicit knowledge embodied in software assets is recovered and represented in models according to certain metamodels. Then various restructuring and refactoring methods are utilized over these models including transformations to a target model. Finally, well-known forward engineering methodologies are employed to regenerate modernized software assets.

Adhering to model-driven principles, the proposed architecture-driven modernization methodology promotes capturing the artifacts that the modernization effort targets as models at any particular abstraction level. It then recommends employing model transformations for modernization tasks. ADM came with a handful of metamodels that cover the artifacts of all three levels of modernization. The abstract syntax tree metamodel (ASTM) (OMG 2011a) and knowledge discovery metamodel (KDM) (OMG 2010) were recommended as the metamodels for artifacts from technical modernization to architecture/data modernization. For business modernization, the semantics of business vocabulary and rules (SBVR) (OMG 2008) and business process model and notation (BPMN) (OMG 2011b) were developed. ASTM is developed for representing software below the procedural level with abstract syntax tree models. KDM, on the other hand, is the cornerstone metamodel that proposes an ontology for all software assets over the procedural level. In the business level, while BPMN provides a notation for graphical representation of business processes, SBVR defines a formal base for business vocabularies, facts, and rules. With these metamodels, ADM furnishes the modernization effort with adequate constructs to capture available assets as models in an abstraction level of preference. The formalized knowledge in models is available for transformations. Query/View/Transformation (QVT) is offered as an OMG standard transformation language that enables specifying transformations between models (OMG 2015). ADM introduces QVT as the means for automation for model transformations in a modernization effort.

In the following sections, the first metamodels for technical and architectural modernization, namely, ASTM and KDM, will be presented. Then, as an example modernization tool that brings these metamodels into play in order to extract knowledge from the existing software artifacts and construct models, Eclipse-based model-driven modernization tool MoDisco (Hugo et al. 2010) will be disclosed. Finally, as an example transformation language, QVT will gently be introduced.

10.2.2   Metamodels

Among the three processes of the horseshoe model, reverse engineering can be claimed as the most important one, because modernization is carried out over the knowledge recovered from the available software assets. KDM offers a standard and integrated way to represent all software artifacts in a certain legacy system. It enables a complete overlook to available assets to understand diverse aspects of the available knowledge. As the archeology requires understanding the civilizing and cultural forces that create available artifacts, reverse engineering depends upon a complete analysis of available artifacts like source code, databases, user interfaces, or repositories as well as the methodologies and infrastructures. So the reverse engineering of software systems is sometimes referred to as software archeology (Moyer 2009).

KDM is proposed as the metamodel to represent existing software and its elements, associations, and operational environments and covers a large and diverse set of application, platforms, and programming languages (OMG 2010). The metamodel is organized in 4 layers: infrastructure layer, program elements layer, run-time resource layer, and abstraction layer. These layers are further organized to packages, each of which corresponds to a certain independent facet of knowledge about the software (Fig. 10.2). There is a KDM model corresponding to each package.

The infrastructure layer specifies the fundamental metamodel element types and constraints. Core, "kdm," and source are the packages of the infrastructure layer.

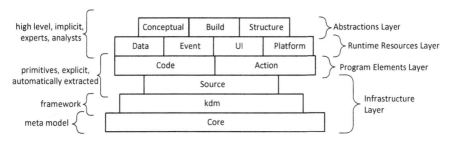

Fig. 10.2   The structure of KDM packages (OMG 2010)

Fig. 10.3 KDM core class
diagram excerpt (OMG
2010)

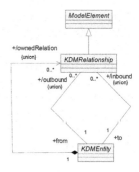

Core and "kdm" packages are not used for a specific model but utilized as the foundation of KDM.

The core package provides a set of base types that are used to derive any metamodel element. Any class in KDM is a subclass of a class that is defined in the core package. Top-level classes of the core package are KDMEntity and KDMRelationship. While KDMEntity is defined as an abstraction for any element of an existing system, KDMRelationship abstracts any semantic association between these elements. Figure 10.3 presents the specification of KDMEntity and KDMRelationship classes in a class diagram excerpt from KDM.

The "kdm" package targets at specifying the structure of KDM instances. It defines infrastructure elements and thus enables describing the organization of KDM. KDM instances constitute *segments*, and *segments* are composed of *models*. A *segment* is defined as a collection of *models* that represent a perspective of the existing system. Model, on the other hand, provides a collection of coherent facts about a given software system.

The source package explicates metamodel elements that represent the tangible artifacts of an existing system, e.g., source files or resource descriptions. The concerns of the source package include identifying the artifacts and their roles (source file, binary file, configuration file), their organization, and their dependencies. It is used to construct an Inventory model. As the top-level generic metamodel element, InventoryItem represents any artifact from the existing system (Fig. 10.4). It is then inherited to further artifact types, e.g., SourceFile, BinaryFile, or Image. InventoryContainer offers a container for InventoryItem instances. Directory is specified as an InventoryContainer.

The program elements layer is composed of code and action packages. They define metamodel elements to provide a language-independent intermediate representation of common programming language constructs. The code model is constructed using these two packages. It represents the implementation-level assets of the existing software system. The code package targets at representing name elements from the source code, and the action package enables representing the behavioral aspects like control flows. Example elements of the code package are PrimitiveTypes, CompositeTypes, ClassTypes, Comment, and

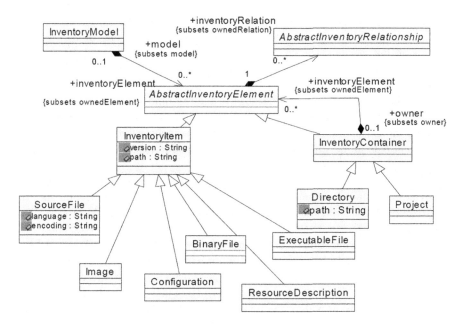

Fig. 10.4 KDM inventory class diagram excerpt (OMG 2010)

Visibility. The metamodel elements ActionFlow, ExceptionFlow, ActionElements, and exception blocks are some examples from the action package. The concerns of the program elements layer include the computation elements of the system, the organization of computational elements, and data types used by the computational elements and the behavior of them. Parser-like tools are recommended to construct a code model.

The run-time resource layer introduces the metamodel elements to describe the operating environment of an existing software system. There are packages in this layer: platform, UI, event, and data. The platform package has metamodel elements to present the run-time environment, like CORBA. The concerns of the platform package include the elements of the run-time environment, the bindings to the run-time environment, the flows initiated by the run-time environment, and deployment configuration of the software systems. It is recommended that the knowledge about the API for the run-time environment or the domain-specific languages, by which the elements of the run-time platform are explicitly defined, can be used for the platform model.

The UI package has metamodel elements that represent information related to user interface. The concerns of the UI package includes the data that originates from the user interface, the organization of the user interface, the dataflows originated from the user interface, and user interface artifacts like images.

The event package offers metamodel elements to represent the high-level behavior of the application. The states, state transitions, and events are some of the elements of this package. The distinct states involved in the behavior of the software system and events that cause state transitions are some of the concerns of the event package.

The data package is the last package of the run-time resource layer to be presented. It defines metamodel elements to represent the structure of the persistent data in the existing software system. Its concerns include the organization of the persistent date in the software system, the information model of it, and the action elements that operate on this data.

The abstraction layer consists of structure, conceptual, and build packages. It provides metamodel elements to represent domain-specific or application-specific abstractions. It also enables to recover information about the build process. The structure package captures metamodel elements for subsystems, layers, and packages and their organization in an existing software system. The conceptual package includes metamodel elements to build a conceptual model for the reengineering effort. Thus, domain vocabulary, scenarios, and business rules can be captured. The build package targets at recovering the information about the build process of the existing system by providing the related metamodel elements. These metamodel elements include build tools, build steps, and libraries.

The abstract syntax tree metamodel and KDM are developed and promoted by the OMG Architecture-Driven Modernization Task Force as two complementary modeling specifications. ASTM is developed for representing software below the procedural level with abstract syntax tree models (OMG 2011a, b). This means that it supports one-to-one mapping of all code-level language statements to the model elements.

The abstract syntax tree is described as the formal representation of the syntactical structure of source code. Formally, it is a finite, labeled, and directed tree. Internal nodes are labeled by the operators, whereas the operands of these operators are represented in the leaf nodes. ASTM accommodates the metamodel elements to compose abstract syntax trees. Thus, it models the constructs within the programming language and provides the bottommost language modeling level. It complements KDM not only with model of syntactic structures using generic model elements common to various languages but also offers specialized modeling elements for particular languages. ASTM is composed of the generic abstract syntax tree metamodel (GASTM), which is the core specification, and specialized abstract syntax tree metamodels (SASTMs), which are a set of complementary specifications that extend the core for a specific language, e.g., relational database manipulation language.

ASTM has three abstract classes for syntactic, semantic, and source property language elements. A set of core modeling elements are derived from the semantic class to represent and derive the basic semantics of the code-level elements. The modeling elements for capturing the properties like source file, starting line, and ending line of any ASTM modeling element are derived from the abstract source class. Finally, modeling elements that represent elements of a programming lan-

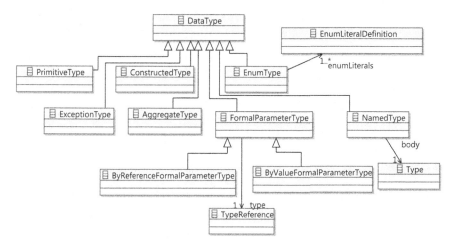

Fig. 10.5   Data type and its subclasses (OMG 2011a)

guage in the form of a finite, labeled, and directed tree are derived from the abstract syntax class. As an example, `Type` is derived from `GASTMSyntaxObject`, and `DataType` is a type of `Type`. `DataType` and its subclasses as proposed in the standard as high-level composite UML class diagram are depicted in Fig. 10.5.

10.2.3   A Reverse Engineering Tool

Reverse engineering is explained as the process of analyzing an existing system with the motivation to identify its components and the relations among them and represent them in a higher abstraction to boost understandability (Chikofsky and Cross 1990). Model-driven reverse engineering (MDRE) is proposed as a methodology that promotes constructing models for the extracted knowledge from a given system based on the required viewpoints (Hugo et al. 2010). As depicted in Fig. 10.6, it is realized in two steps: model discovery and model understanding (Bruneliere et al. 2014). Model discovery is proposed as metamodel driven, which targets at representing the legacy system in raw models with no loss of required information. Model understanding is then explained as model based, which employs model transformations for the generation of new models from the models of the previous step.

MoDisco is a generic and extensible MDRE framework implemented over Eclipse. It possesses three-layer architecture (Hugo et al. 2010). These layers are, namely, infrastructure, technologies, and use cases. The infrastructure layer provides a set of generic components. OMG ADM metamodels like KDM and GASTM are implemented by employing EMF Ecore and the model handling API. While the Discovery provides a simple generic discoverer interface to develop and integrate

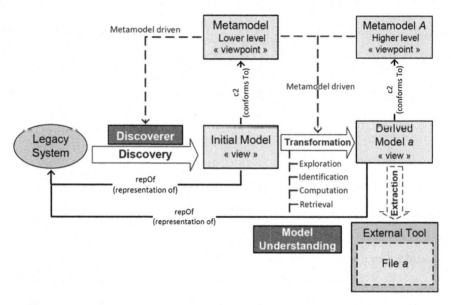

Fig. 10.6 Model discovery and model understanding (Adapted and reprinted from Bruneliere et al. 2014, Copyright (2014), with permission from Elsevier)

discoverers, which generate models to the framework, the Workflow provides a mechanism to define a pipeline by specifying an execution sequence with discoverers, transformations, and scripts. The model browsing component of the infrastructure layer enables to navigate complex models. And lastly, querying and customization components of the infrastructure layer allow registering and executing queries over the models.

The technologies layer, based on the infrastructure layer, provides components for particular legacy technologies. MoDisco supports a number of legacy technologies like Java or XML by offering ready-to-use components. As an example, the technologies layer comes with a Java metamodel covering full abstract syntax and corresponding discoverer to construct a complete Java model out of Java source code. It is also possible to construct KDM "code" models for Java projects with the provided KDM discoverer.

Finally, the use cases layer provides examples based on the technologies layer for a particular reverse engineering scenario. Thus, it introduces how the MoDisco components can be combined and orchestrated for a particular reverse engineering use case. Java application refactoring can be mentioned as one of the example use cases.

10.2.4 A Transformation Language

As the knowledge in the current software artifacts are captured in models, they become available for transformations. Query/View/Transformations (QVT) is an OMG standard transformation language that enables specifying transformations between models (OMG 2015). ADM introduces QVT as the means for automation for model transformations in a modernization effort.

QVT has declarative and imperative parts. The declarative part is composed of two layers, namely, Relations and Core. Relations is proposed as a user-friendly language for complex object matching and object template creation. Core is introduced as a minimal language that allows pattern matching by evaluating the conditions over a flat set of variables. In an analogy with Java architecture, Core is introduced as the Java bytecode, whereas Relations is presented as Java language. Lastly Operational Mappings is promoted as a standard language for imperative implementation of transformations.

Relations defines a transformation between candidate models as a set of relations that need to hold for the transformation. The candidate models are specified with their model types. As in the example below, *simulink* and *uml* are the metamodels of SimpleSimulink and SimpleUML models:

```
transformation simulinkUml (simulink : SimpleSimulink,
                            uml : SimpleUML)
```

The transformations are executed toward the model that is selected as a target. The constraints to be satisfied by the elements of candidate models are specified as relations using when and where predicates. Domains are used to specify patterns which can be described as a set of variables and constraints to be satisfied. While the *when* clause defines the conditions under which the relationship holds, the *where* clause is used to specify a condition that needs to be satisfied by all model elements participating in the relation.

Operational Mappings includes a signature that defines the type of models involved in the transformation by specifying their metamodels and an entry operation as the starting point of execution:

```
transformation Simulink2UML (in simulink:Sim ,out uml:UML) {
    // the entry point for the execution
    main() {
        sim.objectsOfType(Block)->map BlockToActivity();
    }
....
}
```

Mapping operation describes a mapping between the source model elements into target model elements with a guard that is specified using a when clause, a mapping body, and a post-condition using a where clause. Body is composed of **init** section for the code to be executed before the instantiation **population** section for the code to populate the result parameters and **end** section for the code to be executed when exiting the operation.

10.3   Architecture-Driven Simulation Modernization

10.3.1   Extending KDM

With its promise to transform embedded implicit knowledge in the legacy assets to target architectures, the ADM approach is so promising. Considering the large taxonomy of simulation modeling (Silver et al., 2011), there is a wide diversity of methodologies and approaches to specify simulation modeling assets. They basically differ depending on the modeled system behavior (e.g., continuous, discrete, hybrid), focus of the modeler (e.g., activity diagrams, state transition diagrams), abstraction (e.g., agent-based simulation, object-oriented simulation), execution (e.g., activity scanning, event scanning), or model syntax (e.g., declarative, functional). While the formalisms for representing software assets are well captured in standard metamodels like KDM and ASTM as an ontology, Durak claimed that the diversity in methodologies and approaches to simulation modeling prohibits KDM providing adequate meta-definitions to capture knowledge in simulations (Durak 2015). Thereby, he proposed an extension to KDM which he called simulation KDM (SKDM).

SKDM extends KDM with a simulation model package. The simulation model package provides an abstract metamodel used to derive concrete metamodel elements while metamodeling for a specific simulation methodology or approach. As depicted in Fig. 10.7, for the metamodel of a particular simulation modeling methodology or approach, the metamodel developer needs to define their own concrete metamodel elements for the user metamodel via inheriting them from abstract metamodel elements of the simulation model.

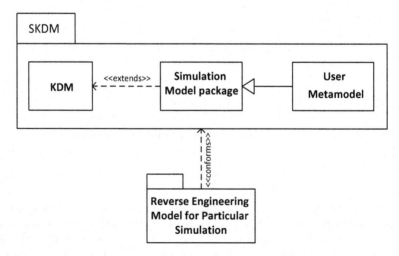

Fig. 10.7 Simulation knowledge discovery metamodel (Durak 2015)

10.3.2   Simulation Model Package

Considering its roots in the theory of modeling and simulation, its expressive power and clarity with a small number of axioms, the system entity structure (SES), which can be described as a schema for knowledge representation of decomposition, taxonomy, and coupling of systems (Kim et al. 1990), is proposed as the basis of the intermediate metamodel in the simulation model package. As briefly introduced in Chap. 9, SES is composed of four node types: (i) entity, (ii) aspect, (iii) specialization, and (iv) multiple aspect (Zeigler and Hammonds 2007). Entity represents real or artificial system components that correspond to a model component. Variables can be attached to entities. The other node types basically specify any relation between their parent and child entities. Aspect nodes introduce the decomposition relationship of an entity. Children of aspect nodes are entities which connect to the parent node in one possible decomposition aspect. Specialization nodes represent the taxonomy of an entity. The children of specialization are variants of their parents. The multiple aspect nodes, finally, represent a multiplicity relationship which specifies that the parent entity is a composition of multiple entities of the same type.

The SES has a set of axioms: *uniformity, strict hierarchy, alternating mode, valid brothers, attached variables, and inheritance* (Zeigler 1984*). Uniformity* dictates that any two nodes with the same labels have isomorphic subtrees. *Strict hierarchy* prohibits a label from appearing more than once down any path of the tree. *Alternating mode* specifies that if a node is an entity, then the successor is either aspect or specialization and vice versa. *Valid brothers* prevents having two brothers with the same label. *Attached variables* notes that variable types attached to the same item shall have distinct names. Finally *inheritance* states that specialization inherits all variables and aspects.

In the simulation model package, SES concepts are provided as metamodel elements for describing metamodel classes for creating a package of a particular simulation modeling methodology or approach (Fig. 10.8).

`AbstractSimulationModelEntity` is derived from `KDMEntity` and proposed as an abstract superclass for concrete simulation model entities. It corresponds to SES entity. While developing a metamodel for a specific modeling and simulation methodology or approach, concepts of the methodology or the approach shall be captured as concrete subclasses of `AbstractSimulationModelEntity`. It has zero or more concrete aspect, multiple aspect, and specialization relationship which shall be inherited from `AbstractSimulationModelAspect`, `AbstractSimulationModelMultiAspect`, and `AbstractSimulationModelSpecialization`, respectively.

`AbstractSimulationModelAspect` is provided as an abstract superclass for concrete SES aspect nodes. For concrete SES specialization nodes, `AbstractSimulationModelSpecialization` is introduced. `AbstractSimulationModelMultiAspect` is an abstract superclass for concrete SES multiple aspect nodes. These three classes are derived from `KDMRelationship`.

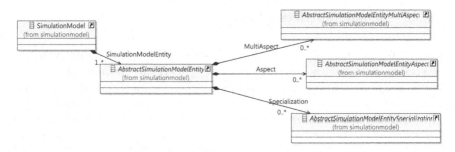

Fig. 10.8 Simulation model package class diagram

10.3.3   Sample Simulation Model Discovery Metamodel

In this section, the approach that is presented by Durak (2015) will be exemplified with a sample simulation knowledge discovery metamodel. The simulation model package will be extended in order to develop a metamodel for a continuous system simulation language (CSSL) (Strauss et al. 1967).

After the introduction of simulation using digital computers, very soon it was recognized that high-level simulation languages decrease the simulation development effort substantially and various simulation languages have been designed (Bausch-Gall 1987). A CSSL was published as the result of the effort on standardization for simulation languages in 1967 and it provided a baseline for future CSSLs. ADSIM is one of these CSSLs that has been developed by Applied Dynamics International for their AD 100 simulation computer (Zammit 1988). The language is still being supported and organizations like the German Aerospace Center (DLR) still possess legacy ADSIM simulations (Klaes 2000).

The intended use case of the CSSL package can be introduced as recovering information from legacy simulations that have been developed with simulation languages like ADSIM which are based on CSSL. This sample metamodel will render a portion of simulation language features that are introduced in CSSL (Strauss et al. 1967) to exemplify metamodel development for a particular simulation methodology or approach.

A set of metamodel elements that capture CSSL constructs and their relations are specified in the CSSL metamodel. The concern of this sample metamodel is to identify how a simulation is structured with respect to CSSL constructs. A parser can be utilized for a CSSL implementation to extract information about the structural constructs from an existing simulation code.

Figure 10.9 presents a class diagram for the CSSL metamodel that is constructed based on the standard (Strauss et al. 1967). To represent the basic unit, `Simulation` is inherited from `AbstractSimulationModelEntity`. It is composed of `Segments` as specified by `simulationDec` that is derived from `AbstractSimulationModelAspect`. `Segments` are introduced as highest-level structural elements that can perform a complete simulation. With `segment-MultiAsp` that is derived from `AbstractSimulationModelMultiAspect`,

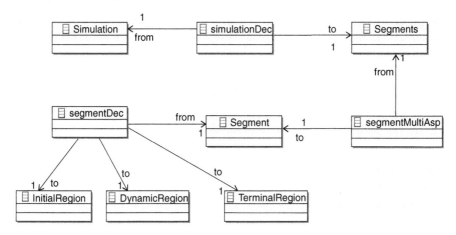

Fig. 10.9 Class diagram from CSSL metamodel

the multiplicity relation between the Segment and Simulation is captured. Segment is defined as the parallel simulation equivalent of closed subroutines from procedural languages. Then, each Segment is decomposed into Initial Region, Dynamic Region, and Terminal Region. The Initial Region is proposed as the simulation program portion of input/output operations and initialization procedures that shall be performed before a simulation run. The Dynamic Region is described as the simulation program portion that simulates the continuous system depending on the integration algorithm and the step size. Finally, the Terminal Region is responsible for the calculations and input/output operations for the termination of the simulation run.

Here with the sample, it can be claimed that the SES abstract classes provided in the simulation model package made the construction of the CSSL metamodel easier. Further, the formalization of the targeted knowledge discovery artifacts in a metamodel which is well aligned with KDM can be helpful in using the tools and methodologies of ADM for simulation reverse engineering.

10.4 Summary

This chapter introduced the simulation evolution and modernization. It embraces and presents software evolution and modernization approaches, particularly ADM. With a gentle summary, the reader is familiarized with the metamodeling languages for technical and architecture modernization, namely, KDM and ASTM. QVT is acquainted as the transformation language of ADM. Then MoDisco is revealed as the example MDRE tool. Further, a recent research, an extension to software modernization approaches is presented to exemplify how the practices and methodologies of the software engineering community can be adopted and enhanced to fulfill the modernization requirements of simulation and modeling. This example also points out a research direction, which can be entitled as model-driven simulation modernization. This direction asks for further interest for identifying and clarifying the particular characteristics of legacy models and simulations, as well as the knowledge extraction and transformation requirements for model and simulation modernization efforts.

References

Bausch-Gall, I. (1987). Continuous system simulation languages. *Vehicle System Dynamics: International Journal of Vehicle Mechanics and Mobility, 16*(1), 347–366.

Bergey, J., Smith, D., Weiderman, N., & Woods, S. (1999). *Option Analysis for Reengineering (OAR): Issues and conceptual approach.* Pittsburg: Carnegie Mellon Software Engineering Institute.

Bruneliere, H., Cabot, J., Dupe, G., & Madiot, F. (2014, August). MoDisco: A model driven reverse engineering framework. *Information and Software Technology, 56*(8), 1012–1032.

Chikofsky, E., & Cross, J. (1990). Reverse engineering and design recovery: A taxonomy. *IEEE Software, 7*(1), 13–17.

Durak, U. (2015). Extending knowledge discovery metamodel for architecture-driven simulation modernization. *Simulation, 91*(12), 1052–1067.

Hugo, B., Cabot, J., Jouault, F., & Madiot, F. (2010). MoDisco: A generic and extensible framework for model driven reverse engineering. In *Proceedings of theIEEE/ACM international conference on automated software engineering* (pp. 173–174). Antwerp: IEEE.

IEEE. (2006). *Software engineering—Software life cycle processes—Maintenance.* IEEE Std 14764-2006. New York: IEEE.

Khusidman, V. (2008). *ADM transformation white paper V.1.* [Online] Available at: http://www.omg.org/adm/ADMTransformartionv4.pdf. Accessed 15 May 2014.

Kim, T., Lee, C., Christensen, E., & Zeigler, B. (1990). System entity structuring and model base management. *IEEE Transactions on Systems, Man, and Cybernetics, 20*(5), 1013–1024.

Klaes, S. (2000). ATTAS ground based system simulator – An update. In *AIAA modeling and simulation technologies conference and exhibit.* Denver: AIAA.

Lehman, M. (1980a). On understanding laws, evolution and conversion in the large-program life-cycle. *Journal of Systems and Software, 1*, 213–221.

Lehman, L. (1980b). Programs, life cycles, and laws of software evolution. *Proceedings of the IEEE, 9*(68), 1060–1076.

Lehman, M., Perry, D., & Ramil, J. (1998). *Implications of evolution metrics on software maintenance.* International Conference on Software Maintenance (pp. 208–217). Bethesda: IEEE.

Moyer, B. (2009). Software archeology: Modernizing old systems. *Embedded Technology Journal,* [Online] Available at: http://www.eejournal.com/archives/articles/20090217_kdm/. Accessed 20 Dec 2015.

OMG. (2003a). *Architecture-driven modernization.* [Online] Available at: http://adm.omg.org/. Accessed 20 Dec 2015.

OMG. (2003b). *Why do we need standards for the modernization of existing systems?* Available at: http://adm.omg.org/legacy/ADM_whitepaper.pdf. Accessed 20 Dec 2015.

OMG. (2008). *Semantics of Business Vocabulary and Business Rules (SBVR) version 1.0.* Needham: OMG.

OMG. (2010). *Knowledge Discovery Meta-Model (KDM) version 1.2.* Needham: OMG.

OMG. (2011a). *Architecture-driven modernization: Abstract Syntax Tree Metamodel (ASTM) version 1.0*. Needham: OMG.

OMG. (2011b). *Business Process Model And Notation (BPMN) version 2.0*. Needham: OMG.

OMG. (2015). *Meta Object Facility (MOF) 2.0 query/view/transformation specification version 1.2*. Needham: OMG.

Paradauskas, B., & Laurikaitis, A. (2006). Business knowledge extraction from legacy information systems. *Information Technology and Control, 35*(3), 214–221.

Parnas, D. (1994). Software aging. In *ICSE '94 Proceedings of the 16th International Conference on Software Engineering* (pp. 279–287). Sorrento: IEEE.

Perez-Castillo, R., de Guzman, I., & Piattini, M. (2011). Architecture-driven modernization. In Modern software engineering concepts and practices: Advanced concepts. In *Modern software engineering concepts and practices: Advanced concepts* (pp. 75–103). Hershey: International Science Reference.

Perry, N., Ryan, P., & Zalcman, L. (1998). Provision of DIS/HLA gateways for legacy training simulators. In *SimTecT 98 conference proceedings* (pp. 227–232). Adelaide: SIAA.

Pullen, J., & White, E. (2003). Adapting legacy computational software for XMSF. In *Fall 2003 Simulation Interoperability Workshop*. Orlando: SISO.

Silver, G., et al. (2011). DeMO: An ontology for discrete-event modeling and simulation. *Simulation, 87*(9), 747–773.

Sneed, H. (2005). Estimating the costs of a reengineering project. In *12th working conference on reverse engineering*. Pittsburgh: IEEE.

Sonntag, M., et al. (2011). *Using services and service compositions to enable the distributed execution of legacy simulation applications*. ServiceWave 2011 (pp. 242–253). Poznan: Springer.

Strauss, J., et al. (1967). The SCi Continuous System Simulation Language (CSSL). *Simulation, 9*(6), 281–303.

Trcka Radosevic, M., Hensen, J., & Wijsman, A. (2006). Distributed building performance simulation-a novel approach to overcome legacy code limitations. *HVAC&R Research, 12*(3a), 621–640.

Visaggio, G. (2001). Ageing of a data-intensive legacy system: Symptoms and remedies. *Journal of Software Maintenance and Evolution: Research and Practice, 13*(5), 281–308.

Zammit, S. (1988). Conversion of existing FORTRAN simulation programs to a general purpose simulation language. In *Flight simulation technologies conference*. Atlanta: AIAA.

Zeigler, B. (1984). *Multifaceted modeling and discrete event simulation* (1st ed.). San Diego: Academic Press, Inc.

Zeigler, B., & Hammonds, P. (2007). *Modeling and simulation-based data engineering: Introducing pragmatics in ontologies for Net-centric information exchange* (1st ed.). Amsterdam: Academic.

Part V
Future Outlook

Chapter 11
Synergies of MDE, Simulation, and Agent Technology

Software agents, modeling and simulation (M&S), and model-driven engineering (MDE) are fields with their distinct body of knowledge and good practices. However, developments in one area can provide new avenues for advancing the methodologies and technical strategies in other fields. This chapter examines the synergies among these three fields by highlighting selected challenges in each area and by delineating how methods developed in each field can mutually be beneficial. We categorize the ways in which the agent paradigm can contribute to critical activities in MDE, and similarly we delineate how domain-specific languages and model transformation strategies can be instrumental in the design, implementation, and management of agent systems.

11.1 Introduction

The use of models in software engineering is pervasive. Yet, models are often used merely as documentation, and they are not properly maintained and synchronized with implementation artifacts. On the other hand, in model-driven engineering (MDE), models and transformations provide an effective and reliable framework for maintaining provenance and synthesizing schematic software (Stahl and Volter 2006). However, despite growing recognition of the utility of MDE, there are still impediments to adoption of MDE methodologies in practice (Mussbacher et al. 2014). The challenges include obstacles in context-sensitive model adaptation (Morin et al. 2009), steep learning curve in model management and transformation (Mussbacher et al. 2014), lack of understanding of the distinction between exploratory and exploitative problem solving with models, uncertainty in environments, and ambiguity in requirements. In this chapter, mutually beneficial synergies between MDE and software agents (Franklin and Graesser 1996; Russell and

© Springer International Publishing Switzerland 2016
O. Topçu et al., *Distributed Simulation*, Simulation Foundations,
Methods and Applications, DOI 10.1007/978-3-319-03050-0_11

Norvig 1996), as well as agent-directed simulation modeling (Yilmaz and Ören 2009), are examined to contribute to addressing the identified challenges.

Intelligent software agent technology has proven effective in developing systems that are capable of deliberative reasoning, adaptation, and learning. Such capabilities allow agents to behave as autonomous components that can monitor and perceive their environments to make decisions and to interact with peer agents for solving complex problems. However, a critical challenge in developing multi agent systems (Wooldridge 2009) is the difficulty of using general-purpose languages to correctly implement complex adaptation, learning, and reasoning models. Mapping such complex methods, which require special expertise in and technical understanding of agent theories, onto general-purpose programming constructs is both labor intensive and error prone. To resolve this issue, domain-specific languages (DSLs) (Fowler 2011) can be used to facilitate developing type systems that formalize the structure, the behavior, and the requirements of cognitive theories, as well as models of agent coordination, adaptation, and learning. Furthermore, by increasing the abstraction levels of agent programming languages, DSLs can improve not only model readability but also productivity of model designers and the adoption of agent technologies.

Similarly, software agents with simulation capabilities (Yilmaz and Ören 2009) can assist MDE as model behavior generators prior to transformation of models into platform-specific code. The reasoning and symbolic understanding (Ören et al. 2013) capabilities of agents can help cope with ambiguous and fuzzy requirements (Rashid et al. 2011; Yilmaz 2015), support the exploration (i.e., exploratory modeling) and management of multiple alternative models before converging to an authoritative problem space representation, provide aid in analyzing models for consistency and correctness, and contribute to synthesis of and experimentation with models (Teran-Somohano et al. 2014). In model transformation, agents can assist in the discovery of transformation rules in the form of formal mappings between metamodels. For instance, machine-learning approaches for syntactic and semantic ontology matching (Doan et al. 2004) along with multi-objective bipartite graph matching algorithms can generate highly plausible mappings between the source and target metamodels.

The objective of this chapter is to systematically examine the characteristics of agents and the MDE process to identify such potential synergies between these fields. The parallels between computational models for the discovery of scientific knowledge and domain model generation are emphasized to propose potential avenues of research in abstraction discovery and model refinement. To this end, the rest of the chapter is organized as follows. In Sect. 11.2, we overview the basic concepts of MDE (Stahl and Volter 2006), DSLs (Fowler 2011), intelligent agents (Franklin and Graesser 1996), and simulation (Law and Kelton 2000; Yilmaz and Ören 2009). Section 11.3 starts with the role of MDE in designing and implementing agent systems. For illustration purposes, we introduce the deliberative coherence-driven agent (DeCoAgent) model and demonstrate how the MDE strategy along with DSL engineering can serve as a framework for developing generative domain architecture for a DeCoAgent (İşçi et al. 2014). Section 11.4 introduces the role of agents for MDE under the categories of exploratory and exploitative modeling, and we conclude in Sect. 11.5 with a summary of recommended future research.

11.2   Background

A synergy between two fields is defined in terms of interactions that benefit both fields. Higher-order synergies emerge when enhanced fields recursively contribute to each other. Figure 11.1 depicts how MDE-enhanced agent models and agent-enhanced MDE methodologies can feedback on each other to provide basis for mutually recursive and continuous advancement in the respective fields.

Next, we provide basic definitions and characteristics of the four major areas of interest for exploring such synergistic interactions.

11.2.1   Model-Driven Engineering

MDE promotes using models as the focal elements and building blocks for software development along with transformations among them as the mechanisms for deriving executable software systems (Stahl and Volter 2006). Model specification, management, and transformation techniques facilitate mapping abstract and

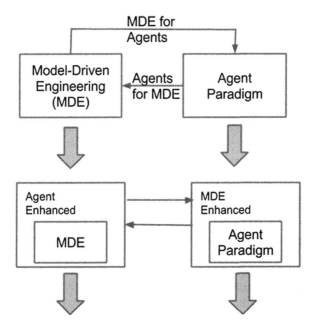

Fig. 11.1 Concepts of synergy and higher-order synergy

platform-independent concepts onto concrete and platform-specific models, including executable code, via multistage refinements. Models can also be transformed into alternative representations at the same level of abstraction to facilitate application of various analysis, verification, and validation tools. The use of models and transformations necessitates explicit representation of metamodels, enabling mappings among them via explicit transformation models. These models are managed along with the application and the domain models, which require modeling languages, called domain-specific languages. For further introduction, please refer to Chap. 2.

11.2.2   Domain-Specific Languages

Domain-specific languages (DSLs) support the MDE process by leveraging computer languages that are based on type systems that can directly express domain concepts and relationships in a formal manner. Unlike general-purpose languages (GPLs), a DSL possesses a domain-specific metamodel (grammar), including its static semantics, and a corresponding concrete syntax. The dynamic semantics gives meaning to the constructs of the metamodel, and automated transformations generate operational and executable specifications that execute the required semantics. By using a DSL, a domain expert is able to focus attention on creating and experimenting with a model. Just as importantly, the modeler is not distracted by the essentially algorithmic problems of realizing a model and does not risk being misled by errors in the implementation.

11.2.3   Agent Paradigm

Intelligent agents are software entities that have capabilities to perceive their environment, assess the situation, and make decisions to act on the environment so as to reach their goals. Goal-directed nature of agents necessitates achieving autonomy via deliberation and knowledge-based reasoning. Agents employ adaptive problem solving strategies when the context (environment) is uncertain and/or ambiguous. In such evolving environments, agents with adaptation and learning strategies improve the resilience of the system by maintaining the desired function. Furthermore, solving complex problems requires explicit models of communication, cooperation, collaboration, and if necessary, conflict resolution among groups of agents.

Developing such sophisticated cognitive agent models in terms of GPL constructs requires significant expertise and is often tedious and error prone. Moreover, in agent-based models, interaction and coordination mechanisms among agents are the subtle and difficult part of a software system where the intended model and the actual implementation often diverge. Model developers are likely to realize varying interpretations of intuitively appealing mechanisms and consequently follow diverse development guidelines. This lack of transparency in the mechanism space of agent-based models is a serious difficulty for end users that need to modify a model.

Model revision is often desirable for investigating problems that, though clearly within the conceptual scope of the model, were not perceived by the original programmer. This leads to high costs, unforeseen and possibly undetected errors, and other substantial problems when end users attempt to modify a model to address new, but related, questions (Yilmaz 2015). As discussed in this chapter, DSL-based MDE principles can mitigate those problems effectively.

11.2.4   Simulation

Simulation is the act of using a simulator to generate a model's behavior over time for the purpose of understanding the referent system. Simulation can also be used for the purpose of education, experimenting, training, or exploring the consequences of the assumptions made in model. The separation of the model from the simulator and the experimental frame allows varying them independently. The simulator interprets the model and generates its behavior according to the experiment plan to answer questions about the referent system.

The M&S community has developed various types of simulators for a diverse set of modeling formalisms to facilitate support for *model experiencing environments (MEEs)* (Mussbacher et al. 2014). Existing advanced distributed simulator algorithms, as well as event and time management mechanisms, can contribute to MDE by enhancing DSL-based model interpretation techniques. MEEs are promoted as examples of futuristic MDE infrastructures, allowing customizable and exploratory simulation of models to facilitate distributed learning, crowdsourcing, community decision-making, and policy analysis. These objectives bring to the fore the need to coordinate and synchronize multiple, distributed models in a coherent manner via advanced simulator technologies with proper time-flow and interaction management mechanisms. This calls for exploring potential synergies between MEE and simulation methodologies to support not only model-driven but also simulation-based software engineering. In the following sections, we examine and give examples to demonstrate potential synergies among agents, MDE, DSL, and simulation.

11.3   MDE for Agents

In this section, we provide an example to make the case for enhancing the agent paradigm with selected MDE principles and practices. First, we introduce an abstract agent architecture that encapsulates explicit learning, deliberation, and interaction models. The utility of MDE-enhanced agent modeling is discussed by means of a concrete DSL syntax to specify a decision-making model based on the deliberative coherence theory of Paul Thagard (Thagard and Millgram 1995).

Developing cognitively sophisticated agents is a nontrivial task. It requires expertise to properly implement learning, decision-making, and interaction mechanisms. These mechanisms are related to each other as shown in the abstract architecture in

Fig. 11.2. As depicted by the architecture, an agent perceives the state of the environment through its sensors and assesses the performance of its behavioral model based on the degree to which it makes progress toward the desired objective state or the level of attained utility. The learning model, which is responsible for making improvements, uses feedback from the critic and determines how the behavior model should be modified to do better. When incremental modifications do not result in improved behavior, the model generator component introduces significant updates to the performance elements to better adapt the agent to its evolving environment.

The behavioral model includes both deliberation (reasoning) and interaction (coordination) mechanisms. Deliberation is needed to make decisions by choosing course of actions that are triggered by the beliefs, desired goals, and available plans and by using methods such as the beliefs-desires-intentions (BDI) (Wooldridge 2009) An alternative method based on the deliberative coherence (DeCo) theory (Thagard 2002) promotes a set of actions and goals that cohere together as a response to the observed state of the environment. Topçu (Topçu 2014) framed the DeCo theory in an agent-based simulation context, focusing the implementation perspective of the theory with a systems engineering viewpoint, to show how a certain form of adaptive decision-making can be realized.

11.3.1 Deliberative Coherence Model of Decision-Making

Coherence can be understood in terms of maximal satisfaction of multiple constraints involving concepts, propositions, goals, and actions. In Thagard (2002), various kinds of coherence and associated constraints are presented to support

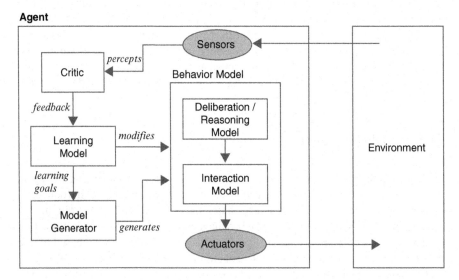

Fig. 11.2 Abstract agent architecture

assessing different types of knowledge. These coherence types include explanatory, deductive, analogical, conceptual, and perceptual coherence. In decision-making, the coherence theory is used in the form of deliberative coherence (Thagard and Milgram 1997) to facilitate making inference to the best plan by choosing compatible course of actions that support the intended goals. The coherence theory of decision-making views the process in terms of choosing sets of goals and tasks that can be accepted or rejected together. The selection process is based on a set of positive and negative constraints among tasks and goals via facilitation and inhibition relations. In the following example, implementation details of this process are shielded by a DSL that provides language primitives to directly express elements of the cognitive theory. The DSL is then transformed into Java code by the generative architecture sketched in Fig. 11.3. The generator also synthesizes an XML definition of the goals, beliefs, tasks, and facilitation and inhibition relations among them. This representation is called the *DeCoNetwork*.

The deliberation mechanism of DeCo is based on a constraint satisfaction algorithm that reaches a reflective equilibrium over a DeCo goal-task network model when a set of goals and coherent tasks linked via facilitation relations are activated above a threshold value.

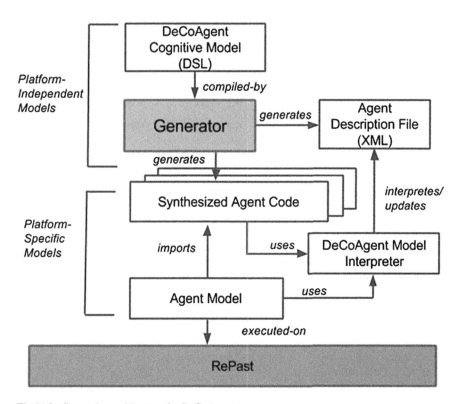

Fig 11.3 Generative architecture for DeCoAgent

11.3.1.1   A Metamodel for DeCo

A connectionist DeCo network model is a graph of relations among the goals and tasks, and the DeCoAgent uses it as the decision-making mechanism. The goals and tasks of a DeCoAgent are represented as nodes while the relations are represented as links among them. The relations include facilitation relation between a goal and a task. A task may facilitate other goals and/or tasks. Evaluation of goals and tasks is based on the computation of the activation values of nodes in the connectionist model.

Figure 11.4 introduces the metamodel that serves as the abstract syntax (grammar) of the DSL. A DeCoModel is comprised of agents, beliefs, and goals. Agents have features (i.e., attributes), actions, as well as beliefs and goals, and they perform tasks that facilitate or inhibit goals. Goals are triggered by beliefs as well as context and activation condition expressions, which are of type constraint. Target condition designates the desired goal state and is evaluated to determine if a goal is satisfied. Tasks and goals are connected to each other through facilitation (excitatory) and inhibition relations, the degree of which is moderated by weight assignments to each directional edge. The essence of the behavioral model is the *DeCoInterpreter* that generates the behavior of the DeCoAgent. The behavioral model is defined in terms of the *DeCoNetwork*. Each node in the network is assigned an initial activation (e.g., 0.01) level. The updated activation level of each node is computed using its current activation, the weights of links to other units to which it is linked, and the activations levels of these linked nodes. At each cycle, the activation level of node j is computed as follows (Thagard 2002):

$$a_j(t+1) = a_j(t)(1-\theta) + \begin{cases} net_j(max - a_j(t)) & \text{if } net_j > 0 \\ net_j(a_j(t) - min) & \text{otherwise} \end{cases}$$

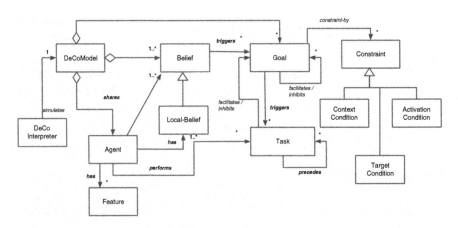

Fig. 11.4 The metamodel for DeCoAgent

Here, d is a decay parameter, min is a minimum activation (-1), and max is maximum activation (1). By using the weight, w_{ij} between unit i and j, the net activation input that propagates to j, is calculated. After all activation levels settle, those nodes with activation levels higher than a threshold are selected and the rest of the units are rejected.

11.3.1.2 The Concrete Syntax for Modeling DeCoAgents

To increase the reliability of the implementation of DeCoAgents and to improve productivity in specifying their cognitive models, a concrete DSL syntax based on the aforementioned metamodel is developed. The *Xtext* (Xtext 2014) platform is used to develop platform-independent specification of a DeCo cognitive model. The template-based transformation strategy enabled the generation of schematic, repetitive code for cognitive model interpretation and the DeCoNetwork updating.

A hypothetical example for the concrete syntax used by a DeCoAgent programmer is shown in Fig. 11.5. The *knowledge-base* keyword is used to list shared beliefs and goals. Goals are parameterized in terms of beliefs used in the constraint statements to express target, activation, and context conditions shown in the metamodel (Fig. 11.4). An agent entity is defined in terms of three sections. The *beliefs* section defines new local beliefs along with references to shared beliefs enumerated in a belief set. The assert function instantiates belief objects that can be used by the expressions declared in the task modules.

The second section focuses in defining *goals*. Each goal is associated with a set of attributes, as well as multiple *inhibits* or *facilitates* relations between the goal and other declared goals/tasks that it is connected with.

The *behavior* component of the agent is similar to a regular class declaration in object-oriented languages. A set of member variables is followed by a declaration of a set of actions. Each action includes *XExpressions* (imperative code fragments in the *Xtend* language) along with a declaration of a list of goals and tasks that it facilitates or inhibits. This information is then used along with the belief and goal declarations to construct a DeCoNetwork, which is synthesized in the form of an XML-formatted agent description file.

A similar study extends Jadex (Braubach et al. 2003), a well-known BDI-based agent development and execution environment, to construct DeCoNetwork models. In this work, Java annotations are used as a concrete syntax and they are extended to enable the definitions of each element (e.g., goal, facilitate, etc.) in a DeCoNetwork. A practitioner may implement DeCoAgents employing this DeCoAgent library (İşci et al. 2014), which is available as open source (İşci and Topçu 2014). The DeCoAgent library (DeCoAgentLib) is also ported to Microsoft .NET[1] development environment (Topçu 2015). Using this library, the DeCoNetwork of an agent is generated automatically by transforming information coming from an external system (i.e., command and control system).

---

[1] http://www.microsoft.com/net, last accessed at Sept. 03, 2015

```
🗋 *DecoDSLTest1.cmdl  ☒    📄 MyAgent.java

    package ausim.decoagent

🔖  import java.util.List

    knowledge-base MAS {
        beliefs {
            belief Block {
                location : Integer
            }

            belief Table {}
        }

        goals {
            goal A [x: Block, y: Table] {}
            goal B {}
        }

    }

⊕ agent MyAgent {
        beliefs {
            belief LocalBlock {}
            belief-set {Block, Table}
            [assert (b1=new Block())
             assert (b2=new Block())
            ]
        }

        goals {
            goal A [x: Block, y: Table] {
                inhibits ((B,0.5))
                priority = 5
                contextCondition {x.location < 10}
            }

            goal B {
                inhibits ((A,0.5))
            }
        }

        behavior {

            name : String
            age : Integer
            bBlock : Block


            action T0() : void {

            }

            action T1() : Integer {

            }

            action T2() : Integer {

            }

        }

    }
```

Fig. 11.5 The concrete syntax

11.3.2 Model-Driven Adaptive Variability Management Strategies for Context-Sensitive Agent Adaptation

The abstract architecture depicted in Fig. 11.2 highlights the significance of adaptation of the cognitive model of an agent. To accommodate an evolving context, agents need to adapt with little or no human intervention. Feature-driven adaptive variability management and product-line engineering are areas of active investigation in MDE. The principles of adaptive and feature-driven variability are adopted here to present a cognitive model of agent adaptation. Adaptation management starts by deriving feature models, which are then extended to incorporate goals, as well as adaptation-related variability, including the notions of context. The adaptation model plays a critical role and needs to capture the variability in the agent's base cognitive model, the variability in the context of the system under study, and the rules that link the changes in the context of the system with the configuration to be used. The elements that constitute the adaptation model are as follows:

- *Dimensions*: A dimension refers to a variation point in the cognitive model of the agent and is associated with one or more alternative variants that can be used for this variation point.
- *Context variables*: The set of context attributes along with their values describes the relevant aspects of the environment of the application. The values or levels of variables specify the context and may suggest specific adaptations. In an agent-based simulation, examples of context variables are the type of signals (e.g., gradient field) and their intensity.
- *Constraint*: The constraints are useful in defining dependency rules that connect context variables to particular variants or features. First-order logic predicate expressions can be used to formalize such dependencies, which can be expressed in the UML object constraint language. For example, a specific variant can only be used if a signal is available in the environment (context).
- *Property*: The properties of the system along with the impact of specific features on these properties need to be captured specifically. For instance, a particular property that involves models of embedded robotic systems is the amount of power consumption. For each related feature in the agent's behavioral model space, the level of power consumption can be specified so that the power consumption of alternative system model configurations can be compared to select a feature set that results in lower power consumption.
- *Adaptation rules*: To enable adaptation via feature selection based on properties requires the provision of rules that link the context to the properties that should be satisfied. These rules allow the expression of adaptation requirements; e.g., if a context variable A is set to a value below critical threshold, then make "minimize power consumption" a high priority goal for the agent's deliberation model.

In this section, we highlighted various strategies for using MDE principles and practices (e.g., metamodeling, DSLs, and feature-driven variability management) to reduce the effort needed for implementing adaptive cognitive models for agents.

The use of domain-specific, theory-driven features and concepts as the constructs of the modeling language helps improve readability and writability of the agent program and the reliability of its simulation via automated and verifiable mappings from the conceptual model to imperative GPL code.

11.4   Agents for MDE

The use of agents for MDE refers to leveraging agent technologies and methods to alleviate the challenges in employing MDE for systems engineering. There are numerous opportunities for agent assistance to improve the tools, the methods, and the theory of MDE and model-driven science (MDS). As shown in Fig. 11.6, based on the purpose of modeling activities, we classify these opportunities under exploratory modeling and model exploitation.

11.4.1   Agents for Exploratory Modeling

Exploratory modeling is more common in the use of models in science, especially due to the need to discover plausible models that can explain the phenomena of interest. Therefore, the search process necessary to converge to an authoritative model is reminiscent of the falsification principle and abductive reasoning models in science, where multiple hypotheses (e.g., models) compete as potential abstractions of the artificial or natural system under investigation. Based on the type of

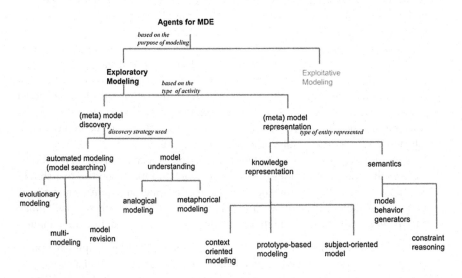

Fig. 11.6 Agents for MDE – exploratory modeling

activities involved, we examine the role of agents under model discovery and model representation.

Model discovery involves various strategies for searching the problem and solution spaces, which are akin to modeling spaces in MDE. As advocated in Klahr and Simon (1999), problem solving can be viewed as a search process. The problem consists of an initial state, a goal state, and a set of operators that transform the initial state (for the initial model configuration) into the goal state, which represents a solution that satisfy problem constraints. The model formulation process is then characterized as a search for a path that links the initial domain knowledge to the desired goal state. Agents can undertake such search processes while adhering to constraints using methods such as *generate and test, hill climbing, simulated annealing*, or *means-ends analysis* (Russell and Norvig, 1993) that aim to use operators that are designed to reduce the difference between the current and goal states. *Planning* is another method suitable for agent assistance and that involves forming an abstract representation of the problem space and then solving the abstracted version by existing search techniques:

- *Automated modeling* techniques that leverage such search processes can further be classified as *evolutionary modeling, model/schema revision*, and *exploratory multi-modeling*. Evolutionary techniques (e.g., creative evolutionary systems) are suitable for evolving an initial model representation using concept elaboration (e.g., mutation) and combination (e.g., crossover) operators to generate varieties of representations. These representations are then put under selective pressure using feedback from engineers (i.e., interactive evolutionary modeling) or well-defined objective functions that optimize a model based on parametric constraints. Targeted model revisions are also feasible by localizing and fixing model anomalies (Craver and Darden 2013) using schema revision strategies suitable for the type of anomaly observed. The applications of such automated modeling methods are not limited to model instances but also to the variation of model schema (metamodels), especially in the evolutionary modeling context, when adaptation of a model's behavior to the evolving context does not produce expected results. In such cases, the metamodel can also evolve to extend the scope and range of exploration by altering problem representation space.
- The *model understanding* strategy for discovery refers to either analogical or metaphorical representations. It involves mapping the conceptual problem space onto previously encountered problems and then selecting plausible models that are suitable for representing the target problem. The recognition mechanism is the most critical aspect of developing analogical solutions, and agent-assisted, analogy-based, or case-based reasoning techniques can be leveraged to contribute to model discovery.

(Meta) Model Knowledge Representation Following the discovery process, further representation and evaluation activities can ensue. This stage involves both knowledge representation and the assessment of the static and dynamic semantics of the generated model(s). The roles agents can play in knowledge representation and management will be more critical as modeling paradigms suitable for explor-

atory modeling are considered. Exploratory modeling requires knowledge representations that lend themselves to efficient and smooth variation in the representation
of problem and solution spaces.

Traditional functional models allow mapping computational units with a name,
but the unit is directly mapped to the concrete procedure implementation without
leaving a choice for variation. The object-oriented view, which is the most common
strategy in representing model components in MDE, adds another dimension for
variation by taking into account the object that receives the message (e.g., behavioral request). On the other hand, context- and subject-oriented views are more suitable for adaptive variation and can use agent assistance:

- *Subject-oriented modeling* (Smith and Ungar 1996) extends the object-oriented
  view by considering not only the request and the recipient but also the sender.
  The behavior varies depending on which source object sends the behavioral
  request. Management and variation of alternative behavioral features can be
  mediated via *broker agents* that serve as run-time decision engines that interpret
  the source and target objects in an interaction scenario.
- *Context-oriented modeling* (Hirschfeld et al. 2008) introduces contextual information as a factor besides the subject, the object, and the model features. Context
  sensitivity enables dispatching behaviors based on context conditions perceived
  in the environment. The perception and understanding capabilities of agents
  make them suitable for monitoring, perceiving, and interpreting such context
  conditions. Consequently, an MDE infrastructure enriched with intelligent
  agents, serving as run-time models for behavior dispatching, will facilitate
  decoupling context evaluation behavior from functional behavior, allowing independent variation and maintenance of both. This view is consistent with the
  adaptive variability management strategy discussed in the previous section and
  clearly illustrates how MDE-enhanced agents can recursively contribute back to
  agent-assisted MDE environments.

The contributions of agents are not limited to knowledge representation mechanisms in model specification. The semantics of such adaptive (meta)models need to
be defined and enforced. The exploratory modeling view and the need for adaptive
run-time management of modeling paradigms call for constraint (assertion) violation
checkers. Constraint reasoning in the form of design heuristics or the way scientists
revise their hypotheses as data become available should be part of the MDE tool suit,
allowing incremental iterative refinement of model mechanisms. The constraint reasoning techniques that can be assisted by agents include qualitative reasoning, qualitative simulation, spatial reasoning, and parameter estimation methods such as found
in metamodel derivation techniques in the design of experiments.

To support exploratory modeling as a search process in the state space of both the
problem and solution domains requires receiving early and iterative feedback on
model behavior, followed by proper revision of models, and if necessary updates to
the schema (metamodels). Agents can assist as model interpreters (Stahl and Volter
2006), which read a model and traverse its abstract syntax tree to perform actions

corresponding the execution semantics of the language. However, in most engineering and scientific problems, the behavior of a model over time is of particular interest. A model can schedule events and activities to occur in the future, and a time advance mechanism is needed to efficiently simulate the specified behavior over time. Time-flow and synchronization mechanisms are essential to generate consistent behavior across multiple models that interoperate together to solve a complex problem. Moreover, as outlined in chapter 2 of (Yilmaz and Ören 2009), agent-directed simulation can facilitate exploration of multiple simulations via multi-simulation techniques, which leverage agents to schedule and intelligently coordinate the execution of multiple alternative contingency models across distinct resolutions, scales, and aspects.

11.4.2 Agents for Exploitative Modeling

The term "exploitative modeling" in this context refers to activities that follow after converging to a plausible problem space representation. Therefore, while exploratory modeling focuses on searching the problem space, exploitative modeling involves using MDE principles and practices to map the problem space representation onto a concrete platform-specific implementation. By exploiting the authoritative model in code generation, experimentation, and decision-making, practitioners can manage the overall engineering process in terms of model-driven problem solving, model-driven experimentation, and model-driven process and management activities. These activities form the basis of classification of agents for MDE and are discussed next. Although the classification shown in Fig. 11.7 is not comprehensive or complete, it provides a context to examine the roles that agents can play to support these different, but related, activities.

11.4.2.1 Model-Driven Problem Solving

The problem space representation discovered in the exploratory modeling phase was aimed to satisfy the problem constraints in the first place and may lack the elegance and simplicity needed to efficiently and effectively apply model-to-model and model-to-text transformations.

Automated Concept Formation To minimize conceptual redundancy and model complexity, the conceptualization, classification, and clustering methods can be applied to further structure the model. *Clustering* is the task of grouping objects into a classification hierarchy so that entities in the same group (cluster) are more similar than those that belong to other groups. As a consequence, the clustering activity creates abstractions that are low coupled and cohesive, resulting in a high degree of modularity. Agent-assisted knowledge discovery methods that measure groups (and ontologies) in terms of syntactic and/or semantic distance functions along with

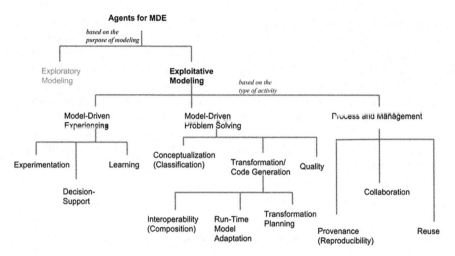

Fig. 11.7 Agents for MDE – exploratory modeling

multi-objective optimization methods that minimize such distance measures can be applied to simplify model representations. Further abstraction and classification can ensue via creating specialization, generalization, and containment hierarchies.

Transformation as Search and Planning In the absence of a well-defined set of mapping rules, model transformation can be viewed as a search process across the metamodel and constraint spaces of the source and the target language. By viewing the source model instance as the initial state, transformation can be construed as the application of a sequence of operators that gradually translate the source state into the target state, representing the model instance in the target language. Similar to classification and control problems, the state space transformation strategies can be complex and need to be discovered and optimized in a multidimensional space while adhering to problem constraints. Planning strategies for model transformation can resort to dynamic programming, reinforcement learning, and combinatorial optimization.

Run-Time Model Adaptation In stable environments with known models, transformation can be performed offline, as is done in model-driven software engineering. With the growing interest in run-time models and the need for dynamic and adaptive variation due to uncertainty in system contexts, techniques for run-time model adaptation are becoming vital. Agent and complex adaptive systems theories provide a multitude of learning and evolutionary adaptation techniques that can be leveraged to transform models online. Developments in symbiotic adaptive and autonomic introspective systems (Mitchell and Yilmaz 2008) suggest that agents can be used as introspective models that serve as a reflective layer over the run-time application layer. Retaining system models at run time and connecting them to agents that can introspectively change or tune models based on contextual information open new vistas for dynamic system adaptation. Dynamic transformation planning strategies may also be applicable in this context, as plans need to be continuously updated as the perceived environment and context conditions change.

Agent-Assisted Composability and Interoperability   As the complexity of problems increase, so does the need for integrating multiple models of the phenomena at different resolutions, scales, and aspects. While technical integration of models across different platforms is often feasible via adapters and wrappers, meaningful exchange and correct interpretation of data across simulations are still a challenge. Provision of ontological assumptions and schema constraints in a form that can be interpreted by agents can alleviate such challenges (Yilmaz and Paspuletti 2005). While dynamic composability, interoperation, and run-time extensibility in models are highly sought, contemporary solutions often lack mechanisms for (dynamic) selection and assembly of models, as well as meaningful run-time interoperation among models. In particular, they are limited in dealing with (1) dynamically evolving content (i.e., data, model) needs of existing federated applications and (2) run-time inclusion of new models into a federated system with their own encoding standards and behavioral constraints.

In prior work (Yilmaz and Paspuletti 2005), we have introduced an agent-based meta-level framework that supports interoperation over the modeling infrastructure via explicit separation of run-time interoperation and composition mechanisms from the model execution environment. In decoupling interoperation with a meta-level agent framework to support flexible model integration and composition among models within a model-driven run-time system, the following are the minimal requirements:

- *Administration* is the process of managing the information exchange needs that exist between models. Administration involves the overall information management process for the model-driven system architecture. Location, discovery, and retrieval of model content are critical tasks of administration.
- *Management* involves identifying, clarifying, defining, and standardizing the meaning of content as well as their relations.
- *Alignment* ensures that the data to be exchanged exist in the participating models as an information entity or that the necessary information can be derived from the available models.
- *Translation* is the technical process of aggregation and/or disaggregation of the information entities of the embedded models to match the information exchange requirements.

11.4.2.2   Model-Driven Experiencing Environments

Capabilities afforded by models, besides software development, are well recognized. The term model experiencing environment (Mussbacher et al. 2014) is promoted as an expression to acknowledge the promising contributions of model-driven experimentation, game-based learning, decision support, and policy analysis. For instance, goal-directed reproducible experimentation with models and practical, but rigorous, optimization of the system being simulated are currently significant challenges. The underutilization of design of experiments (DOE), limited transparency in the collection and analysis of results, and ad hoc adaptation of experiments and models continue to hamper reproducibility and hence cause a credibility gap.

An agent-assisted strategy can leverage higher-order synergies between intelligent agent technology, DOE, and feature-oriented variability modeling to support development of a generative domain architecture and software system for model-driven experiment management. To this end, explicit and distinct experiment models can be introduced for experiment synthesis and execution. Feature-based variability modeling can be leveraged to design a family of experiments, which can be interpreted by experiment orchestration agents to execute experiments. Experiment adaptation via intelligent agent recommendations can facilitate model updating as objectives shift from validation to variable screening, system exploration and evaluation, and, ultimately, system optimization.

11.4.2.3 Agent-Assisted Process and Management

The three areas for which agents can add value for MDE processes and model management activities include *collaborative model development*, *model provenance and reproducibility*, and *model reuse*. In this section, we only highlight selected issues in collaborative model development.

Collaborative model development with global and distributed teams requires situational and context awareness across team members. As model artifacts evolve, possible constraint violations need to be monitored and inter-model consistencies should be enforced. Furthermore, proper notification mechanisms need to be implemented to coordinate and synchronize multiple interdisciplinary teams working on different aspects of the problem. Since the activities of teams are interweaved and depend on other teams' contributions, proper synchronization and control mechanisms need to be available. A generic and customizable collaborative model development environment can leverage project-specific explicit synchronization models interpreted by agents to mediate coordination and cooperation across multiple teams. This view opens new vistas for model-driven process management of MDE activities.

11.5 Summary

This chapter examines potential synergies among the agent, simulation, and MDE methodologies. We advocated exploitation of such synergies toward emergent higher-order synergies. Such synergies include MDE-enhanced agent theories that in turn are leveraged to advance the state of the art and practice in MDE. To this end, we first illustrated how cognitive agent architectures can be programmed by using a DSL that offers language primitives based on the constructs and concepts of a cognitive theory.

Model-driven science, or the exploratory use of models in computational science, is discussed to develop arguments for model discovery using automated modeling techniques inspired by how scientists and engineers explore plausible models before converging to an authoritative model. Agent-assisted model understanding and model searching are proposed as potential areas for further investigation. Also, the potential role of agents in context-oriented, subject-oriented, and prototype-based modeling is highlighted. Finally, we proposed potential research issues and selected agent-based solution strategies for exploitative modeling, including automated concept formation, transformation planning, run-time model adaptation, and interoperability.

References

Braubach, L., Lamersdorf, W., & Pokahr, A. (2003, September). Jadex: Implementing a BDI-infrastructure for JADE agents. *EXP: In Search of Innovation (special issue on JADE), 3*, 76–85.

Craver, F. C., & Darden, L. (2013). *In search of mechanisms: Discoveries across the life sciences.* Chicago/London: University of Chicago Press.

Doan, A., Madhavan, J., Domingos, P., & Halevy, A. (2004). ch. Ontology matching: A machine learning approach. In *Handbook on ontologies international handbooks on information systems* (pp. 385–403). Springer Verlag: Heidelberg, Germany

Fowler, M. (2011). *Domain-specific languages.* Upper Saddle River: Addison-Wesley.

Franklin, S., & Graesser, A. (1996). Is it an agent, or just a program?: A taxonomy for autonomous agents. In *Third international workshop on agent theories, architectures, and languages.* Heidelberg: Springer.

Hirschfeld, R., Constanza, P., & Nierstrasz, O. (2008). *Context oriented programming.* [Online]. Available: http://www.jot.fm/issues/issue200803/article4/

İşçi, S., & Topçu, O. (2014). *DeCoAgent library.* [Online]. Available at: http://sourceforge.net/projects/decoagentlibrary/. Accessed 19 Dec 2015.

İşçi, S., Topcu, O., & Yilmaz, L. (2014). *Extending the jadex framework with coherence-driven adaptive agent decision-making model.* In IEEE international conference on Intelligent Agent Technology (IAT'14), pp. 48–55.

Klahr, D., & Simon, H. (1999). Studies of scientific discovery: Complementary approached and convergent findings. *Psychological Bulletin, 125*(5), 524–543.

Law, A., & Kelton, W. D. (2000). *Simulation modeling and analysis* (3rd ed.). New York: McGraw-Hill Higher Education.

Mitchell, B., & Yilmaz, L. (2008). Symbiotic adaptive multisimulation: An autonomic simulation framework for real-time decision support under uncertainty. *ACM Transactions on Modeling and Simulation, 19*(1), 31.

Morin, B., Baras, O., Jezequel, J. M., Fleurey, F., & Solberg, A. (2009, October). Models at run-time to support dynamic adaptation. *IEEE Computer*, pp 44–51

Mussbacher, G., Amyot, D., Breu, R., Bruel, J.-M., Cheng, B. H. C., Collet, P., Combemale, B., France, R. B., Heldal, R., Hill, J. H., Kienzle, J., Schottle, M., Steimann, F., Stikkolorum, D. R., & Whittle, J. (2014). The relevance of model-driven engineering thirty years from now. In *MODELS 2014*, pp. 183–200.

Ören, T., Kazemifard, M., & Yilmaz, L. (2013). Machine understanding and avoidance of misunderstanding in agent-directed simulation and in emotional intelligence. In *SimulTech'13: 3rd international conference on simulation and modeling methodologies, technologies, and applications* (pp. 318–327). Setúbal: ScitePress.

Rashid, A., Royer, J.-C., & Rummler, A. (2011). *Aspect-oriented model-driven software product lines*. Cambridge/New York: Cambridge Press.

Russell, J. S., & Norvig, P. (1996). *Artificial intelligence: A modern approach*. Englewood Cliffs: Prentice Hall.

Smith, B. R., & Ungar, D. (1996). A simple and unifying approach to subjective objects. *TAPOS Special Issue on Subjectivity in Object-Oriented Systems, 2*(3), 161–178.

Stahl, T., & Volter, M. (2006). *Model-driven software development: Technology, engineering, and management*. Chichester/Hoboken: Wiley.

Teran Somohano, A., Daylbas, O., Yilmaz, L., & Smith, A. E. (2014). Toward a model-driven engineering framework for reproducible simulation experiment lifecycle management. In A. Tolk, S. Y. Diallo, I. O. Ryzhov, L. Yilmaz, S. Buckley, and J. A. Miller, (Eds.), *IEEE/ACM winter simulation conference* (pp. 2726–2737). Piscataway: IEEE.

Thagard, P. (2002). *Coherence in thought and action*. Cambridge, MA: A Bradford Book.

Thagard, P., & Millgram, E. (1995). Inference to the best plan: A coherence theory of decision. In A. Ram & D. B. Leake (Eds.), *Goal-driven learning* (pp. 439–454). Cambridge, MA: MIT Press.

Thagard, P., & Milgram, E. (1997). *Inference to the best plan: A coherence theory of decision*. [Online]. Available: http://cogsci.uwaterloo.ca/Articles/Pages/Inference.Plan.html

Topçu, O. (2014, July). Adaptive decision making in agent-based simulation. *Journal of Simulation: Transactions of the Society for Modeling and Simulation International, 90*(7), 815–832.

Topçu, O. (2015). DeCoAgent Web Site. [Online] Available at: https://sites.google.com/site/okan-topcu/DeCoAgent. Accessed 19 Dec 2015.

Wooldridge, M. (2009). *An introduction to multi-agent systems*. Chichester: Wiley.

Xtext. (2014). [Online]. Available: https://eclipse.org/Xtext/documentation/

Yilmaz, L. (2015). Toward agent-supported and agent-monitored model-driven simulation engineering. In *Concepts and methodologies for modeling and simulation: A tribute to Tuncer Oren*. Cham: Springer.

Yilmaz, L., & Ören, T. (2009). *Agent-directed simulation and systems engineering*. Weinheim: Wiley.

Yilmaz, L., & Paspuletti, S. (2005). Toward a meta-level framework for agent-supported interoperation of defense simulations. *Journal of Defense Modeling and Simulation, 2*(3), 161–177.

Index

© Springer International Publishing Switzerland 2016   271
O. Topçu et al., *Distributed Simulation*, Simulation Foundations,
Methods and Applications, DOI 10.1007/978-3-319-03050-0

Printed in the United States
By Bookmasters